Reflexions
on
Poetry & Poetics

Reflexions
on
Poetry & Poetics

Howard Nemerov

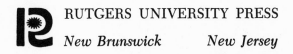

RUTGERS UNIVERSITY PRESS

New Brunswick   *New Jersey*

Copyright © 1972 by Rutgers University, the State University of New Jersey

Library of Congress Cataloging in Publication Data

Nemerov, Howard.
  Reflexions on poetry & poetics.

  1. Poetry—Addresses, essays, lectures. I. Title.
PN1136.N43   808.1   74-185396
ISBN 0-8135-0727-8
Manufactured in the United States of America

Grateful acknowledgment is made to the following for permission to use material originally published by them:

   The American Scholar: "Speculative Equations: Poems, Poets, Computers." Re-
printed from The American Scholar, Volume 36, Number 3, Summer, 1967. Copyright
© 1967 by the United Chapters of Phi Beta Kappa. By permission of the publishers.
   Atlantic-Little, Brown and Company: "Thomas Mann" and "William Butler Yeats."
Reprinted from Atlantic Brief Lives edited by Louis Kronenberger, by permission of
Atlantic-Little, Brown and Company. Copyright © 1971 by Little, Brown and Company.
   Basic Books, Inc.: "Attentiveness and Obedience." Reprinted from Poets on Poetry
edited by Howard Nemerov. Copyright © by Howard Nemerov. Basic Books, Inc.,
Publishers, New York.
   The Carleton Miscellany: "The Difficulty of Difficult Poetry." Reprinted from The
Carleton Miscellany, Volume V, Number 2, Copyright © by Carleton College.
   The Christian Science Monitor: "The Sweeper of Ways." Reprinted by permission
from The Christian Science Monitor. Copyright © by the Christian Science Publishing
Society. All rights reserved.
   Graduate Journal: "Two Ways of the Imagination: Blake & Wordsworth." Spring,
1967.
   The Kenyon Review: "Randall Jarrell (A Myth about Poetry)." Fall, 1969.
   McGraw-Hill Book Company: "Owen Barfield." From Poetic Diction: A Study in
Meaning by Owen Barfield. Copyright © 1964 by McGraw-Hill Book Company. Used
with permission of McGraw-Hill Book Company.
   The New Leader: "One Last Midrash," "The Fascination of What's Difficult," "The
Language of Praise," "Instant Opinions of Poetry," "Chinoiserie, New Idioms, Middle
Biedermeyer," "The Theory and Practice of What," "Polonius as Polonius." Reprinted
with permission from The New Leader. Copyright © by The American Labor Con-
ference on International Affairs, Inc.
   Northwest Review: "A Response to the Antiphon." Reprinted from Volume I, Number
2 (Summer, 1958).
   Salmagundi: "Poetry and the National Conscience," "The Protean Encounter." The
essay "The Protean Encounter" appeared under the title "Poetry" in the Fall 1971 issue
of Salmagundi.
   Sewanee Review: "James Dickey." Winter, 1963. "Everything, Preferably All at
Once: Coming to Terms with Kenneth Burke." Spring, 1971.
   The Virginia Quarterly Review: "Bottom's Dream: The Likeness of Poems and
Jokes" (Autumn, 1966), "On Metaphor" (Autumn, 1969), "Poetry, Prophecy, Predic-
tion" (Spring, 1971).

to Allen Tate
with affection and admiration

To Allen Tate

Dear Allen,

Here is a collection of essays. I especially hope you will like it, because you've been gracious enough to accept the dedication without having vetted the contents, save for such of them as may have fleetingly passed into your view on their flight to the periodical oblivion from which the present book designs to save them for a time.

It is conventional for a book of essays to have a preface, in which the author either claims a—frequently somewhat occulted—programmatic character for the essays he simply happened to write in the course of several years, or else, scorning to be so pedestrian, goes all cavalier and boldly flaunts the miscellaneous and indeed opportunistic nature of what he has done. It is tempting, on the basis of this distinction, to divide writers into two camps and burn the camps; but, as is not unusual, I seem to be somewhere in between, and think to do best by making my prefatory confession directly to you, and only through you to Them, the Others, the hopefully Happy if certainly Few (and may they be Fit).

The first thing to face is that after fifteen books I am nowhere near being able to make my livelihood by writing; I've got to teach, though I've had the good luck to find teaching a reasonably congenial way of getting along in the world. So some of these pieces were originally worked out and worked up for lectures in class. That may in part account for an element of conversational informality in the manner, which I don't mind and hope you won't either. It seems to me a fair object for the written language to carry, if it can, the liveliness of the spoken; not a good recipe for anyone who wrote like an angel and talked like Poor Poll, which is what Garrick said Goldsmith did; but I do neither. Maybe the slogan is the one I give my students: Write English, not English Department: reserving for the graduate student

this other one: Write like one of the grownups, but not like most of
'em.

But if it's impossible to make a living directly from writing—and I
fear the predicament will have been familiar to you—one can come
surprisingly close to doing so by accepting invitations to talk to people
about books, about writing, about, above all and O dear, *the creative
process;* invitations one would not have had without having written
the books. But I mustn't be, and indeed could not becomingly be,
nasty about the creative process, for if it's a cant term, and it is, it
nevertheless covers a multitude of more or less fascinating sins, and
on the evidence I've fallen for some of its temptations, I hope not to
the extent of becoming what our friend Karl Shapiro calls "a language
nut."

In a couple of ways, I think, the essays here have a thematic center
that makes them less miscellaneous in their relations with one another than the ones in my earlier book *Poetry & Fiction* (1963). For
one thing, this book contains few reviews—I made my enemies early,
and left off perhaps not early enough—, and where it does treat of
individual authors the attempt has been in the main to consider, for
the most part very briefly, their work as a whole. Thus the second section, Epitomes (1), is about a number of authors I care for, and is balanced by the fourth, Epitomes (2), a sort of vaudeville interlude taking
up some items now and seemingly always on the scene that I find less
than admirable. Maybe these two groups will be regarded as those
pages of illustrations that Wallace Stevens casually assumed would
always be where they ought to be.

The first, third, and sixth sections, while they don't join one another
in any plain logical consecution from premise to conclusion—my
mind just doesn't seem to go that way over the long distance—might
all the same be thought of as variations on a theme, or, as I should prefer to say it, variations looking for their theme and sometimes finding
it. So they begin with the exploration of some internal and constructive aspects of lyric poems, such as metaphor and the humble enough
comparison of poems with jokes. And they progress to some reflexions
on the place of poetry in the world.

I should have liked to complete my design by paralleling "Bottom's Dream: the Relation of Poems and Jokes" with a lofty ending
far out in the intense inane; that one was to have been called "Prosper's Art: the Relation of Poems & Dreams." But alas, the unconscious,
that unrespective sink, has so far refused me the needed evidences,
and that might have to be the subject of another book.

We are left with section five, which is about the self poetizing. I have tried to be clear about what things the poet may be able to say of his poem that others could not say, in comparison of what things the poet may know less about in his poem than any other reader whatever; but success in making this distinction perhaps belongs in the second category.

Anyhow, on this section alone, dear master, you will have to take a part of the responsibility, for having yourself so attractively introduced the fascinating if somewhat risky theme of Narcissus as Narcissus, one of so many examples, in poetry and in prose, wherein you have led and — let us both hope — illuminated your friend and faithful scholar.

Affectionately,
Howard

Contents

IV   Epitomes (2)

V

VI

I

Bottom's Dream: The Likeness of Poems and Jokes

The poetic attempt to say the world, to name it rightly, is perhaps a matter altogether too mysterious to be talked about. When someone, behaving "poetically," looks into the landscape and tries to speak it, this mystery turns inward and takes the form of an anxious searching and striving, until (sometimes) the mind by some wild reach having an evident relation with insanity produces a phrase, and this phrase— somehow—*expresses* . . . whereupon some quiet click of accurate conjunction tells us that what has happened is somehow reasonable.

Yet this moment of expressiveness itself occurs at a crossing point, and tells us that something in language is not linguistic, that something in reason is not reasonable. It speaks of a relation between inside and outside, an identity between inside and outside, but this relation, this identity, is itself unspeakable:

> Suddenly, I saw the cold and rook-delighting heaven. . . .

That has no meaning, strictly, that can be expressed otherwise, or translated. How, then, to someone who for a long time entertains the phrase as a sort of empty and objectless talisman, a piece of jade turned over in the hand, does it—suddenly, as the poet says—come to identify one alone sort of weather, one alone sort of poetry, that quality the poet wanted, he said elsewhere, of "cold light and tumbling clouds"?

Echo answers. Which is not to say that nothing answers, for it may be by a species of radar that intelligence moves through the world. We might say of expressiveness itself, of the irreducible phrase, that first it is, and then it finds a meaning in the world. Or else: Whatever the mind invents, it also discovers. Or again: Whatever is revealed, in poetry, plays at being revealed.

It is that element of play that I wish to talk about as an essentially poetic quality. This quality, I think, somehow exists in all language, in language considered as an unstable fusion of practicality and dream, in language which is in so large part an instrument for repeating, but in some small part an instrument for inventing and discovering what is invented—which is only to say, perhaps, that epic poems and systems of theology are all written by people who, whatever their talents, could not have been the first to say "cat," because it had already been said for them.

Though this poetic quality exists in all language, it will most often and most easily be visible in expressions which time or custom has set free from the urgencies of exhortation and the immediate claims of life: inscriptions on tombs, the proud dominations of antiquity, Ozymandias in his desert—surely the superfluity I mean has its relations equally with the ideal and the idea of death. Yet it may as certainly be identified in the most trivial examples. If you remove, say, the headline from an advertisement and let it dry in the sun until it shrivels out of context, it will grow other and rather surprising relations:

> . . . new shades of youth. . . .

Its valency, standing thus alone, is other than what it is when you put it back in its intentional place as an incitement to buy something called Ogilvie Creme Hair Color Foam. The tonality of *shades*, for instance, is more Stygian.

So in seeking to identify, if possible, something of the quality of expressiveness called "poetic" you might start, not with the sublime, but down at the humble end of the scale, with such things as that, with appearances of this quality in misprints, newspaper items, jokes . . . working your way up in Horatio Alger style to see how far your descriptions will take you (whether in the end you will marry Sophia, holy wisdom, the boss's daughter). In doing this we shall rely on the help of Freud—in some particulars on his fine joke book, "Wit and Its Relation to the Unconscious," and in general on his attempt to demonstrate systematically how mental life is continuous with itself in all its manifestations, from slips of the tongue to systems of philosophy and the visions of religion.

Also of Shakespeare, who in giving a title to these remarks gives also an instance of the quality we are trying to say something about. When

Nick Bottom wakes in the forest from the true dream in which he wore an ass's head and was adored by Titania, he speaks of what has happened in language whose comic effect has much to do with its tone of reverence, its being so full of garbles from scripture, and so on; and he says:

> It shall be called Bottom's Dream, because it hath no bottom.

Probably there can be no better definition of poetry—no better definition, I am tempted to say, of anything that matters to us—, though all the same it is clearly better for Bottom than for the rest of us.

Something of the quality I mean may be discovered in misprints. The mathematical probability must be quite large that any misprint, such as the omission or addition or substitution of a single letter, will produce merely a moment of nonsense in the result, and indeed that happens often enough. But given this preponderant possibility it is surprising to notice how often misprints make a curious other sense, and surprising, too, how economically such transformations may be effected. Here are a few examples:

a. The Russians are dredging what will be "the largest man-maid lake in the world." Nearly nonsense, and not quite; though not quite witty, either. Between man and lake the idea of mixed bathing has intervened to pervert the spelling by the nicest economy so that it gives another sense which hovers between the appropriate and the absurd; perhaps this secondary sense is not quite strong enough, and that may have to do with the fact that we cannot hear the difference but have to see it or spell it.

b. A reviewer of one of Kinsey's reports was made to say, "The sexual urge in females is demonstarted by" . . . Who would bother reading the rest of the sentence? Not only does "demonstarted" make sense instead of nonsense; it makes a sense which is as it were subversively appropriate to the serious discussion which was supposed to be going on.

c. A girl escaping from East Berlin "swam the icy river to be with her finance in the West." One imagines a Communist reading this with deepest satisfaction, since it confirms what he has always believed about love and money in the West. And the compositor was so taken with his invention that he used it again in the next sentence,

while giving the finance's name. One observes, too, that the pertness
of the criticism is enhanced by the somewhat ballad-like romance of
the subject.

The effect common to all three examples is that one reality gives
place to another, and a tension is revealed between them: the world
of information and, we might say, the symbolic world, reflect one
another in this tension. Moreover, the reality revealed by inadvertence is in each instance subversive of the reality intended; this is not
so surprising in the first example, since we generally expect the sexual
to be the hidden reality in statements, as it is in the second and third,
where sexual and marital concerns themselves give way to themes of
deeper mystery and deeper obsession still, theology of sorts, and
money.

As to the relation of all this with the quality of the poetic, which
many have called "vision," it is the first effect of Freud's demonstrations, on errors, dreams, jokes, to show that vision begins with a fault
in this world's smooth façade.

The examination now of a few rather more complicated and elaborated examples will perhaps enable us to go further in our description
of this quality and its mechanisms.

In "A Handbook of Arms and Armor," by Bashford Dean, I read that
Japanese feudal warfare was especially rough on horses because they
were not armored; there followed this sentence: "Not until the Tokugawa period, when warfare disappeared, was the horse given adequate
armor."

This statement takes the mind away from arms and armor, but not
entirely away. It combines with the subject another subject, of symbolic reflexions and resonances, in which the sentence bears a sadly
ironic truth (everything is always too late) without in any way losing
its pleasant and somehow Oriental flavor of bland paradox calmly
mastered (as in the report of an English-language Japanese newspaper, that "the entire aircrew climbed out on the wing of the burning
plane and parachuted safely to their death"). It would be possible,
no doubt, to appreciate intellectually the wit of the proposition alone,
dismissing all that was not abstract as irrelevant; but that would be
to lose the nice particularity of "the Tokugawa period," the elegant
coup de grâce given in "adequate," and the fine intricate play of
sounds (r and w especially) and internal rimes (like that between
"period" and "disappeared") which stitches the words together and
gives decisive character to the entire statement.

The second example is an AP dispatch reporting that a former lawyer of Al Capone's is convicted of income tax evasion. "I have in mind that you've suffered enough," said the judge, who also said, "Ten years ago . . . you were a well-to-do man. Now you're a man without means because of the debts you incurred in paying off the taxes. You've lost your law practice. This is a strong reminder that the power to tax is the power to destroy."

Something here, maybe the biblical austerity of the last sentence especially, strikes me as bearing the quality of expressiveness I am after; something both tragic and funny, featured by the judge's deadpan style — is he aware, right there, of the comparison implied between gangsters and governments? — and the whole rather complicated situation of the feelings wants only a touch of arrangement, a little bit of pointing, to be brought out. I imagine the former lawyer brooding on what has been said to him:

> Ten years ago, I was a well-to-do man,
> Now I am a man without means.
> I have received
> The strong reminder.
> The power to tax is the power to destroy.
>
> The lesson of the State's Do What You Can,
> That is what the law means
> Though we are deceived,
> O strong reminder
> Of Alcatraz, my master, my joy.
>
> Out here beyond the average life span
> The end no longer means
> What it did. Reprieved
> By the strong reminder,
> I get up the ante and go to destroy.

My last example is also a news item, reporting that a jet plane was shot down by its own gunfire. It is probably interesting enough to know that we live in a world in which this has become possible, but the thing sticks in the mind as well as the throat. An admiral and what the *Times* called "other Navy experts" explain: "The shells left the cannon traveling 1,500 feet a second faster than the airplane. After entering their trajectory they immediately began to slow down and fall because of air resistance and gravity. Meanwhile, (the pilot), going into a steeper dive, began a short cut across the shells' curved course. About two or three miles from the point at which the shells were fired, they reached the same point the plane had achieved. . . ."

This may already be a poem, finished and impossible to meddle with, though the newspaper's account is a little dispersed on the page for my entire satisfaction, and stuffed with irrelevant details. All the same, the relations expressed between murder and suicide are splendidly and as it were secretly there: "a short cut across the shells' curved course" is in itself a fine piece of virtuosity, giving the truth of the human situation with a decisiveness not so easily matched in poetry, though surpassed in this of John Webster: "Like diamonds we are cut with our own dust."

So it seems that this episode of the jet shot down by its own gunfire may be only the last playable variation on a theme poets have constantly handled; the particular comparison which comes to mind is with Hardy's "The Convergence of the Twain (Lines on the loss of the 'Titanic')" where the likeness and prospective identity of ship with iceberg are guaranteed at last by their literally coming together: the point of the joke, which Hardy calls "consummation."

Not trying for the moment to demonstrate the relation of such things to poetry, I shall say instead what characteristics my examples have in common.

Each is a thing in itself, a something decisive which the mind easily recognizes and detaches from the context in which it occurs. To say almost the same thing in another way, each example has the intention of giving information, but is received by the mind as giving something else; the statement, as it is made, crosses over from the practical realm into another, the realm of the superfluous and ideal, where it becomes a focus for meditations on the human condition under the figure of armored horses, aged lawyers, jet pilots who shoot themselves down.

This crossing over, this relation between two realms and the process of moving between them, is perhaps comparable with the relation, in poetry, between letter and allegory, between the picturesque and the symbolic.

The examples have, though in varying degrees, a reflexive character or one in which contradictions resolve; they are, again in varying degrees, increasingly from first to last, about retributive justice, and it may be this which gives them their quality of decisiveness and finish. This reflexive character could be put another way, as a principle of economy: they use their materials twice. And they all three, rather unexpectedly, exhibit the pathos of the obsolete, or obsolescent; they are all about something's being caught up with, something's being over.

Our next step will be to see if the mechanism of a joke in any way illuminates that of a lyric poem; we shall limit ourselves to brief examples.

One critical resemblance between the two will be clear to anyone who has ever tried to make up either—(by the way, how do jokes get made? I do not know that anyone has seriously studied this question) —and this is the problem of the ending. Anyone can begin a poem, anyone can begin a joke (the pointlessness of doing that is very clear, it seems, but many people begin poems). As Plato says in the Laws, "The beginning is like a god, who while he lives among men redeems all." There is a grand feeling of liberty about beginning anything, for it looks as though any gesture in the whole world will do. But, in the difficult world of forms, the gesture you elect will entail consequences good and bad, seen and unseen. Sooner or later, you have to ask yourself how to stop, what it means to stop, what it is that has finished. This is the question we will now examine, first with reference to a few jokes.

a. A riddle. How do you catch the lions in the desert? Answer: you strain off the sand, and the remainder will be lions.

b. From Shipley, "Dictionary of Word Origins," s.v. Strategy. A Chinese general sent his advance guard up to the edge of a forest. To find out if the enemy were in ambush there, he ordered each man to throw a stone into the forest, and if birds flew up there were no men there, so that it would be safe to advance. All this was done, birds flew, the army marched forward—and was captured. For the opposing general, also as it happened Chinese, had said to *his* soldiers: Men, I want each of you to grab a bird, and let it go when they throw those stones.

These instances are perhaps directed against the intellect's characteristic wish to simplify situations so as reductively to bring out logical structure at the expense of everything else in experience, the wit being that this same essentializing structure is employed to bring out the absurdity of logic in this world. Both jokes make use of the same almost absolute economy, using as much as possible in the response what was given in the stimulus, merely revising the elements of the relation in an "impossible" way.

The pleasure we get must come from the fulfillment of an expectation that the resolution in both instances will make use very purely, indeed exclusively, of the given materials, plus our surprise at the use made, which as straight men for the occasion we should not have thought of. But note that although we should not have thought of the reply, the very fact of its employing *only* terms already used gave us a not quite explicit sense that we might have thought of it in another instant; that though we did not in fact think of it, our minds were playing with the possibilities of lions-deserts, stones-birds, so that the answer, as a matter of timing, seemed "right" or "inevitable," responsive to a wish on our part for symmetry and economy together with a certain shock, the compounded fulfillment of fairly definite formal expectations with a material surprise. We might compare what happens with what happens in music, eighteenth-century music, say, where to a strict and relatively narrow canon of harmonic possibility, including certain clichés of cadence, is added the composer's originality at handling his materials within the convention.

c. From Freud, "Thoughts for the Times on War and Death" (1915). A husband to his wife, "If one of us should die, I would go and live in Paris."

Here we observe, as with so many jokes, and especially those bearing on sex and marriage, that the sentiment itself is about as unfunny as it could be, setting the death of one partner against the pleasure of the other and leaving no doubt of the choice that would be made. The wit, we suppose, the element which allows us to laugh, comes from two circumstances: first, that the wish expressed is one very widely entertained but usually concealed; second, that it breaks from its concealment so economically, using as its means a very slight grammatical displacement of the solemn, "objective" statement, with its air of entertaining the worst contingencies, which the husband must have consciously intended.

Thus, like our misprints earlier, this remark makes a revelation of sorts. A revelation can be only of that which is hidden, what is hidden is secret, what is secret is so because it is, or is thought to be, evil, shameful, taboo (sacred); finally, this evil represents something we believe to be true. So that the revelation is subversive of the usual order of appearances, beneath which it shows another order, one that gains its reality from the comparison of the two.

d. A last example, not a joke, but from Freud's analysis of one of his own dreams. He dreamt of a place called Mödling. No amount of personal association gave any reason for its presence in the dream, until he went through the following process of dream etymology or even archeology: Mödling, from earlier Mödelitz, from the Latin Mea Delicia (my joy) = mein Freud.

Though not strictly a joke, this instance purely illuminates a vital quality of wit, which takes the longest way round only as the shortest way home, whose beginnings and endings seem to be disposed upon a circle, not a straight line. This quality has to do with that economy we mentioned earlier in connection with our first two examples, to which it adds, however, the further consideration that this economy may tend to be reflexive, to turn back on itself and use itself again in a new sense (here quite literally a translation into another language and back). This is in itself a very poetical idea about the nature of forms, that they are like human beings who in seeking the world find themselves, like Odysseus who encompassed a vast world simply by trying to get home (this aspect of the journey is finely brought out in a beautiful poem by Cavafy, "Ithaka"). So also Donne, "Thy firmnesse makes my circle just, And makes me end where I begunne." (The example suggests another and more recondite possibility, that dreamer, poet, and wit are somehow endeavoring to say the world as a form of their own name. "When Thou hast done, Thou hast not Donne." This would only rarely, if ever, be demonstrable, though I have observed my own name, only slightly concealed, in my contention that the poet is a "namer of" the world. But it is in this sense that Shakespeare, with a "profound" or "abysmal" pun, has Bottom say of his night in the enchanted wood, "It shall be called Bottom's Dream, because it hath no Bottom.")

Summing up what we have so far: our examples tell us about the effect and mechanism of jokes that they depend on a strictly limited material, which they resolve surprisingly in terms of itself. Freud would remark that this economy is itself a source of our pleasure, and adduce such terms as remembering, recognition, recurrence, as analogous; and would add, what we discovered from one of our examples, that hostility may also be a pleasure-bearing part of wit. For, after all, a smile, physiologically speaking, is a step on the road to a snarl and a bite (cf. "sarcasm," a "biting remark").

So we have: economy of materials.

       sudden reversal of the relations of the elements.

       introduction of absurdity, but

       the apparent absurdity, introduced into the context of

          the former sense, makes a new and deeper sense;

       the hidden is revealed.

We may suspect that makers of jokes and smart remarks resemble poets at least in this, that they too would be excluded from Plato's Republic; for it is of the nature of Utopia and the Crystal Palace, as Dostoevsky said, that you can't stick your tongue out at it. A joke expresses tension, which it releases in laughter; it is a sort of permissible rebellion against things as they are—permissible, perhaps, because this rebellion is at the same time stoically resigned, it acknowledges that things are as they are, and that they will, after the moment of laughter, continue to be that way. That is why jokes concentrate on the most sensitive areas of human concern: sex, death, religion, and the most powerful institutions of society; and poems do the same. We might consider in this connection how grave a business civilization must be, to require professional comedians. Or, as Mr. Empson said (in a poem), "The safety valve alone knows the worst truth about the engine."

In general, to succeed at joking or at poetry, you have to be serious; the least hint that you think you are being funny will cancel the effect, and there is probably no lower human enterprise than "humorous writing." Still, there are poems which clearly also are jokes, yet by no means light verse, and one of these may serve for a bridge between the two realms; the inscription on the collar of a dog which Alexander Pope gave the Prince of Wales:

> I am His Highness' dog at Kew.
> Pray tell me, sir, whose dog are you?

This couplet possesses fully the characteristics we have distinguished in jokes: the sentiment itself is tendentious, might even come near to being savage were it not spoken by a dog with an air of doggy innocence; by cleverness it gets away with the sort of revelation of how societies exist which might at various times and in various realms cost a man his life or liberty; it works economically, by transformation of the given material. Probably, to be pedantic, the wit consists in getting us to accept the literal meaning of "dog" in the first line, so that we receive the metaphorical "dog" of the second line with surprise, but a surprise conditioned by expectation, for it is after all the same word.

The example raises another point, that one mechanism of economy in joking is the pun, either in the use of one word in two senses, as here, or in the use of two words of similar sound which mean different things but still somehow establish a resemblance beyond that of the sound. Notice that in the archaic economy of poetry it frequently happens that a resemblance in sound is, though cryptically, a resemblance in sense, as in the kind of logical connection hinted by a rime, or in these examples:

> For ruin hath taught me thus to ruminate (Shakespeare)

> O Attic shape! Fair attitude! (Keats)

We may add this as well. The "purely formal" arrangements of poetry, such as measure, rime, stanza, which it appears not at all to share with the joke, are in fact intensifications of a characteristic we have already noticed in jokes: the compound of expectation with a fulfillment which is simultaneously exact and surprising, giving to the result that quality sometimes thought of as inevitability, or rightness. Observe, too, that many jokes show a rudimentary form of stanzaic progression, by being arranged in a series of three, with similar grammatical structure, so that the hearer correctly anticipates the punchline as coming the third time a character says something, does something, and so forth.

Here is an example in which the humor is overtly savage, and any responsive smile might be accompanied by some gnashing of teeth; it is from Swift's "Satirical Elegy on the Death of a Late Famous General"; he means the Duke of Marlborough:

> Behold his funeral appears,
> Nor widow's sighs, nor orphan's tears,
> Wont at such times each heart to pierce,
> Attend the progress of his herse.
> But what of that, his friends may say,
> He had those honours in his day.
> True to his profit and his pride,
> He made them weep before he dy'd. . . .

What is possibly the oldest joke in the world says, "With friends like that you don't need enemies." Its present form seems to be Jewish, but I have found it in Tacitus, who remarks on the persecutions under Nero, "Those who had no enemies were betrayed by their friends."

And now, to climax this sequence, an example from whose grim strength all the laughter has fallen away; and yet it seems that the mechanism of the joke remains unchanged. It is Housman's "Epitaph on an Army of Mercenaries."

These, in the day when heaven was falling,
    The hour when earth's foundations fled,
Followed their mercenary calling
    And took their wages and are dead.

Their shoulders held the sky suspended;
    They stood, and earth's foundations stay;
What God abandoned, these defended,
    And saved the sum of things for pay.

Among so many fine things here, we single out the splendid economy of wit which remembers "and took their wages" from the first
stanza to bring it back in a savage reversal as "the sum of things."

But by now you may have the serious objection that I am being unduly free with the idea of a joke. Engrossed in my pedantries, I seem
to have forgotten that the first thing to see about a joke is that it makes
us laugh; whatever doesn't do that cannot really be likened to a joke.

I should reply as follows. There is a great range of jokes whose
intent is indeed to make us laugh. But can you really distinguish these
as absolutely separate from and in no way resembling the range, at
least as great, of such artifacts of speech as: riddles, proverbs, apho-
risms, epigrams, gnomic sayings, anecdotes, parables . . .? Jokes, it
is reasonable to claim, have often been the instruments of moral
teaching, and even religious revelation. Their humor may be far
indeed from laughter (consider the other meaning of "funny": strange,
wrong), or may be close to it without invoking it, as in the riddles of
the Zen Koan or those Tales of the Hasidim collected by Martin
Buber. To take one example only, with what sort of laughter does one
respond to this joke by Nietzsche: "The last Christian died on the
Cross"?

I think I may continue to claim that poems and jokes resemble one
another, laughter or no; and that the essential characteristic, in virtue
of which the resemblance obtains, is not the laughter but, far rather,
the quality of decisiveness and finish, of absolute completion to which
nothing need be added nor could be added: not laughter, but the
silence with which we greet the thing absolutely done.

You may go on with examples from a more ambiguous realm, where
the quality of the response may be hovering and doubtful. Here is
Herrick, on Julia weeping:

She by the River sate, and sitting there,
She wept, and made it deeper by a teare.

Its delicacy, its reticence, are not without humor; probably its miniature aspect asks for a smile. And yet, to even a moment's contemplation, it grows very large and the thin, molecular film of that tear spreading over the river is enough to express the world's sorrow; just exactly as in that saddest joke of all, where one rabbi comes to another who is weeping for the death of his son.

"Why do you weep," asks the one, "seeing it does no good?"
"That is the reason," says the other, "I weep because it does no good."
And the first rabbi sat beside the other, and wept with him.

There are poems by William Blake in which the feeling seems to be resolved actually by ambiguity, or by the maintaining a tension (a balance?) between two possibilities of feeling. This is difficult to explain, but less difficult to demonstrate. In "The Chimney Sweeper," a boy is the speaker; he tells of his and his friend Tom's wretched life, and of Tom's beautiful dream, in which an Angel opens the coffins of all the chimney sweeps and sets them free; then the poem ends:

> And so Tom awoke and we rose in the dark
> And got with our bags & our brushes to work.
> Tho' the morning was cold, Tom was happy & warm,
> So if all do their duty, they need not fear harm.

My point is this: one first reads the last line as spoken by the child, and spoken straight. Yet one cannot fail to catch, I believe, another voice, that of William Blake, who is also speaking the same line at the same time, in a tone of righteous indignation, in a snarl of woe against Church and State. And the same thing happens in "Holy Thursday," where, after describing the poor children being walked to church by beadles, and how their songs were "like harmonious thunderings the seats of heaven among," he finishes with the moral: "Then cherish pity, lest you drive an angel from your door." Again, you can read it straight: pity the poor children, for their angelic prayers really are powerful in heaven; or it is possible to sneer it, as if it meant to say: what sort of pity is it, that allows children to be poor? If you try reading the poems aloud, I think you will see that this tension is there. It is a tension which Blake expresses explicitly in one of his jokes, one of those quatrains which read like nursery rimes until they explode in your face, taking most of the moral world with them:

> Pity would be no more,
> If we did not make somebody Poor;

> And Mercy no more could be,
> If all were as happy as we.

The course of an argument will normally be thus, that many matters from the roots come together in a single trunk, a thought which can for a certain time be sustained; but inevitably, at last, the trunk divides in branches, the branches in twigs, the twigs bear leaves, and the leaves fall. Perhaps we are just now arriving at the place where the trunk divides and becomes several instead of one, and I ought to say here that I am not trying to show that jokes and poems are one and the same thing throughout the range. We have the same problem with metaphor generally, where the assertion that A is like B implies that A is also other than B, and not the same thing at all. "To thee the reed is as the oak." The poet meant, not that there was no difference, nor that both reed and oak are plants, but that the differences, to Imogen as dead, were a matter of indifference.

Or else you might say that at a certain point in an argument the thought, which had seemed identifiably one, begins to become in-distinguishable from a good many other thoughts — as though we had gone a long way round only to discover ourselves back in quite familiar territory. Here are some of the landmarks of that territory, which perhaps our journey at best has but allowed us to see for a moment as though they were new.

The real resemblance, the illuminating one, is that poems and jokes to succeed must do something decisive; which may seem to mean that their endings are somehow contained in their beginnings. This of course is precisely the magical, illusionist, or religious character of art, which has customarily rested on the assumption that God in creating the world did something coherent although mysterious, and that therefore history, at the last great day, would be seen as "like" a drama. So that poetic art has concerned itself characteristically with doubleness, and with what oneness can possibly or impossibly be made out of doubleness: with freedom and necessity, with change-lings, with going out and coming back, with echo, mirror, radar, with serious parody; here we approach Aristotle's notions of recognition and reversal, and may see them operant not only in the major forms of tragic poetry, but also and equally in the minute particulars of the poet's art, e.g.,

> With eager feeding food doth choke the feeder,

or,

> Property was thus appalled,
> That the self was not the same;
> Single nature's double name
> Neither two nor one was called.

We see also that the mechanism we have attempted to describe is like that of the plot in a story, also a magical device for dealing with time as though it were eternity, a way of doing two things — at least two! — at once, a way of handling appearance and reality as mirror images of one another. As Rebecca West says, "I am never sure of the reality of a thing until I have seen it twice." The mechanism we mean is what gives us this power of seeing a thing twice: it is like those striking moves in chess, called generally double attack — the pin, the fork, double check, disclosed check —, which show the contrapuntal effect of getting two moves for one and thus, as it were, making time stand still.

Our examples thus far have been chiefly epigrammatic in nature anyhow, and so the resemblance to jokes has been clear enough. But a poem is, for one thing, more ambitious than a joke; literally, it takes more world into its ambit. So for a conclusion let us look at two somewhat larger instances.

> Glory be to God for dappled things,
> For skies of couple-colour as a brindled cow;
> For rose-moles all in stipple upon trout that swim;
> Fresh firecoal chestnut-falls; finches' wings;
> Landscape plotted and pieced — fold, fallow and plough;
> And all trades, their gear and tackle and trim.
>
> All things counter, original, spare, strange;
> Whatever is fickle, freckled (who knows how?)
> With swift, slow; sweet, sour; adazzle, dim;
> He fathers forth whose beauty is past change:
>   Praise Him.

This poem of Hopkins' seems not only to illustrate the relation we have been discussing, but also to take this relation for its subject: it gives a religious guarantee, which is perhaps the only guarantee available, for the real resemblance between particular and generality, between detail and meaning; it so relates the unique with the universal as to show them the same and not the same; its transaction seems to define metaphor for us as: the exception caught becoming the rule.

And a last example:

The Collar-Bone of a Hare

Would I could cast a sail on the water
Where many a king has gone
And many a king's daughter,
And alight at the comely trees and the lawn,
The playing upon pipes and the dancing,
And learn that the best thing is
To change my loves while dancing
And pay but a kiss for a kiss.

I would find by the edge of that water
The collar-bone of a hare
Worn thin by the lapping of water,
And pierce it through with a gimlet, and stare
At the old bitter world where they marry in churches,
And laugh over the untroubled water
At all who marry in churches,
Through the white, thin bone of a hare.

By the romance of the beginning we are drawn into one sort of world, a belief in one sort of world; of which the decisive emblem at the end offers a sudden and absolute vision. The change could not be more abrupt, but neither could the harmony be more convincing, and one is a function of the other, and both are mysterious. As though to say once more, "It shall be called Bottom's Dream, because it hath no bottom." But now the leaves begin to fall.

The Difficulty of Difficult Poetry

Part One

1. The problem of difficulty in poetry, or "obscurity," is often thought to be exclusively a modern problem. When I began to study poetry the common assumption was that somewhere about 1910 poetry, which had formerly been clear and easy, became obscure and hard. More recently, a poet whose work I admire said that modern poetry stood to the poetry of the past as algebra did to arithmetic. Remembering my agonies with algebra, I shudder; but I don't believe this statement of the case to be entirely accurate, as I'll try to show.

2. "Obscurity" has always been, it seems, a standard accusation, even against some of the most famous poets and celebrated poems in our language.

Here is Dr. Johnson writing of Milton's "Lycidas":

It is not to be considered as the effusion of real passion; for passion runs not after remote allusions and obscure opinions. Passion plucks no berries from the myrtle and ivy, nor calls upon Arethuse and Mincius, nor tells of rough satyrs and fauns with cloven heel. Where there is leisure for fiction, there is little grief.

And again, a page after:

> We drove afield, and both together heard
> What time the grey fly winds her sultry horn,
> Battening our flocks with the fresh dews of night.

We know (says Dr. J.) that they never drove a field, and that they had no flocks to batten; and though it be allowed that the representation may be allegorical, the true meaning is so uncertain and remote, that it is never sought, because it cannot be known when it is found.

Among the flocks, and copses, and flowers, appear the heathen deities; Jove and Phoebus, Neptune and Aeolus, with a long train of mythological imagery, such as a college easily supplies. Nothing can less display knowledge, or less exercise invention, than to tell how a shepherd has lost his companion, and must now feed his flocks alone, without any judge of his skill in piping; and how one god asks another god what is become of Lycidas, and how neither god can tell. He who thus grieves will excite no sympathy; he who praises will confer no honor.

Of "The Rime of the Ancient Mariner," which is now read, very badly, in high schools, the *Monthly Review* had this to say: It "seems a rhapsody of unintelligible wildness and incoherence, of which we do not perceive the drift, unless the joke lies in depriving the guest of his share of the feast."

The same magazine sums up the poetry of John Keats with three epithets: "singularity, obscurity, and conceit." And *Blackwood's* speaks of Shelley's poetry as "a melange of nonsense, cockneyism, poverty, and pedantry." And of Wordsworth's poem "The Excursion," Jeffrey wrote in the *Edinburgh Review*, "it is often extremely difficult for the most skillful and attentive student to obtain a glimpse of the author's meaning, and altogether impossible for an ordinary reader to conjecture what he is about." Even Coleridge, defending Wordsworth's poetry from critical attack, gives some time to a discussion of those faults which he considered his friend to have rapidly outgrown; and what these faults are—"arbitrary and illogical phrases, at once hackneyed and fantastic, which hold so distinguished a place in the *technique* of ordinary poetry," "harsh and obscure construction"—he shows by quoting a passage from Wordsworth's earliest poetry:

> 'Mid stormy vapours ever driving by,
> Where ospreys, cormorants, and herons cry;
> Where hardly given the hopeless waste to cheer,
> Denied the bread of life, the foodful ear,
> Dwindles the pear on autumn's latest spray,
> And apple sickens pale in summer's ray;
> Ev'n here content has fixed her smiling reign
> With independence, child of high disdain.

Few readers now, I think, would care to defend these lines against any charge whatever, yet few readers now would have thought of calling them obscure—in fact, that word "construction" is not now very often heard among objectors to "obscurity," since many modern poems, very complicated in the relations of the imagery, are at the same time quite simple, sometimes even primitive, in the structure of their sentences. We see after a moment some of the things at least that Coleridge must mean: that when we have sorted out the pear and apple as subjects of the middle lines we may still be bothered by the suggestion that these fruits dwindle and sicken for want of the "food-ful ear"; and the family relations suggested among Content, Independence, and Disdain may fairly be called "arbitrary . . . at once hackneyed and fantastic." But perhaps because we are careless readers in this respect we refuse to be disturbed very much, and might be inclined to say that it's all very well to quibble but the general idea is quite clear. In other words, and if I am right in supposing that many modern readers would feel about the passage something like what I have described, we go through a process of extracting the "sense" from a construction, and from figures, whose particular life or want of it we tacitly agree to disregard in the interests of statement; and the statement of the lines is of course clear enough when we have subtracted all that for better or worse forms their individual quality.

3. Two relevant generalities, I think, can be drawn from the consideration of these examples. The first is historical, the second critical and philosophic.

a. What one age finds obscure sometimes, not always, comes to seem perfectly plain to a later age. Note that if that very difficult poem "The Ancient Mariner," which seemed to contemporary opinion "a rhapsody of unintelligible wildness and incoherence," is at present taught in schools, that is because it is believed to be not a difficult poem at all but a very easy poem.

Tastes change, then; but not by themselves, not automatically. Proust, in a passage of his novel which I have not managed to find again, says of Beethoven's last quartets something to this effect, that if, after being played once and being called "insane" by critics, these works had been hidden away in silence for seventy-five years and then played again, they would still be called "insane" by critics — because they would not, in that time, have formed, slowly, in the audience the canons of style in whose light they had to be read.

In other words, difficult work, harsh and at first sight unpleasing work, work which offends against the taste of the age in which it appears, such work — sometimes, again, not always — slowly forms new elements of sensibility, inspires meditation and imitation until at last it is assimilated into the general complex of culture and a later audience is surprised and amused to find that this work once baffled and

offended serious intelligences. This process may be observed in our
own time to have brought "The Waste Land" from a poem of appalling obscurity to one which may be read, with a little help, by fresh-
men; and, even more striking, the resemblances between "The Love
Song of J. Alfred Prufrock" and a monologue by Browning—the "Toc-
cata of Galuppi's," for instance—have gradually come to seem as pro-
nounced as the differences must have seemed in 1917.

b. My second point is this, that poetry always exists in a tension
between polarities which have been very variously named: between
reason and mystique, between order and passion, between prose and
music, between diagnostic and vatic or sybilline. Historically, the
tradition of this tension is very old, going back to Aristotle with his
accent on construction and composition, as over against Plato who em-
phasizes frenzy and inspiration, and Longinus who cares pre-emi-
nently for the Sublime, or for what is liberated from construction and
composition. This tradition goes back further still, and its doubleness
can be seen in the Bible, and back beyond our tracing, in those tribal
chants which seem to combine prophetic raving with inventories and
account books.

In English poetry this tension has generally been most visible in
the manner of conceiving and making metaphors; that is, at some times
metaphor is thought of and employed as an illumination or adornment
of a discourse which essentially is regarded as existing separately, and
as able to be perfectly understood, though less pleasurably understood, without the metaphors; at other times metaphor is regarded as
itself the essence of poetry, and is thought to produce meanings which
could not be arrived at by rational discourse at all.

The distinction is beautifully presented in a passage quoted
by De Quincey from a conversation with Wordsworth, who said:
"it is the highest degree unphilosophic to call language or diction
'the dress of thoughts'" and for "the dress of thoughts" he substitutes "the incarnation of thoughts." De Quincey comments thus: "the
truth is apparent on consideration; for, if language were merely a
dress, then you could separate the two; you could lay the thoughts on
the left hand, the language on the right. But, generally speaking, you
can no more deal thus with poetic thoughts than you can with soul and
body. The union is too subtle, the inter-texture too ineffable, each co-
existing not merely *with* the other, but each *in* and *through* the other.
An image, for instance, a single word, often enters into a thought as a
constituent part. In short, the two elements are not united as a body
with a separable dress, but as a mysterious incarnation."

The taste of poets at present is so set toward "incarnation" against "dress" as a way of describing figurative language, that we shall do well to remind ourselves of how powerful the other view has often been, as for example in Dryden and in a good deal of Pope, and in Dr. Johnson. But since it is Shakespeare who is finally the example of "incarnation" in poetic speech, I shall illustrate the idea of metaphor as "the dress of thoughts" from his great opposite Dante, who in the 25th Chapter of his *Vita Nuova* sets himself to answer the question how he can speak in poetry of Amor, Love, as a person, seeing that everyone knows Love is not a person but occurs as "an accident in substance." He replies that this is a liberty justly and traditionally allowed to poets, and cites ancient examples from Virgil, Horace, Homer, Ovid. But he finishes with this stern warning: "it would be very shameful for anyone to hide his thoughts under the garments of figures and rhetorical colors, and then be unable, on demand, to strip his words of those garments in such a way as to produce a true understanding."

Something like this, I think, is what stands behind Dr. Johnson's attitude to the elaborate traditional expansions of Milton's "Lycidas," a poetry deeply bound in the past and the particular; what Dr. Johnson wants, and does not find, is *meaning* detachable from the language of the poem: "and though it be allowed that the representation may be allegorical, the true meaning is so uncertain and remote, that it is never sought, because it cannot be known when it is found." To balance up this matter for the moment, we may place beside "Lycidas" an elegy of which Dr. Johnson might presumably have approved, though I do not know that he mentioned it; it is Dryden's "To the Memory of Mr. Oldham":

> Farewell, too little and too lately known,
> Whom I began to think and call my own:
> For sure our souls were near allied, and thine
> Cast in the same poetic mold with mine.
> One common note on either lyre did strike,
> And knaves and fools we both abhorred alike.
> To the same goal did both our studies drive:
> The last set out the soonest did arrive.
> Thus Nisus fell upon the slippery place,
> Whilst his young friend performed and won the race.
> O early ripe! to thy abundant store
> What could advancing age have added more?
> It might (what nature never gives the young)
> Have taught the numbers of thy native tongue.

> But satire needs not those, and wit will shine
> Through the harsh cadence of a rugged line.
> A noble error, and but seldom made,
> When poets are by too much force betray'd.
> Thy generous fruits, though gathered ere their prime,
> Still showed a quickness; and maturing time
> But mellows what we write to the dull sweets of rhyme.
> Once more, hail, and farewell! farewell, thou young,
> But ah! too short, Marcellus of our tongue!
> Thy brows with ivy and with laurels bound;
> But fate and gloomy night encompass thee around.

The Roman gravity and austere sweetness of these lines are no less moving than their simplicity (it is sad to think, by the way, that many people now would find them impenetrably obscure by reason of the "allusions," and would rather rest in that opinion than find out about Nisus in Virgil and Marcellus in any dictionary of antiquity). But it will be fair of us to acknowledge that this simplicity is as much a means of rhetoric, devoted to a particular end, as Milton's labyrinthine grandeurs.

Part Two

Before returning to the general problem of difficulty in poetry, I shall mention a few of the forms such difficulty may take, and give examples. What follows, of course, is but a sketch, and not a complete catalogue.

1. There is a sort of reader who finds everything difficult if it happens to be written in verse. This need not keep us long, and would not need to be noticed at all were it not for the voluble arrogance with which such complaints are often expressed. Such readers really have a very simple problem: they don't like poetry, even though some of them feel they ought to; and they very naturally want poems to be as easy as possible, in order that there may be no intellectual embarrassment about despising them. These readers get their entire pleasure, not from reading poems, but from wrangling interminably over "communication," as though each of them lived in his own telephone booth.

2. There is a corresponding difficulty on the poet's side: the periphrastic habit which comes from the wish to make common matters singular, easy matters hard, and shallow thoughts profound; what Pope calls "the Art of Sinking in Poetry," and describes ("Dunciad") as a way of "obliquely waddling to the mark in view." Here is a mod-

ern American example, in which the poet, asking himself "How does the mantis pray?" replies:

> Does he not fix his dark Silurian eye,
> Stark ebony, on the revolving day,
> His mechanism pulleyed and well-strung,
> And with precise antennae cautiously
> Tuned all a-twitch to his predacious wing,
> Drink the charged space with vast humility?

The mechanism of the verse is also pulleyed and well-strung but even the competence of its maneuvering works against it since the pretentious diction cannot disguise the triviality of the statement.

3. The syntactical resources of poetry can get the unwary practitioner into very ridiculous situations, as this of William Nathan Stedman will show:

> . . . upon your dainty breast I lay
> My wearied head, more soft than eiderdown,

where departure from the prose order of the sentiment seems literally to have induced a softening of the brain. But Stedman's difficulty here comes from the misuse of precisely the sort of rhetorical and musical variation which properly belongs to poetry and distinguishes it from prose. This rearranging of the elements of the thought, these syntactical inversions and grammatical economies, are true sources of power in, for instance, Milton, Hopkins, Yeats, Cummings. And here is Shakespeare imitating a rising anger struggling with control, the passion perhaps which makes people more rather than less elaborate in their phrasing (it is Goneril addressing her father):

> Not only, sir, this your all-licens'd fool,
> But other of your insolent retinue
> Do hourly carp and quarrel, breaking forth
> In rank and not-to-be endured riot. Sir,
> I had thought, by making this well-known unto you,
> To have found a safe redress; but now grow fearful
> By what yourself too late have spoke and done,
> That you protect this course, and put it on
> By your allowance; which if you should, the fault
> Would not 'scape censure, nor the redresses sleep,
> Which, in the tender of a wholesome weal,
> Might in their working do you that offence,

> Which else were shame, that then necessity
> Will call discreet proceeding.
>
> (Lear, I iv 223 . . .)

Whether you find this difficult or not will depend on how familiar the passage is to you, but I have known people to blink on seeing it for the first time. A closer acquaintance reveals its complexities as forming a marvel of clarity, though very tightly packed.

4. A common metaphoric form is A:B::C:D, and when plainly stated in this way it gives no trouble, as often in Dante, e.g. As the cranes go singing their song . . . so I saw the shades come, uttering cries. A slight complexing of this relation, or ambiguity in the placing of its terms, can cause us difficulty, as in this of Yeats:

> Things out of perfection sail,
> And all their swelling canvas wear,
> Nor shall the self-begotten fail
> Though fantastic men suppose
> Building-yard and stormy shore,
> Winding-sheet and swaddling clothes.

5. Probably the difficulty which most vexes most readers, modern readers at any rate, has to do with the content of poems, and the quantity of knowledge required to make some poems intelligible. It is the poet's assumptions about his readers' information which have provoked the angriest outcries against modern poetry, as most particularly shown by those who were enraged against the author of "The Waste Land" for using materials which they had not available—and even more enraged at him for making these materials available in the form of notes. One poet once said scornfully to me, "Why, if there were any value in all this esoteric stuff I could be much more esoteric than Eliot; I once translated Rumanian Folk-epics, and I could put in a lot of allusions to them."

This is a problem not to be solved once and for all by any general principle. It is hard indeed for anyone to know just what his neighbor includes under the heading of knowledge, or culture. Every day, in newspapers and magazines, we all receive masses of information, all of which is perfectly public and available to all, yet any detail of which, employed in a poem, would be perfectly obscure except to such readers as accidentally remembered its source.

The prevailing comic-ironic tendency of a good deal of poetry also plays its part in this matter. We can see from the works of the past, that tragedy tends to the universal, comedy to the local and particular, comedy makes its jokes of things quickly forgotten, which after the lapse of years or centuries are made available again only by the archaeological diggings of scholars; in this sense, though in this sense only, *The Alchemist* is a far more difficult work to read than *Hamlet* is. And I do not know how much we should make of *The Divine Comedy*, beyond vague inspirations, were it not for the devotion of generations of readers who, not content with broad outlines only, traced the meaning and the source of innumerable details, and made their results available in the form of notes.

And here we must return to our general argument, and the suggestion that there are two more or less distinct types of poetry, which I named by some pairs of opposed terms. We may now add a new pair of terms: reason and history, or reason and tradition.

Aristotle brought this matter up, only to dismiss it unequivocally, in a famous remark in the *Poetics*, that poetry is a more philosophic and excellent thing than history, since poetry deals in what is general and universal, while history deals in the particular and expedient. This sentiment has affected our whole tradition with respect to the problem of difficulty in poetry. Dr. Johnson, when he says that "Lycidas" is full of "mythological imagery, such as a college easily supplies," is clearly on Aristotle's side, and poetry for Dr. Johnson consists in the illumination of universal principles of reason by perspicuous metaphors; but—here is the catch—history for Dr. Johnson consists in much the same thing, and when he writes in his own poem "The Vanity of Human Wishes," of Charles XII,

> He left the name at which the world grew pale,
> To point a moral, or adorn a tale,

we need no information about Charles XII other than what is supplied in the poem itself, to realize that he appears not as a character but as an example, indeed "to point a moral, or adorn a tale."

The sort of poetry represented both theoretically and in practice by Dr. Johnson has great achievements to its credit, not the least of them the poem from which I have just quoted. The virtues of this poetry are simplicity, dignity, and rational force, depending, however, on somewhat narrow assumptions as to the nature of experience, the stability of societies, languages, meanings, and the way in which particulars and generalities are connected; historically, for Dr. Johnson as for John Dryden, these virtues are thought of as the result of an affinity for Imperial Rome and the tradition of didactic, moralizing and satiric poetry in Juvenal and Horace.

But there is another side to poetry, of course, and this other side regards poetry not simply as detailing the relations of principles to particulars in an ultimately rational world, but as coming prophetically out of a tradition, a history, an organic growth, of which it is the living voice; for this poetry the possible rationality of nature or history is of negligible interest compared with the philosophically absurd and irreducible brute fact that nature exists and history happens. For this poetry, at the extreme case, the particular must not be exhausted in generality, must not be prejudged in accordance with a moral scheme, must, if necessary, live on the page quite alone, without assistance from philosophy, which in some sense it seems to replace. This poetry, which is almost invariably difficult, is so at its best because it wrestles with mystery; at its worst, because the poet has but substituted dream for thought, or has not thought hard enough about his dream.

I have defined this problem in an extreme way to make it as visible as I can. It is evident that almost any poem has elements of the one and the other faction, and is characterized by the domination of one or the other.

There are in our tradition a few poems which hold the mystery of the art; they are altogether difficult, they are altogether fine; and they must be known for themselves alone, since neither will information solve their intricacies, nor interpretation reduce to plain sense the antinomies they contemplate. Shakespeare's "Phoenix and Turtle," Donne's "Nocturnall," Blake's "Mental Traveler," Coleridge's "Kubla Khan," Yeats' "Byzantium"—these seem to me fit examples, and I think there are few others so reckonable.

We do not **live** in those intensities always, nor rise to them often; yet those absolute poems, in which the opposed pressures of great energies produces harmonious forms and a controlling calm, represent the extreme range, and the extreme range is what makes the simpler poetry possible. Such works are perhaps not entirely rational, they issue in mystery; but their existence is an extension of the area in which reason may work, they summon thought beyond itself to think not on what already is, but on what may be.

Part Three

Beyond any limited and technical question concerning poetry stand the unlimited and possibly insane questions, "What Is Poetry?" and "What Is Poetry for?" It is clear enough that these questions cannot be resolved to everyone's satisfaction, which alone should be enough to suggest that poetry is many things and is for many things.

Thus truth, so rarely acknowledged nowadays, is finely spoken by the ancient Chinese poet Lu Chi in his prose poem on "The Art of Letters":

1. Lyrical poems are the outcome of emotion and should be subtle elaborations: prose poems are each the embodiment of an object and so should be transparently clear.

2. Inscriptions on monuments should cloak the art with simplicity: funeral elegies are tangled skeins (of grief) and so should be cries of distress.

3. Dedications on ritual bronzes are both comprehensive and concise but should be warm (in tone); admonitions are to make a break (in conduct) and so should be forthright.

4. Panegyrics should be expatiations on admirable qualities, with a balanced elegance; dialectical essays deal with subtle points and should be clear and comprehensive.

5. Memorials to the throne should be easily intelligible along with their polished elegance; expositions of theories are very illuminating — and deceptive.

6. The marked-out territories being in this fashion, the styles none the less all ban evil and restrain licence.

7. (and) since it is essential that the language be understandable, and reasoning well-maintained, there is no point in being long-winded. (tr. E. R. Hughes, Bollingen XXIX).

Nevertheless any talk whatever about poetry involves a response to these questions, which I want to attend to now directly, and reply to personally. My answers will be something to this effect.

1. Poetry is a means of contemplation, and it produces objects which help people to contemplate reality: objects in the same class with ikons, mirrors, prayer-wheels, and those glass paperweights containing, say, shells, pebbles, fish-hooks or feathers, common enough things which become uncommon by being sunken deep in a transparent medium.

2. So far as poetry is *for* anything beyond contemplation, we may say that it exists for the purpose of producing more poetry.

I say that my answers will be "something to this effect" because I have made them into parables, and a parable, like a poem, is a way of seeing what the world has to say about what you believe you have to say. But before presenting these fables, a few general reflexions.

The flat statement that poetry is or ought to be communication, even if it happened to be true, would be uninteresting. Some poetry, not necessarily the most interesting sort, has the clear intention of communicating — meanings. Other poetry has the clear intention of deepening the silence and space about itself ("The Tyger," for example, or the 12th chapter of *Ecclesiastes*).

There is a poetry for the world, and a poetry in which one talks to oneself (and this latter sort the world, like a child who wants only what he can't have, comes to value more highly than the other).

Meanings, generally speaking, are derived from the world and meanings are communicable; but is the world communicable? The work of art imitates in the first place world, it does not immediately imitate meanings except as these occur in the world (the opinions of Polonius, of Laertes, of Hamlet). Sometimes it appears to candid reflexion that great works of art give no meaning, but give instead, like the world of nature and history itself, materials whose arrangement suggests a tropism toward meaning, order and form; give, often in a tantalizing way the prospect of meaning somewhere beyond, beyond. What, finally, does Hamlet mean?

And this word "finally," doesn't it suggest something a trifle overbearing in the idea of meaning? as though all argument were conducted under the imminent promise or threat of the Judgment Day? whereas we observe instead that the argument simply continues.

Archimedes, inventing the lever, cried, "Give me a place to stand and I will move the world."

Much later, Kierkegaard gave to the decisive commitment of Christianity — Incarnation, the idea that one's eternal happiness might depend on something which happened in history and in nature, at a time, in a place — this same name of The Archimedean Point.

The problem for poetry, as for all disciplines which interpret the world, resides likewise in the idea of the Archimedean point. Poems issue out of world, and then it is possible critically to refine further and think of meanings as issuing out of poems, but poems also flow back into world and become part of the continuum they sought to interpret; they suffer under and make the most of the Uncertainty Principle.

If poetry reaches the point which chess has reached, where the decisive, profound, and elegant combinations lie within the scope only of masters, and are appreciable only to competent and trained players, that will seem to many people a sorry state of affairs, and to some people a consequence simply of the sinfulness of poets; but it will not in the least mean that poetry is, as they say, *dead;* rather the reverse. It is when poetry becomes altogether too easy, too accessible, runs down to a few derivative formulae and caters to low tastes and lazy minds — it is then that the life of the art is in danger.

I should like to redeem Narcissus from the contempt heaped on his pretty head by psychoanalysts, and I think to do this by telling you over a piece of his fable omitted by other authors, a piece in which he is allowed to talk back from beyond the grave.

It was Tiresias, according to Ovid, who being asked if Narcissus would live to old age replied, "Yes, so long as he doesn't know himself" (Si non se noverit). Tiresias might be the psychiatrist, who cryptically tells the child's worried parents, "He'll be fine once he gets over his narcissism," which would be most difficult if one happened to be Narcissus in the first place (we have the same problem with Oedipus, who having killed his father and married his mother could not have suffered from an unresolved Oedipus complex). But let me imagine Narcissus' reply.

"Alas, how reputation fades, how uncertain a thing is fame, when even a timeless legend proves mortal as to its meaning; it was better for me in the sixteenth century, when I was a foolish boy but at least a beautiful one, and my end could produce a tear instead of derision; whereas now I no longer exist except in the pallid ghost of an adjective of myself. Narcissism! I am as disgusted as you are by the sneaky, self-cuddling hypocrisy of that word, epithet for that worst of men who, pretending friendship to all, in fact believes in none, who in his room alone adores with smug satisfaction the image he is in fact destroying.

"Let me defend my contention that I was not in the least like that. When I looked into the still pool, and saw my image, I was not deluded into believing it was the image of another. I knew myself, you see, and on that account, as Tiresias said, I was doomed to die young. Let me remind you how it is when one looks into the still pool.

"First, there is the water, already hard to describe except for what you see in it, just as it is hard to say what time is except by saying what happens in it. All the same, just as with time you know it is there, a medium in which something happens. You see the water, you see into the water, you see things in the water and things reflected on its surface, all at once and indistinguishably. You see the bottom of the pool with its loathsome dark murk of leaves, twigs, branches, reeds. You see reflected the leaves of the tree which has dropped, for so many years those dead leaves; the tree itself, rooted in a foot or two of water, goes up into the air and down into the pool in a tension equal and opposite; and the shadow of the tree swings slowly about that axis all during the day. Beyond this, there is the sky with its sailing clouds, the sun; or the moon and stars. And in, of, on, rove through all this shimmering spectacle you see your own face, your eyes are searching into your own eyes, which hold also the sky, the water-floor, the doubled tree, and the tension of the surface itself. A fish or a frog swims by, a strider dimples the film of the surface, a drop of water falls from a leaf above, or a breeze arises. The image is troubled, it wavers, vanishes, reappears.

"What I seemed to see, what seemed to me to demand such profound, long and loving regard, was this: that mortal men lived in the world as they were reflected in the pool, their fleeting images rove through the stuff and fabric of the creation by whose means alone they might define themselves; likewise, then, a breath of air could destroy instantly this beautiful and living tension. Studying the pool, one's own image not more nor less essential than the simultaneous imagery of tree and sun and star, of water-floor and water itself, seemed to me a figure for what poets tried to do; and poetry in turn a figure for the contemplation of truth.

"So, if I may draw the moral which I consider to be appropriate, I gazed at the double and ungraspable image of myself in the world until I died of it; which is what all men do. And after death I sprung up again as a flower; which again, allowing for the poetical ornament—it might have been as grass—is what all men do."

As to the question what poetry is for, here is my fable, about the monkish medieval poet Caedmon.

Caedmon, a stupid man by nature, became a poet by divine visitation in sleep; waking, he found he could remember quite well the verses to the glory of the Creator which he had been inspired to sing in sleep during the night, and he wrote them down. He spent the rest of his life versifying passages from Scripture, which others had to translate for him—the Exodus from Egypt, the Passion of Christ, and so on. Now concerning all these things, which the present taste does not even find very beautiful, scholars believe, first, that they were not written by Caedmon; second, that nothing from his hand has come down to us, and third, that no such person, it may be, ever lived. What remains, then? Poets ought to consider it well. There remains only the voice in the night: "Caedmon . . . sing the beginning of created things."

On Metaphor

While I am thinking about metaphor, a flock of purple finches arrives on the lawn. Since I haven't seen these birds for some years, I am only fairly sure of their being in fact purple finches, so I get down Peterson's *Field Guide* and read his description: "Male: About size of House Sparrow, rosy-red, brightest on head and rump." That checks quite well, but his next remark—"a sparrow dipped in raspberry juice"—is decisive: it fits. I look out the window again, and now I *know* that I am seeing purple finches.

That's very simple. So simple, indeed, that I hesitate to look any further into the matter, for as soon as I do I shall see that its simplicity is not altogether canny. Why should I be made certain of what a purple finch is by being led to contemplate a sparrow dipped in raspberry juice? Have I ever dipped a sparrow in raspberry juice? Has anyone? And yet there it is, quite certain and quite right. Peterson and I and the finches are in agreement.

It is like being told: If you really want to see something, look at something else. If you want to say what something is, inspect something that it isn't. It might go further, and worse, than that: if you want to see the invisible world, look at the visible one. If you want to know what East really is, look North. If you have a question concerning the sea, look at the mountains. And so on.

I say that is a simple example in part because the finches were visibly there. Even so, the matter is complicated by the presence of language. It is not alone a matter of seeing, but of saying as well, of the power of the word whether in Scripture or Dictionary. I might paraphrase Hamlet's observation: "Nothing is but saying makes it so." Seeing and saying, the dictionary tells me, were perhaps originally related; and "a saw" is still "a saying." As to this power of the word, whose limits are unknown, Erich Heller gives this wise instruction as from teacher to students: "Be careful how you interpret the world, it *is* like that."

In speaking of metaphor, I wish to be free to develop the term as far as I am able, as well as to place it with reference to other words in the series of which it is a part, of which it is perhaps the middle term, standing between the utmost expansion and the utmost compression, between the story or fable at the expanded and the symbol or name at the compressed end.

For this very reason of a proposed freedom, however, it will be well if I apply now to the dictionary to ask about the strict construction of the term metaphor: in Rhetoric, metaphor is one of the four tropes, the others being synecdoche, metonymy, and irony, and is described as "Use of a word or phrase literally denoting one kind of object or idea in place of another by way of suggesting a likeness or analogy between them." Examples: "the ship *plows* the sea; a *volley* of oaths." The examples are suspiciously like those that Pope, in "Peri Bathous," collects under the head of catachresis, or "The Variegating, Confounding, or Reversing Tropes and Figures": Mow the Beard, Shave the Grass, Pin the Plank, Nail my Sleeve. Which is worth remarking only for this reason, that as metaphor depends upon a compound of likeness and difference not always stable in the fashions of thought one man's metaphor may be another man's foolishness. The dictionary, for instance, illustrates catachresis with a rather famous example: "To take arms against a sea of troubles," which some have tried to justify by the example of Cuchullain among many other heroes of fable who tried to fight the sea; if that is fair pleading one may see by it how the metaphor is a highly compressed and allusive rendering of a dramatic episode.

The dictionary goes on about metaphor with a useful distinction: "A metaphor may be regarded as a compressed simile, the comparison implied in the former (a marble brow) being explicit in the latter (a brow white like marble)."

I found that most helpful, for somehow at school I had regularly been taught that the difference between the two terms was that simile used "like" or "as" and metaphor did not, but seemed rather to assert something like identity. I had never been able to understand that distinction very well; to say, as some do, that "he is a lion" is more ferocious or leonine than "he is like a lion" did not impress itself upon my mind as making a real difference. But the dictionary distinction is useful as leading to a further thought: the simile isolates for you the likeness in virtue of which the comparison is made; the metaphor leaves it up to you to isolate the likeness or for that matter not to isolate it. In the given example, I didn't think of "white like marble" at all; the expression "a marble brow" brought into my mind fleeting thoughts of heaviness, coldness, hardness, pallor, a monumental quality associated with the tomb.

Even under the strict construction of a dictionary definition, therefore, the metaphor reveals rather mysterious properties. As though — and these are metaphors — it were a nucleus that held to itself an indeterminate number of particles, a tone to which a not quite random series of overtones responded, a sound that echoed from some surfaces but not from others. Compared with the simile, the metaphor is both more implicit and less selective, less abstract, and more multivalent. It doesn't give itself away, but awaits, if it doesn't indeed demand, the reader's participation for its fulfillment. In this sense, it belongs to leisure, philosophy, and contemplation, rather than action.

Here is an instance, possibly a foolish, and certainly a trivial, instance. If we are at dinner and I say "Please pass the salt," the entire sense of the communication is absorbed at once; you pass the salt, and that finishes our business together. But if we are not at dinner, and neither table nor salt is available, you will think me extremely silly for saying "Please pass the salt." Let us suppose, though, that for some reason you value my good opinion, and that I insist on repeating my silly request. What happens? I think what happens is that your mind begins to play with such symbolic or metaphorical possibilities as learning has acquainted it with on the subject of salt — such things as being the salt of the earth, taking things with a grain of salt, sitting below or above the salt — and that these resonances will come to seem to you expressive of something not necessarily simple about the relations between us: I may be acknowledging our equality, doubting or pretending to doubt something you have just said, or accepting you into my tribe.

But here is, I hope, a better example. At the entrance to the Zoo in Washington, D.C., I read the following notice:

All persons are forbidden to cut, break, injure, remove, or pluck branches, flowers, or plants of any kind, or to have in their possession while in the park any tree, shrub, plant, or any part thereof.

I suppose this message must have a practical use, or it wouldn't be there. All the same, without the message the thought of doing any of all those things would probably not have crossed my mind at all, and I stood there a little amazed, first at the somewhat pedantic detail of the commandment (imagine the dialogue: "I didn't cut it." "Well, you

broke it." "No, I did not break it." "Anyhow, you injured it"), but
beyond that at the poetical depths and ranges to which the sign invited, or even compelled, anyone who stopped to consider it. The
Garden of Eden and man's first disobedience. The wood at Nemi
where the challenger plucked the golden bough. Aeneas finding his
way to the underworld. Dante in the Wood of the Suicides, where the
torn branches screeched at him, "Perchè mi schianti, perchè mi
sterpi?" What would happen if one had the temerity to cut, break,
injure, remove, or pluck . . .?

So far the relation is not quite metaphorical, merely a parade of
harmless educated commonplaces. But that the sign should be at the
entrance to a Zoo seemed to add the necessary deepening to the complex of resemblance. For surely the Zoo, or Zoological Garden, expresses in imagery something of our feeling for the Earthly Paradise,
where Adam gave the beasts their names, where we had nothing to
fear from these gorgeous or powerful or merely odd emanations of our
as yet undivided nature; even while by its bars and cages and other
enclosures it expresses that this feeling is conditioned by the Fall,
and that the animal kingdom with its gruntings and brayings and
howlings and hissings is a presentation to us of the divisions of our
nature, a kind of natural hell externalized.

That leads to something else I want to suggest about metaphor,
though quite uncertain of being able to demonstrate it as a law: that
one resemblance, insufficient in itself, reveals another. Not that the
second is *deeper,* as they say, for one human thought is perhaps no
deeper than another; but that there is a gradient between them,
shallow or steep, and the revelation of its existence is surprising but
somehow just. Another silly example: the words "prenatal" and
"parental" are anagrammatic arrangements of one another. That isn't
much by itself, but it expresses something of the operation of metaphor to see the mechanical resemblance as it were warranted by
another, that the two words belong to the same cluster and have to do
with a single subject matter.

One more example here may help. In E. O. James's book, *Pre-
historic Religion,* I read that with certain exceptions the people of
Ancient Mexico "were destined to pass at death to the dreary sub-
terranean region, Mictlan, 'a most obscure land where light cometh
not and whence none can ever return.' There they were sunk in deep
sleep, but class distinctions were maintained, the lords and nobles
being separated from the commoners in the nine divisions into which
it was divided. At the end of the fourth year of residence in this

cheerless abode the ninth division was reached, and in this its deni-
zens were annihilated."

If I am reading this for information only, to pass a test, say, in a
course on the subject of Primitive Religion, I shall probably absorb
the "facts" and read on. But if I stop for only a moment, certain
mechanical resemblances will very likely make me think of a college
or university, and I may try rereading the passage to see how it works
when that way regarded. The major mechanical resemblances are,
of course, the four years and the class distinctions; the latter might
have to do about equally with grades and honors and Dean's Lists,
and with fraternities, athletic achievement, popularity, or any other
way of becoming a lord instead of remaining a commoner.

But there it will stop, *unless* I happen to be in a mood either vi-
ciously critical or sadly despairing of what goes on in universities and
colleges. If I am in either condition, I shall go on to develop the allegory suggested by the obvious and mechanical resemblances, and
read the passage with the other reference as far as I am able to: "Yes,
it's true, there is no light here and once the students arrive they can
never go back. They are indeed sunk in deep sleep with reference to
the intellect, and aroused only by a perpetual snobbery or squabble
over 'class distinctions.' But no matter, when they pass through the
eight divisions (corresponding to semesters in four years) they will
all be annihilated, they will become alumni — which by a foolish etymology would be derived from a (privative) + lumen (light), out of
the light."

And so the factual passage has become a metaphor, and far removed
from the author's intentions. But for this to happen, I repeat, the
factual, mechanical, numerical likenesses were not enough; they had
to be reinforced by an attitude, which in this instance I brought to the
material. In poetry, most likely, this attitude would in great part be
supplied by the context, which would specify the field of application
as well as something of the tone of voice.

Resuming what has been said so far about metaphor, I have ascribed
to it the following characteristics. 1. The instance of the purple finches
suggested there was something uncanny about metaphor, a sleight-
of-hand sort of thing wherein the word is quicker than the eye. 2. A
metaphor may be a compressed story — much as a joke that appeals to
a group of friends need not be told in full whenever some application
of it turns up in talk: the last line, or even a single catch-word, will
be plenty. 3. The metaphor leaves implicit a complex of resemblances,
where the simile will isolate one and make it overt. 4. Metaphor works

on a relation of resemblances; one resemblance draws another, or others, after it. 5. Exaggerating, one might say that any piece of language is capable of becoming metaphorical if regarded with other than a literal attention.

The last point most likely has to do also with the circumstance that language is, or seems to be, as Owen Barfield says, nothing but "an unconscionable tissue of dead, or petrified, metaphors." That these metaphors may be not dead but only sleeping, or that they may arise from the grave and walk in our sentences, is something that has troubled everyone who has ever tried to write plain expository prose wherein purely mental relations have to be discussed as though they were physical ones. When I read long ago in college, for example, that Descartes believed the pineal gland to be "the seat of the soul," I heard nothing literal in "seat." Only years later I found out that he supported the belief by identifying two little dents in this gland as the marks of the soul's behind.

Student writing, not unexpectedly, is particularly productive of examples, I suppose because the student is confronting for the first time consciously the fact that mental relations may be quite complex, and because he is often not conscious of the dormant metaphorical life in words that look harmlessly abstract, or safely dead. Thus, "Richard III is impervious to the pitfalls of disappointment because he has no honor to prevent his stooping to find another way out. His wits, sharpened to deadliness on his hump. . . ." This was a hump, indeed, that another writer could not get him over: His hump is an insurmountable burden. Once in a great while, though, such things become great treasures, they confirm Blake's idea that if a fool persists in his folly he becomes wise, and the plain foolishness of the fact becomes the mysterious truth of metaphor: "Man is descended from the man-eating ape."

It goes with this, and with the complexly associative nature of metaphor, that you cannot reason by means of metaphor or similitude for any length of time without running into trouble. A metaphor in a discourse ought to be like the sudden bursting of a flare, so that you see for an instant not only the road ahead but also its situation in the terrain around. Maybe that is why the best imagist poems are so very short; if the poet puts himself under the deliberate limitation of never specifying applications, never moralizing or drawing the general conclusion, but proceeds only by giving illustrations and leaving his auditors the option of saying, if they can, what the illustrations illustrate, he will do best to stop at that mysterious place where perception shows signs of turning into thought. Even in the more traditional discourse of poetry, where argument is not excluded, there is the danger that if you plant your metaphors too thick none of them will grow. Dante seems to have been aware of this, by his way of clearing a space to either side of his formal and extended figures. But once again the difficulty may be identified by anecdote; this one is said to have been Einstein's reply to a request for a simple explanation of relativity:

A blind man was walking with a friend on a hot day; the friend said, "O, for a nice drink of milk." "Drink I know," said the blind man, "but what is milk?" "A white liquid." "Liquid I know, but what is white?" "White is the color of a swan's feathers." "Feathers I know, but what is a swan?" "A bird with a crooked neck." "Neck I know, but what is crooked?" The friend took hold of the blind man's arm and stretched it out. "That is straight," he said, and then, bending the arm, "That is crooked." "Aha!" cried the blind man. "Now I understand what milk is!" (after Graves and Hodge, *The Long Weekend,* p. 88).

II

In what follows I should like to develop the idea of metaphor with a more particular reference to poetry, saying what I am able to of its uncanniness on the one hand, and of its relations with meaning on the other. If I find it next to impossible to talk about what metaphor is and does except in metaphors, I hope you will take that as a difficulty of the theme itself, and not as my mere wilfulness; the word itself, after all, is a metaphor, as you can see from its odd but exact survival in our word "ferry." And when you look into the derivation of Greek φέρειν and Latin *ferre* you find them associated with our verb "bear," arousing the wildly metaphorical suspicion that what is hidden within the word is not only the notion of "carrying across" or "transferring" something from one place to another, but the idea of being born, of how thoughts, like children, come out of the nowhere into the here: an ancient and traditional idea concerning the production of thoughts, such as may be seen from Socrates' considering the philosopher's business as that of the midwife, or from this of Shakespeare's Richard II:

> My brain I'll prove the female to my soul;
> My soul the father: and these two beget
> A generation of still-breeding thoughts,
> And these same thoughts people this little world
> In humours like the people of this world. . . .

I suppose we shall never be able to distinguish absolutely and with a hard edge the image from the metaphor, any more than anyone has so distinguished prose from poetry or perception from thought (these are instances, not necessarily parallels). We shall very often be able to tell, just as we can very often tell the difference between snow and rain; but there are some weathers which are either-neither, and so here there is an area where our differences will mingle. If the poet says, simply, "The red bird," we shall probably take that as an image. But as soon as we read the rest of the line — "The red bird flies across the golden floor" — there arise obscure thoughts of relationships that lead in the direction of parable: the line alone is not, strictly, a metaphor, but its resonances take it prospectively beyond a pure perception, if perception could ever be quite that. Metaphor stands somewhat as a mediating term squarely between a thing and a thought, which may be why it is so likely to compose itself about a word of sense and a word of thought, as in this example of a common Shakespearean formula: "Even to the teeth and forehead of my fault."

So I assert that the procedures of metaphor resemble the procedures of magic. And if the physical sciences have a relation to magic with respect to the material world, so that men can on their account now do many things that before could only be thought, or dreamed, so I should say that poetry has a relation to magic with respect to the ideal world. Poetry has of course always been associated with magic, though latterly the idea appears as merely sentimental; as people do not "believe" in magic, it may be no more than an honorific way of saying that poetry no longer matters. Yet I wonder if there may not be a more specifiable sense to this metaphor about metaphor.

Speech and light have most commonly been the vehicles of magic art, and it is easy to see why: both share the capacity to act across distances and through an invisible medium. The idea of comparison is like that. And the rhythmical character of poetry, that cosmic and physiologic piety whereby things change while the form remains, is also characteristic of ritual incantations for magical purposes. But it is possible, I think, to go further than this.

In *The Golden Bough* Fraser tells us that magic is based on two principles: "first, that like produces like, or that an effect resembles its cause; and, second, that things which have once been in contact with each other continue to act on each other at a distance after the physical contact has been severed." The first sort he calls Homeopathic, or Imitative, Magic; the second, Contagious Magic. Here is a Malay example that combines both principles: "Take parings of nails, hair, eyebrows, spittle, and so forth of your intended victim,

enough to represent every part of his person, and then make them
up into his likeness with wax from a deserted bees' comb. Scorch
the figure slowly by holding it over a lamp every night for seven
nights. . . . After the seventh time burn the figure and the victim will
die." The likeness of the victim draws upon the Homeopathic principle, the materials drawn from his body on the Contagious principle.

Transferred to poetry, I imagine that the first principle, of likeness,
appears at first glance easy and probable, while the second appears
neither easy nor probable. Yet let us try to follow the comparison for
a little; if we do, I think we may see mysteries, not merely problems,
emerge.

Here is a metaphor from *The Divine Comedy:*

> Noi siam vermi, nati a formar
> L'angelica farfalla.
>
> We are caterpillars, born to become
> The angelic butterfly.

Specified in its context, simple in its statement, this figure allows of
little if any doubt as to its meaning, though that it should have a
meaning doesn't in the least clear up its mysteriousness, which is as
much inherent in the metamorphosis of caterpillar into butterfly as it
is in the parallel relation of body to soul, or of this life to the next.

Here is a modern example, however, of the same relation: a caterpillar looks at a butterfly and says, "Waal, you'll never catch me in
one of those durn things" (Marshall McLuhan, "Understanding
Media," p. 34). Though the relation is constant, the applications
may be several, though all of them on the lines of Ophelia's "We
know what we are, but not what we may become." The figure parodies
an old joke about flying machines, the caterpillar's locutions make
him out to be a country bumpkin, the story behind the figure may
be about growing up, about technological change, or still about the
relation of body and soul. In fact, in its context it is used to illustrate
"the principle that during the stages of their development all things
appear under forms opposite to those that they finally present."

Now both examples are metaphorical: the metamorphosis of an
insect illustrates a proposition about human beings. But equally in
both the metaphorical relation takes place between two symbols,
and at least in the example from Dante the relation is so ancient and
widespread in tradition that the symbol of the butterfly alone, in an
appropriate context, would carry the sense. So, once again, a meta-

phor is a kind of condensed myth, and the symbol is its emblem, which conveys sufficient knowledge to those familiar with the story behind it. In the same way, the early Athenians are said to have worn as a badge or totem the golden image of a cicada in sign of their having been autochthonous and self-begotten just as they supposed the cicada to be. So there you have the contagious principle at work: the likeness between an Athenian and a cicada is not self-evident, but requires the knowledge of a tradition behind it, a tradition which must have said that the original Athenians *were* cicadae before the symbol said that Athenians resembled cicadae in virtue of a particular trait held in common.

A metaphor may show signs of being the compact, allusive form of a story or fable; and the symbol, in turn, may be the even more compact precipitate of a metaphor. We might extend these relations in either direction, though I suspect we should come round in a circle by doing so: from story, to metaphor, to symbol, to the name itself. This is not an historical account, for you have to have names for things before you can tell stories about them, and surely the process may work both ways; so that name, or image, might stand equally at either end of the series. The everyday working of such a process of expansion and reduction may be seen in the fact that we have for our convenience *names,* which stand for immensely complex sets of events: your name, my name, the names of Hamlet and Lear, such names as DNA, The Age of Reason, the universe. So do great trees grow from little seeds with the apparent purpose of producing little seeds, and it may be, as I think Samuel Butler was the first to say, that a chicken is but an egg's way of producing another egg.

Something of this may be seen by contemplating for a few moments the mystery of names and naming.

What sort of word is a name? I remember being told in school that a name was a proper noun; an answer chiefly valuable for discouraging a further question. But in later years that word "proper" became a little less empty, and I was able to see that in its curious equivocations lies the traditional answer to my question. A name is a *proper* or correct noun because it belongs to, or is the property of, what it names. The two senses attest to a capitalistically profound respect for possessions (and for being possessed, too, perhaps), and run almost indistinguishably close together: as in the Latin *proprie,* which means both "each for himself, singly," and "correctly, or strictly speaking"; the difference being perhaps no more and no less than that between our verb "appropriate" and our adjective "appropriate."

A name, then, is supposed to be *peculiar* to the thing named (peculiar being also a word of property, *pecunia,* referring to the calculation of wealth in cattle); it is no mere arbitrary label but is felt to bear within itself some real distinguishing essence. If that is so, then naming things will have been the privilege of a very great, even magical, insight or power, such as seems to be ascribed to Adam at the creation: "And out of the ground the Lord God formed every beast of the field, and every fowl of the air; and brought them to Adam to see what he would call them; and whatsoever Adam called every living creature that was the name thereof" (Genesis, 2.19). Nor were these names given by Adam merely arbitrary; on the contrary, it was believed at least as late as the eighteenth century that Adam "came into the world a philosopher, which sufficiently appeared by his writing the nature of things upon their names; he could view essences in themselves, and read forms without the comment of their respective properties" (Robert South, *Sermons Preached Upon Several Occasions*, Oxford, 1742; quoted in Aubrey L. Williams, *Pope's Dunciad* p. 67n.).

So it seems to have been thought that names were essences, that things would reveal their names, which is to say, metaphors about their natures, to the discriminating eye, thereby revealing also, according to the Doctrine of Signatures, their usefulness or menace to man; as the heart-shaped leaves of the fox-glove make apparent that the extract of this plant will be the specific for angina pectoris; concerning which Scott Buchanan observes: "This is a classic illustration and it is usually cited to show the primitive imagination correlating shapes of organs and shapes of herbs by magical impulse. Actually it is the mnemonic distillate of what must have been considerable experience. . . . Two things should be noted about it: its truth value is not zero: its truth value can be increased by more knowledge" (*Doctrine of Signatures*, pp. xi–xii).

One further consideration will lead us back to metaphor, magic, and our Homeopathic and Contagious principles.

Rabelais tells us, in a passage of most learned fooling with derivations (*Le Tiers Livre*, Chapitre L), that plants get their names in one or another of eight ways:

1. from their first finder, or cultivator, as "panacea, de Panace, fille d'Aesculapius."
2. from their country of origin.
3. by ironic antithesis ("antiphrase et contrariété"), "comme absynthe, au contraire de pynthe, car il est fascheux à boire."
4. from their powers or functions, "comme aristolochia, qui ayde des femmes en mal d'enfant."
5. by their distinctive qualities, like heliotrope.

6. after people metamorphosed into them, "comme daphné, c'est laurier, de Daphné."
7. metaphorically, "par similitude," as "iris, à l'arc en ciel, en ses fleurs" (and men reciprocally take their names from plants, as Cicero from "des poys chices," or chick-peas).
8. morphologically, "de leurs formes," "comme trefeuil, qui ha trois feuilles."

From that chapter, which is one of the lessons in the great uncompiled handbook of the poetic art, we may learn something of the primacy of the contagious principle of metaphor over the homeopathic principle which at first seemed so much more obvious. In only a very small number of Rabelais' categories do names "make sense," without further knowledge, to present observation and rational reflexion. We can see why a plant with three leaves might be called a trefoil, but no amount of unaided thought will tell us why a plant is called artemisia. In most of the categories, even those based, like antithesis and contrariety, upon formal relations, we cannot understand a name until we understand something else; and that something else is most often a unique and particular something else, something that happened, or is said to have happened, only once, and which therefore does not enter language as a generality; it has to be remembered to be understood, and if it is not remembered it cannot be derived by reason and cannot be known; it is a part of history, or tradition.

Hence, whether names are or are not in the first instance arbitrary, they bring something arbitrary into discourse, something obstinately unyielding: bringing in the individual, they bring in history, or tradition, and the stern idea of a world in which things happen once and for all.

So names are compressed fables, or histories.

And the evocative power of names, whether or not they are recognizable as distorted, combined, or corrupted words, depends upon the strange relation they make between the real world of happening and the ideal world of reason. Names relate to language as human beings relate to possibility, or as, for Dante, Beatrice related to Virgil, and the realm in which Beatrice was the guide related to the realm in which Virgil was the guide.

In general, and without even touching upon, much less trying to solve, the mystery of which came first, we may divide the matter this way, that the Homeopathic principle reflects nature, while the Contagious principle reflects history. And as to what in all this matter of the metaphorical expansion of names or condensation of fables is magical, only this, that although many metaphors propose a relation verifiable to the reader, a relation between objects whose natures are known (the legs of a table, the shoulder of a mountain) another sort of metaphor proposes a relation not verifiable by any living person, between two objects only one of which is known, as for example in "Care-charmer sleep, son of the sable night, Brother to death," and so on, or in the verse of Dante quoted before. There what is known is proposed as a presumptive demonstration of what is not known, what can be seen as a reflexion of what cannot be seen.

Poetry in the hands of the great masters constantly tends to a pre-occupation with the second sort of figure, making statements about invisible mysteries by means of things visible; and poems, far from resting in nature as their end, use nature as a point from which they extrapolate darkly the nature of all things not visible or mediately knowable by the reason — the soul, society, the gods or god, the mind — to which visible nature is equivocally the reflexion and the mask. Such poetry is magical, then, because it treats the world as a signature, in which all things intimate to us by their sensible properties what and in what way we are. Poetry is an art of naming, and this naming is done by story-telling and by metaphorical approximations and refinements, according to the two principles of magic I have described.

II   Epitomes   (1)

Thomas Mann

Of Thomas Mann I find it especially hard to say much in a little space, perhaps because since boyhood I have admired his works so very much, even while sometimes acknowledging those doubts of which Erich Heller gives so convincing an account in his *Dialogue on The Magic Mountain.* Mann stands for me as an illumination singular in its purity of the truth that a great modern artist must be a monster, absorbing the whole world and transforming it by means of his few obsessions into the illusion of the whole world again. So much thoroughness, so much explicitness, so drastic an analysis! and at the end all is magic and mystery still.

Through the vast range of his stories and settings, through his powerful grasp of the particulars of the many knowledges, these obsessions remain clear and form his thematic center, his peculiar realm of the problematic. The kinds of question he examines through a long and spendid development remain visibly constant from *Buddenbrooks* through *Doctor Faustus,* from mythological Egypt *in illo tempore* to mythological Europe enthralled by the demonisms and dynamisms of the twentieth century. Of this thematic center I shall try to give a swift overview.

The genetic inheritance of Mann's artist heroes, like his own, comes as the result of a series of opposites: from the father, all that is Northern, stern, mercantile, puritanical; from the mother, all that is Southern, relaxed, artistic, passionate, and indulgent. Through the whole range of his fictions, art is regarded as a seduction from the clear duties of life, a giving-in, a giving-over of the self to a realm dubious, enthralling, disgraceful, yet necessary with its own unique and untranslatable necessity. In art there are nightmare, disease, criminality, madness, and death; but also exaltation—"heightened metabolism"—power, courage, and even grace. To the perils of this course the artist must expose himself at the cost of health, reason, even life—but especially at the cost of love. And what saves him, if anything does—

what saves Mann himself if it saves all but none of his heroes, the lone exception being Tonio Kröger – is, oddly but appropriately, the bourgeois virtue of the forbidden father: *work.*

For a writer so much at home in the realm of the aesthetic and the morally questionable, this one commandment – work! – appears strangely as an absolute which must never be questioned. Mann's heroes are protected by routine, and the disasters which form their stories almost without exception overtake them when – and because – they go on a vacation. If this vacation be in the northward direction and the direction of home, as with Tonio Kröger, they may get away with it, experiencing their revelation at no greater cost than that of a certain dreamlike embarrassment; but if it is in a southward direction, and away from home, the result will be devastation, disease, madness, diabolism, whether they are then reborn or whether they die. Indeed, in Mann's stories, to go south *is* to go to the devil: Aschenbach to Venice, Castorp to his mountain, Joseph to Mizraim, Leverkühn to Italy and the pact with Satan.

Only toward the end of his life, speaking of Chekhov and finding as always in his subject chiefly himself, did Mann become explicit about this: "If the truth about life is by nature ironical, then must not art itself be by nature nihilistic? And yet art is so industrious! Art is, so to speak, the very paradigm of all work, it is work itself, and for its own sake." Developing the point with reference to Chekhov, he breaks in a few lines later: "Chekhov has fellow sufferers today, too, writers who do not feel at ease with their fame because they are 'amusing a forlorn world without offering it a scrap of saving truth' . . . These writers, too, are unable to say what the value of their own work is; nevertheless, they go on working, working to the end."

Mann goes on to speak of the protective, talismanic, regenerative powers of work in terms proper to his essay. But in his novels, it must be said, what work protects against is life itself, and the abruption of work leads dramatically through a disastrous love affair, often involving a child, to the death of artist or of child. In several of the early stories this prohibition against love, and penalty for daring to love, shape the action, Aschenbach's fatal love for Tadzio in *Death in Venice* being the best example. *The Magic Mountain* gives a more fragmented or dissociated version: Hans Castorp's love for Madame Chauchat, the immediate cause of his disease, refers itself to an early passion for a schoolmate; while the chief epiphany of the novel, his vision in the snow, makes the charm of an idyllic world depend upon a secret chamber where in darkness hags dismember and devour children. In the late novel *Doctor Faustus* the motif becomes explicit: Leverkühn's nephew is destroyed by Leverkühn's love for him.

Through the many metamorphoses of this central relation of artist and child I think to see in abstractest terms one of the poignant and recurring questions of modern literature: May the artist ever grow up and resume his rightful place among the fathers, or must his revolt be doomed from its beginning to irresponsible folly and he himself be numbered forever among the children? The subject is a secret presence throughout Mann's oeuvre, as it is an open one in Joyce and in Kafka. And for the most part Mann's answer would appear to be no. The artist can never re-enter with full adult authority the world of action. When Castorp goes back to the flatland it is as a private soldier, and in the infantry. Leverkühn in adult life duplicates as far as possible the scenes and even the persons that surrounded him in childhood. Joseph, though he gains great authority in the world, and though he is the adequate hero of a very great story, does not receive the father's blessing at the end; that belongs to the more serious and more limited Judah.

But I should not leave the subject without at least mentioning one happier resolution of this critical question. *The Confessions of Felix Krull,* originally a memoir left unfinished in 1911 but resumed at the end of the author's life and left, alas, unfinished again — we have one volume of a projected three — seems to represent that transvaluation of all values that stands the whole world on its head to make it right again, the satyr play that in the Greek theatre crowned as it concluded the tragic sequence, dealing in the same persons, the same materials, but now in a spirit of absolute license and irreverence. If heretofore the artist for Mann had been *like* a child, *like* a criminal, and guilty on that account, the solution at the last is to embody the spirit of art in one who actually *is* a child and actually *is* a criminal, and who consequently has no reservations, and especially no feelings of remorse, about being both the one and the other. Here, it may be, is epitomized the wisdom of art, to which representing is "a higher and holier thing than merely being," and of which the artist said: "The wisdom meant was a tragically ironic one, which out of artistic instinct, for the sake of culture, holds science within bounds and defends life as the highest value on two fronts at once: against the pessimism of the calumniators of life, the apostles of an afterlife or of Nirvana; and against the optimism of the rationalists and reformers who preach their fables of justice and happiness on this earth for all men, and who prepare the way for a socialist uprising of the slaves."

Mann says that in description of a proposition Nietzsche inherited from Schopenhauer. Or so he says. But, again, that is the way with those great monsters, the great artists. Everything they touch becomes them.

William Butler Yeats

W. B. Yeats, widely agreed to be the greatest poet of the modern age, was not in any obvious way a *modern* poet at all; those who like their histories consistent may profitably consider his example. For if the identifying traits of "the modern" are what they are so often said to be, liberalism, secularism, rationalism or scientism, appearing in poetry as tending to freedom of form, nervousness, the dominance of image over discursive thought, and a certain metropolitan concession to chaos, Yeats is at almost all points opposed: conservative, aristocratic, religious—though with neither god nor creed save what he made for himself—and minded to magic, which he thought of not as domination over nature but as the evocation by symbols of the prophetic soul of the wide world dreaming on things to come. His universality, far from being cosmopolitan and direct, as in Eliot, for instance, or Pound, is frequently mediated through the local and parochial materials of Irish myth, Irish history; and his poetry for the most part, from first to last, holding out against "free verse," comes locked in rhyming stanzas, because, he says, "all that is personal soon rots; it must be packed in ice or salt."

In one essential respect, however, his work is in agreement with that of such contemporaries as Eliot, Pound, and Joyce: its theme is the confrontation with the wonder and terror of history; and his attempt, like theirs, is to find a form for this immense force with the aid of mythological figures, stories, symbols that might exalt, dignify, and direct the chaos of the personal and contemporary. With this object, it may be said, he was able to view even the politics of the struggle for Irish independence as Athenian, and he drew up into the ambit of timeless traditions his own life and the lives of those around him, becoming in a sense at last the archetype of himself; for "on the throne and on the cross alike," he wrote, "the myth becomes a biography."

This remarkable attempt at remaking the self required of the poet an austerity and energy no less remarkable, a conscious turning away, in middle life, from a style already formed, and the conscious rejection of a character already formed. He writes of an early poem, "dissatisfied with its yellow and its dull green, with all that overcharged colour inherited from the romantic movement, I deliberately reshaped my style, deliberately sought out an impression as of cold light and tumbling clouds. I cast off traditional metaphors and loosened my rhythm, and recognising that all the criticism of life known to me was alien and English, became as emotional as possible but with an emotion I described to myself as cold." At the same time he gives up all thought of finding the self—

> That is our modern hope, and by its light
> We have lit upon the gentle, sensitive mind
> And lost the old nonchalance of the hand

—in favor of seeking definition in all that is most opposite to self, "the mysterious one," summoned by symbol, who will look

> . . . most like me, being indeed my double,
> And prove of all imaginable things
> The most unlike, being my anti-self . . .

Rejecting the moods of distance and nostalgia for lost fairylands that characterize his early work, the qualities he seeks henceforth are hardness and coldness; like Dante, he will "set his chisel to the hardest stone," and find "the unpersuadable justice." Instead of forlorn lament, the poetic posture will be one of pride, recklessness, fury, and tragic gaiety. And although remaining unalterably opposed to science, technology, commerce, and other characteristics of a leveling age, he makes, with magical and occult help as well as the help of tradition, a system of his own which is oddly scientific-looking in its appeal to strange geometries and arrangements of numbers, as well as in its capacity for generating incredible complexities from apparently simple principles. This system, described in several versions of the book called *A Vision,* formulates recipes for describing psychology, history, and metaphysics in their largely deterministic relations, and Yeats told several contradictory accounts of its provenance, the most famous being that it was dictated to his wife by unknown instructors who said at the outset, "We have come to give you metaphors for poetry." To the question whether he "actually believes" in the literal truth of his visionary designs, however, he replies: "I

can but answer that if sometimes, overwhelmed by miracle as all
men must be when in the midst of it, I have taken such periods literally, my reason has soon recovered; and now that the system stands
out clearly in my imagination I regard them as stylistic arrangements
of experience, comparable to the cubes in the drawing of Wyndham
Lewis and to the ovoids in the sculpture of Brancusi. They have
helped me to hold in a single thought reality and justice."

It is commonly thought nowadays that no man can make himself
into a great poet by consciously willing to be so, or by the construction
of systems however ingeniously elaborated, and what we have said
of *A Vision* might make it appear merely a curiosity of literature, save
for one thing, that Yeats did become a great poet, and by all the signs
he managed to do so in a remarkable degree by the force of his will
and the energy of his intelligence applied to the systematic exfoliation
of a whole world from a few themes and relations, based chiefly on
the thought of the relation of opposites deriving in the first place from
the images of sun and moon. It remains to say briefly in what consists
the greatness of the work, and that is not easy. But something like
this.

Order and force are the limiting terms of art, the opposites that
together compose the world. To these forms of art correspond two
limiting desires of the spirit, for death and for life. It is as though for
Yeats the contemplation of these polar opposites released immense
energies in the form as it were of an alternating current of desire; to
stand at one pole was at once to wish passionately for the other. As
Yeats put this movement between extreme terms, "I am always, in
all I do, driven to a moment which is the realisation of myself as
unique and free, or to a moment which is the surrender to God of all
that I am."

This is a simple-appearing idea, perhaps, but it puts one at the
center of his poetic creation. In the timeless golden stasis of his
Byzantium, his "artifice of eternity," his clockwork golden bird can
find but one subject for his song: history, or what is past, or passing,
or to come. Any retirement from the brute violence of life into the
heaven of pure idea induces a brutal and violent return. The key
poems that stand as emblems of this mental flight are "Sailing to
Byzantium" and "Byzantium," but the agon itself is given full expository form in "A Dialogue of Self and Soul," where after all the Soul's
eloquent persuasion to death and the dark of the absolute the Self
looks steadily at the filth and horror of life and affirms its will to live
it all again. As Yeats put it aphoristically, in a late poem looking back
over his career,

> Players and painted stage took all my love,
> And not those things that they were emblems of.

By some such magic of the opposites the poet many times in a long life renewed himself into a tragic joy transcending the stoicism and pessimism at its natural base. To see and hear this happening in the poetry is for the rest of us a source of life.

One Last Midrash

T. S. Eliot, *Collected Poems 1909–1962.*

Here once again is the old and new and familiar Book, like a new edition of the Bible, this time with Apocrypha in the form of a few occasional pieces, and, among the Ariel Poems, "The Cultivation of Christmas Trees." That comparison with the Bible will hold equally for its believers, its atheists, and its apostates; those for whom it is a sacred book, and those for whom it used to be, as well as those for whom it wasn't ever. To open it is to be at once in a realm of memories and misremembered commentaries; there on the first page of text stand the proud and guilty words of Guido da Montefeltro, probably better known in American colleges than anything else in the *Comedy,* even *Lasciate ogni speranza.* . . . When I was a sophomore I wrote an "analysis" of that passage as it related to Prufrock, to Mr. Eliot, to me, and was given a C+ for being too ingenious. And so—

> Let us go then, you and I,
> When the evening is spread out against the sky
> Like a patient etherised upon a table. . . .

The figure always used to worry me. I accepted the guarantee of the learned that it was "metaphysical wit," and I believed devoutly that such things could not be read by "inveterate visualisers," but secretly feared I must be one of those contemptible persons, for I kept seeing that patient as on a great billboard advertising some monstrous anemia of the spirit. A mere quarter-century later I think of the lines as fairly competing to replace a couplet by Robert Montgomery—

> The soul, aspiring, pants her source to mount,
> As streams meander level with their fount—

which is quoted in *The Stuffed Owl* with Macaulay's judicious comment: "On the whole, the worst similitude in the world."

You mustn't weep or get mad, Spinoza said, but try to understand. There came the time I began to teach, and tried — how hard I tried! — to understand the *Four Quartets*. And, if understanding is comprised in commentary, there came the time that I did understand the *Four Quartets;* at least I was easily able to occupy an hour expounding upon the very first passage: "Time present and time past / Are both perhaps present in time future," etc. I could do this with diagrams, with illuminating reference to *The Family Reunion,* with descriptions of Eternal Return, and with the feeling that something had been accomplished when I got done.

There came the time, too, that I started doing this in class and got no further than "perhaps" before starting to giggle, something I had not at all expected. The class was a trifle upset, for however Mr. Eliot may have disagreed with Arnold about poetry's replacing religion, his poems, and especially those *Quartets,* had for many years made a fair show of doing the replacing — certainly they had more religion in them than most sermons, as well as offering, some said, a wider choice of religions — and the normal classroom expectation was reverence all the way.

When I got through behaving badly I tried to explain, as much to myself as to my pupils, what had happened. I said that for many years, beginning when I was a pupil, I had looked on these poems as on The Word, that the reverence I had felt for them was freely given, and that I no longer felt it. Also that a part of this reverence, as experienced first by a very young man somewhat snobbishly inclined, was based on the difficulty of the poems, a trait in the intellectual realm corresponding to austerity in the spiritual, and that I no longer saw the poems as difficult. Finally, that I did not see it as fit for me to introduce them to the poems, since I saw no reason to think my present opinion better than my earlier opinion only because I had it later. It seemed better that the students should read the poems on their own and care for them, if necessary, ignorantly, than that they should learnedly dislike them under my direction.

The students were very good about all this, but I don't know just what I could have done that would have been right. (RESIGN   RE-SIGN   RESIGN   But there I am quoting that man again; see "Difficulties of a Statesman".)

Mr. Eliot was our hero, and he did a great deal for us (by "us" I mean largely but not exclusively people about my own age, especially those who tried to write poetry); that "great deal" will be the subject

of the few observations I have now to make. But first it is useful to
add a couple of definitions:

1. What a man does for you he also does to you.

2. To be a hero is also to be a villain; both of them indistinguishably
do the damage that later will be written down as history.

We have heard it is natural, or at least necessary, or anyhow that it
happens, for sons to rise and slay their daddies, even their spiritual
daddies; and in the poetry business, with particular reference to
Mr. Eliot, we have seen Karl Shapiro get into the arena and have a go.
Not only Karl Shapiro, of course, who is the most recent (as of last
week, anyhow); for years and years, an annual young poet was led
to the altar with poison ivy on his brow and ritual fadimans on his
feet, and a voice would intone something about his being destined
to "lead modern poetry out of the waste land." We will omit the *ubi
sunt* which ordinarily would come at this point in the service, and
proceed to the acknowledgment of our indebtedness; though Mr.
Eliot might reasonably protest that every last derivative poem of it
had already been paid many times over. I speak particularly to poets
and teachers, considered either separately or together.

1. He set us an example of the art of poetry, which by its seriousness
and ambition successfully pressed the claim of poetry itself to be
taken seriously in the world. For better or worse, there must be ever
so many of us who would not have attempted poetic composition
except for that example, that voice, the somewhat dour and wry ascetic
charm which it conferred upon the art.

2. He gave us, by precept and demonstration as well as by example,
an idea of what the art of poetry was. Indeed, though the first impression made by his work was one of diffuseness and great difficulty, its
later function was to concentrate and simplify the readers' notions
of what poetry attempted, as well as what it achieved. The canons
of his art, as expressed not only in poems but in criticism, may now
seem narrow and rigid; they did not seem so when we began, but, on
the contrary, appeared to open a world of exciting possibility.

3. To persuade us out of our parochialism into this world, he invented a great tradition for poetry, so that even as beginners we might
know ourselves not bounded by an English country churchyard (to
which his *Quartets* nevertheless return), but entrants upon the fair
field full of folk entire; part of a grand, minutely articulated human
enterprise. For one example only, without the glamor of *The Waste
Land,* how many, brethren, would have got up enough hit-or-miss
Italian to read Dante?

4. It is impolite, as well as a little ludicrous, to have to mention

this in company; but such as our living is, we have made it off him for years, those of us who teach or who have taught; except for the influence of his poetry, with its special sort of perplexities, it is likely that nothing so altogether unintentional as a "young poet" would ever have seen the inside of the Faculty Club. As to those of the brethren who do not teach, have not taught, and never will teach—those frequent lectures they give against "the academic" sufficiently indicate a similar indebtedness, one stage removed.

It goes with this that if I broke down on what may well have been my seventy-third "close reading" of the *Four Quartets,* it was my hopeless commentary that I giggled at, more than the poems. I hope so, anyhow. For it is natural enough that if you use language you will sooner or later use it up; and Mr. Eliot's work has had both the advantage and the related disadvantage, all in a very few years, of the kind of attention even Shakespeare and the Bible might presently, after centuries, be exhausted by. For behind the particular problem of Mr. Eliot's work there arises, revealed to us by the relentless efforts of so many clerks and scribes, the general problem that might be thought of as the assault of language upon mind, whereby the much-multiplied effort of our age to find "the meaning" of something leads out time and time again to where the ghostly meaninglessness of everything beckons to despair—for these journeys end only with the desert or the sea. But that is another story.

Meanwhile, I may have said enough in reminder of how much a very reckonable attempt both in poetry and thought has mattered to us. We ought not to value familiarity only for its proverbial power of breeding something else. It may be that we attend now upon that strange process whereby a work loses its immediate necessity and becomes "a classic" for those who live afterward, and that again is another story. It remains for me to thank Mr. Eliot, something I have never done, for his book, and end by paraphrasing—something so many of us have found it so hard not to do—a remark of his: of course we know more than he does, and he is what we know.

Owen Barfield

Owen Barfield, *Poetic Diction: A Study in Meaning.*

    This book first appeared in England in 1928, and was reissued there in 1952 with the addition of a new preface that helped to specify the application of its author's argument to views of the subject that had in the interval become more explicit, more brutal, and more unthinkingly accepted by scholar and layman alike, than had previously appeared possible.

    Mr. Barfield and his book have been very little heard of in the United States during all this while. But I should add that among the few poets and teachers of my acquaintance who do know *Poetic Diction* it has been valued not only as a secret book, but nearly as a sacred one; with a certain sense that its teaching was quite properly esoteric, not as the possession of a few snobs but as something that would easily fail of being understood by even the most learned of those jugheads whose mouths continually pour forth but whose ears will serve only for carrying purposes.

    It is not for the prefator to anticipate the arguments of the book, which the reader perhaps should already be learning at first hand by abandoning me in favor of Mr. Barfield; maybe the only preface worth having would be one such as I saw in a manual of Buddhism: that said, in effect, if you have read this far, throw the book away, it's not for you. But it may be appropriate to introduce the American edition of Owen Barfield's book with some reflexions on its subject, and on the situation of that subject at the present time.

    It seems as though there are two main ways of taking poetic diction as a subject of study. In the first of these, it is a technical matter belonging to the art of poetry, or, more exactly, to the craft of poetry, hence of interest only to poets, perhaps especially to young poets who learn according to their natures a certain boldness, or a certain fastidiousness, pertaining to what is possible and what is forbidden in the art when they first begin to practice it. At present, for example, the poet in his character of angler will not allow himself to speak about fish as "the finny prey." He would feel silly if he did, and quite properly so; he would *be* silly if he did.

But even at this early stage a little reflexion may cause him to ask himself why, if "the finny prey" is now impossible, prohibited, *out,* could it ever have been *in?* How could it ever have appeared to any poet seemly, appropriate, and—in a word that raises at once more questions than can be answered—*natural?*

If the poet is of a reflective and inquiring disposition—there is no guarantee that this is poetically a good thing for him to be—he senses very soon that a question of this kind, if he will pursue it, is going to take him into some very queer and even perilous places. "For," he may say to himself, "here is my language, that all this time I have just been using as if—as if—as if what? Why, as if it were natural, as if the words really belonged to the things, as if the words were really the 'souls' of things, their essences or Logoi, and not by any means the mere conventional tags they are so often said to be."

At this point the first way of regarding poetic diction, as a study in technique, goes over into the second, where the subject becomes psychological, metaphysical, and extremely problematic. Here the poet, especially if he is still young, may find it best to abandon the inquiry in favor of writing poems while he yet is able to, agreeing with something Mr. Barfield says in another connexion: "The fact that the meanings of words change, not only from age to age, but from context to context, is certainly interesting; but it is interesting solely because it is a nuisance."

But when the poet is older, if he has continued to write, it is at least probable that he will reach a point, either a stopping point or a turning point, at which he finds it necessary to inquire into the sense of what he has been doing, and now the question of poetic diction becomes for him supremely important, nothing less than the question of primary perception, of imagination itself, of how thought ever emerged (if it did) out of a world of things. There is some evidence that poets reaching this point—I think for example of Yeats, Valéry, Stevens— may feel acutely their want of formal philosophical training, so that they either abandon poetry and turn to study for a time, or else direct their poetry itself toward this study. And yet it seems their want of formal training may be not altogether a disadvantage, so that any regret they may express on the subject will perhaps have something of the irony of Socrates, who introduces his own reflexions on names and natures by saying, "If I had not been poor, I might have heard the fifty-drachma course of the great Prodicus, which is a complete education in grammar and language — these are his own words — and then I should have been at once able to answer your question about the correctness of names. But, indeed, I have only heard the one-drachma course, and therefore I do not know the truth about such matters." (Cratylus, 384b).

Now this development of the subject of poetic diction in the individual poet, as it were from five-finger exercises to questions of life and death, shows an odd and suggestive correspondence with a part of the course of poetry in English. It might be said that in the youth of our poetry the imagination was mysterious but not problematic, while later on, roughly from the time of the French Revolution, the problematic nature of imagination, the making explicit of its mystery, began to be the chief preoccupation of poets and even the subject of their poetic meditation; for example, *The Prelude,* a poem about writing poetry, Blake's *Milton* or his *Jerusalem,* Keats' Grecian Urn Ode.

In Shakespeare's time, as Rosemond Tuve has taught us (*Elizabethan and Metaphysical Imagery*), poetic diction was scarcely distinguished as a subject by itself, but belonged to the study of rhetoric, the making of tropes and distinguishing of figures, and was learned by the poets, as by other men, of school masters, and in the grammar school. Consciously, by analysis of the devices of speech, the student learned the recipes appropriate to the producing of particular effects, of grandeur, violence, sweetness, or whatever. The sturdy common sense of the attitude is delightfully represented by Ben Jonson: *Ingenium,* "a natural wit and a Poeticall nature in chiefe," is indeed his first requirement of a poet, but the others all have to do with conscious technical mastery. *Exercitatio* is one: "If then it succeed not, cast not away the Quills yet, nor scratch the Wainescott, beate not the poor Deske, but bring all to the forge, and file again; tourne it anew. There is no statute Law of the Kingdome bids you bee a poet against your will; or the first quarter. If it come, in a yeare or two, it is well." *Imitatio* is another: "to bee able to convert the substance or Riches of another Poet to his owne use." And last is *Lectio,* "exactnesse of Studie and multiplicity of reading. . . . not alone enabling him to know the History or Argument of a Poeme and to report it, but so to master the matter and Stile, as to shew hee knows how to handle, place, or dispose of either with Elegancie when need shall bee."

The immense distance of this attitude from most modern attitudes to the study of poetry is as impressive as it is obvious; when Jonson adds that a man must not think to become a poet "by dreaming hee hath been in Parnassus, or having washt his lips, as they say, in Helicon," the modern student may think with a profitable amazement of this warning in relation to, say, Shelley, Baudelaire, Verhaeren, Rilke, and so on.

In the seventeenth and eighteenth centuries it would appear that prose and poetry, which had formerly been rather close together in their choice of language, were decisively differentiated from one another, and there gradually grew up a kind of language special to poetry and not admissible in prose except on most exalted occasions. This language gives, historically, the first separable meaning to the term "poetic diction." And for a long while it is assumed that this state of affairs is natural, necessary, and reasonable; nor do poets much inquire why it should be thus and not otherwise. When Pope writes, "We acknowledge Homer the father of poetical diction, the first who taught *that language of the Gods* to men" (his italics), the second clause does not appear to him, though it does to us, as requiring elaboration. Just as early modern historians had perforce to pretend that the peoples they studied had suddenly appeared out of nowhere and begun to be "historical," so Pope sensibly assumes there is no point in staring at the darkness inside that phrase about the language of the Gods, and decides instead to look at Homer's diction, which is something he can see.

But it may be that the truly "modern" thing about the modern age, the nineteenth century and the twentieth, its really diagnostic trait, is the interest in beginnings, in origin, in aetiology: when we try to say what something *is* — witness Darwin, for example, and Freud — our way of doing it is to go back and talk about how it got to be the way it looks now. Or it might be said that with the eroding away of the assumptions of the first chapters of Genesis, other mythology had to be supplied, mythology in the fashionable scientific language, if only in order to fill up what began to appear as the dark backward and abysm of time.

The great change in the consciousness, or self-consciousness, of the western world that is usually dated to the French Revolution appears simultaneously in letters as the Romantic movement, or revolt; and this revolt has first and last a great deal to do with poetic diction in the first, or technical, sense; it is a revolt against a conventional language that has precipitated out conventions of feeling and belief. To Wordsworth, writing in 1800, the term itself is a sort of insult: "There will also be found in these pieces little of what is usually called poetic diction; I have taken as much pains to avoid it as others ordinarily take to produce it."

But it belongs to the understanding of Romanticism that you cannot rebel merely against the technical, or craft, part of poetry without rebelling also against something deeper and of more generally human concern, the belief about the world and the place of mankind in the world that produced the technical conventions you find intolerable; and this rebellion, if thoroughly pursued, involves the rebel in making his own creation myth, his own story of how things came to be as they are.

In an appendix to his "Observations Prefixed to the Second Edition of Lyrical Ballads," Wordsworth elaborates on the subject of poetic diction, and his way of doing it takes him back to first things: "The earliest poets of all nations generally wrote from passion excited by real events; they wrote naturally, and as men: feeling powerfully as they did, their language was daring, and figurative." William Blake, a few years earlier, testifies in a similar way: "The ancient Poets animated all sensible objects with Gods or geniuses, calling them by the names and adorning them with the properties of woods, rivers, mountains, lakes, cities, nations, and whatever their enlarged and numerous senses could perceive." One of his examples is Isaiah, who is made to say, about the divine vision, "I saw no God, nor heard any, in a finite organical perception; but my senses discover'd the infinite in everything. . . ."

About these earliest and ancient poets, Mr. Barfield has much to say, which I must not anticipate; it is enough to make my present point if I add that the subsequent intellectualizing imitation of the supposed practice of the supposed earliest poets produces, for Wordsworth, the corruption of language that he means by "poetic diction," and, for Blake, systematic abstraction, priesthood, scientism, the loss of the good of the imagination.

For the great Romantics, then, poetic diction becomes a subject of the first importance, because out of their efforts to reform this highly specialized diction and reach back instead to "nature" arose the deeper question of the extent of the imagination's role as creator of the visible and sensible world. For Blake that extent was total: Imagination is the Savior. For Wordsworth the relation was a more tentative and balancing one, in which world and thought we mutually adjusted one to another, a solution about which Blake wrote: "You shall not bring me down to believe such fitting & fitted. I know better & please your Lordship." For both, and for their great contemporaries, the primacy of imagination was a point of considerable anxiety, too, because the view opposed, the view of a universe of independently and fatally moving *things*, the view named by Alfred North Whitehead as "scientific materialism," was so evidently triumphant in imposing its claims upon the general mind of Europe and America.

That view has continued triumphant, though disturbing questions are ever more persistently raised about its foundations. And in the situation of poetry at present, in the United States, it appears as though one after another outbreak of "modernism" which regards itself specifically as anti-romantic presently reveals that it is but another variation on superficial aspects of the Romantic movement, while something submerged and unfinished about that movement remains largely untouched. Poetry and criticism, with a few honorable exceptions, either disregard the question raised about the imagination, or else seem to assume implicitly, without saying much, some positivist or behaviorist or mechanist resolution of it, and one result in particular is apparent: a poetry enthralled by the false realism of the reason, spellbound to the merely picturesque, imposed upon, Blake would have said, by the phantasy of the angel whose works are only Analytics, and so prevented, in spite of all its claims and manifestoes, from dreaming deeply or other than the common dream.

It is to the student willing to open this question of the imagination again to a candid exploration that Owen Barfield's book is directed.

A Response to the Antiphon

Djuna Barnes, *The Antiphon.*

The new work by the author of *Nightwood, Ryder,* and *A Night Among the Horses,* is a play, and written in verse; beyond this, not easy to characterize. To me, it seems to combine under extreme pressure several elements distinctive in a good deal of work which defines for us the term "modern," and these might be outlined under the following heads:

1. An art of serious parody.

2. A breaking-up of surfaces; destruction of the conventional sequences and coherencies of "plot"; a return to something of the "insanity" of Greek tragedy, if you will take a fairer sample of Greek tragedy than is provided by the few popular works (*Agamemnon, Oedipus Rex, Antigone*) conformable to nineteenth-century ideas on this theme.

3. Treatment of language as an independent value.

Before discussing these matters, some description will be necessary. The persons are six (some extras appear, but do not speak), the time is "during the war of 1939," the place is Burley Hall in the township of Beewick, in England; the house, "formerly a college of chantry priests," has been in the Burley family since the late seventeenth century.

On one evening, in this ruin, there meet the members of the family, all at least in middle age, and two of them old: Augusta Burley Hobbs, the mother; her brother Jonathan Burley; the daughter Miranda (in her late fifties); and two sons Dudley and Elisha. The sixth person, traveling with Miranda, is disguised as a coachman under the name of Jack Blow, but is at the last revealed to be the third son Jeremy. These people debate what life has brought them to, receive certain revelations on this subject; at the end, mother and daughter, who have been mysteriously seen throughout as interchangeable, or identical, fall dead. The progression of the play, the external order of its coming to pass, suggests close comparison with Greek forms: after the prologue of Act I, Act II consists of a series of agons and an epiphany, Act III of a pathos, sparagmos, and threnody. The theme is that of the curse upon the house.

The curse upon the house, that wound in nature *ab illo tempore,* is an ancient convenience of tragedy; in the eating of Thyestes' children there spoke the arbitrary prophetic voice of necessity, to which the human actions of Agamemnon, Klytaimestra, and Orestes would freely conform themselves. Shakespeare, it seems, thought rarely or not at all of plots so deeply laid in the past; his prophecies, though they serve a similar function of suspension which the tragic event resolves, are more immediate to the person concerned, as in *Macbeth;* their depth is not in time, but inward. For contemporary poetic drama the theme again becomes vital, but now it is not only the tragic occasion, it is also the tragic subject, as it is in Eliot's *The Family Reunion,* for instance, and in Yeats' *Purgatory.* The tendency of this theme, as it is crystallized in *The Antiphon,* is to a generalized form of tragedy, in which the tragic flaw is neither more nor less than life itself. As there is no superficial "story" in Miss Barnes's play, with immediate purposes, psychological motivations of the people, neither is there any particular curse or local purpose, but the doom here disputed is from the beginning the general one, the bond of generation and death, or original sin inferred (as in Kafka's *The Trial*) from original punishment. There is in other words very little "machinery"; as in the story of Job before it was fitted out with a prologue in heaven, the human sufferers debate the secret cause without aid from the secret cause itself.* And the sort of probing into motive, nature, and destiny, which it is the traditional work of the action to carry on, must now be supplied by the strike and reach of the language, enriched or at least complexed in this play by allusion, symbol and a kind of chiaroscuro of systematic allegory.

To return now to the three points I outlined earlier—

1. An art of serious parody. Travesty may be the better word. Eliot's introduction to *Nightwood* called our attention to "a quality of horror

---

* The terms "human sufferer" and "secret cause" belong, of course, to James Joyce, and come from the place in the *Portrait of the Artist* at which Stephen glosses Aristotle's remark in the *Poetics* about pity and terror.

and doom very nearly related to that of Elizabethan tragedy"; here we have rather Jacobean qualities, free, excessive, and often grotesque in style, ever full of random brilliancies, morbid and mordant:

> It's true the webbed commune
> Trawls up a wrack one term was absolute;
> Yet corruption in its deft deploy
> Unbolts the caution, and the vesper mole
> Trots down the wintry pavement of the prophet's head.

When it is good it is splendid; when it is bad it is absurd; but it is almost always fascinating. Considered only technically, it is a *tour de force* as brilliant as Nigel Dennis's parody of late Shakespeare in his novel *Cards of Identity;* but this is a great deal darker, and of more persistent intention. It is as though the author would deliberately assert the connexion of tragedy less with life than with a certain exalted and strained condition of language. It is parody not as Shelley's "Swellfoot the Tyrant" is parody, but the parody proceeding from desperation, as in Eliot's "Fragments of an Aristophanic Melodrama," or in the music ascribed to Adrian Leverkühn in Mann's *Dr. Faustus:* "all the methods and conventions of art today are *good for parody only.*" Style mocks at itself in the mirror, and the idea of the art-work itself, the exquisite and finished product endeared to a century of "well-made plays" which no one wants, is broken.

2. Breaking-up of surfaces; destruction of the conventional sequences and coherencies of "plot." *The Antiphon* is a play almost without a literal level to its action; allegory, moral and anagoge are made to emerge as by a kind of Cubist handling from the shattered reflexions of "story." I find this richness sometimes confusing (no more confusing, really, than I find *Hecuba* or *The Bacchae*), and am still mighty hesitant about such understanding as two readings have produced, but will risk a brief note of interpretation.

The doom on the house is allegorically the fall of civilisation—Let us speak of Beewick as our country," says Augusta—and the end of history: the pathos of Augusta and Miranda in Act III is as it were the lament of Eve looking back upon centuries.

Augusta's dead husband, Titus Higby Hobbs of Salem (Mass.), is seen as Jehovah, who created the world and repented of his creation and left his progeny to suffer its destruction; unless they can find security in the doll's house shown to Augusta at the epiphany by her son Jeremy, the disguised and ineffectual redeemer: this doll's house is called "Hobbs' Ark," and through its windows are revealed the mysteries of generation, which the mother, however, is unable to accept.

Morally, the play represents the soul seeking life and finding death, and finding death a mercy. Yet there is in this an obscurely redemptive movement, if it is not to be read as a further sarcasm: among the many symbolic properties which furnish Burley Great Hall are the two halves of a gryphon, "once a car in a roundabout." At the beginning of Act III the two halves have been brought together under a crown, and here Miranda lies sleeping. To Augusta, the gryphon seems to move: "We have a carriage!" she says, and the two women thus begin their elegiac journey through past ages. Now this gryphon, I suppose, refers us to the gryphon seen by Dante in the Earthly Paradise, where its double nature, eagle and lion, figures forth incarnation, duality resolved, divine and human nature made one. It is upon this car that Augusta and Miranda, who are also one, finally fall.

It may be that the parable here embodied is the anagogical bearing of the play: the failure of both the Old Law and the New. Or, since Augusta and Miranda are one, or interchangeable—"I am she, and she Miranda," "Miranda's all Augusta laid up in Miranda"—it may be that the paradigm is more complicated, telling how the old covenant under the Father was revoked by the new covenant with the Son, and how this in turn was revoked for modern times by the Puritan revolution (the house was a college of chantry priests, but has been in the family since the seventeenth century). "This history," says William Blake, "has been adopted by both parties"; but maybe the difficulty of interpretation here springs from the entrance of a third party, for it has been rare in literature for "this history" to be told us by a woman.

3. Treatment of language as an independent value. I mean by this that the extreme violence and dense compaction of the words is constantly taking us away from immediate action, away from narrative, away from the solidity of things ordered, and involving us instead in a dimension specifically poetic rather than dramatic, a complicated vast web of relation in which the threads are spun among dissolving objects, as if you were to have constellations without stars. This is how Shakespeare tends to work at moments of the greatest intensity; save that with Shakespeare you have always the feeling of being anchored to solidity in the action. Miss Barnes works this way all the time, and her handling of the style seems in consequence to be sometimes hysterically strained.

It may be mentioned here that the language employed about sex in the play is particularly bitter, grotesque, and affecting. When Shelley brought out *The Cenci* someone wrote in Blackwood's that it was composed "in the vulgar vocabulary of rottenness and reptilism," and our surviving nineteenth-century spirits may have similar things to say about this work (compared to which *The Cenci* reads very innocent), so I will record in anticipation my view that the kind of shock administered in Miss Barnes's language is entirely appropriate to her play.

How *The Antiphon* will do on the stage I don't feel qualified to say. The first act is exciting, especially as being our introduction to a language and rhetoric not often heard in our theater, but we form no judgment of it alone; all is expectation. The second act seems very long and sometimes turgid. But the third I found immensely moving. Altogether the work compels a deep attention; it rides over its faults heroically, speaking to us with a lonely and sometimes savage nobility. In a world full of angry young men writing their manifestoes in favor of decorum, it is heartening to hear again the old prophetic voice talking audacities.

James Dickey

James Dickey, *Drowning with Others.*

Coming to know an unfamiliar poetry is an odd and not so simple experience. Reviewing it—conducting one's education in public, as usual—helps, by concentrating the attention; perhaps, though it is a gloomy thought, we understand nothing, respond to nothing, until we are forced to return it actively in teaching or writing. It is so fatally easy to have opinions, and if we stop there we never reach the more problematic, hence more interesting, point of examining our sensations in the presence of the new object.

The following notes have to do with coming to know, with the parallel development of sympathy and knowledge. Undoubtedly they raise more questions than they can answer; and they may strike the reader not only as tentative but as fumbling and disorganized also, for the intention is to record not only what happened but something as well of how such things happen.

The situation of reviewing is a special case, narrower than merely reading, and nastier, certainly at first, where one's response is automatically that of a jealous cruelty. Hmm, one says, and again, Hmm. The meaning of that is: How dare anyone else have a vision! One picks out odds and ends, with the object of making remarks that will guarantee one is A Critic. Little hairs rise on the back of the neck. One is nothing if not critical. For instance:

> I spooned out light
> Upon a candle thread . . .

Triumphant sneer. Surely this is too ingenious by far? Has he no self-control?

But already I have suspicions of my behavior. I am afraid that a great deal of literary criticism amounts to saying that mobled queen is good, or bad.

Despite myself, I observe that I quite like Mr. Dickey's characteristic way of going: a line usually of three beats, the unaccented syllables not reckoned, or not very closely reckoned; it offers an order definite but not rigidly coercive, allowing an easy flexibility and variation. Although the line so measured will tend to the anapest often, it doesn't lollop along as that measure usually does, maybe because the poet is shrewd enough not to insist on it by riming:

> The beast in the water, in love
> With the palest and gentlest of children,
> Whom the years have turned deadly with knowledge . . .

All the same — give a little, take a little — an indulgence in riming makes hash of this procedure. Mr. Dickey once indulges, in (mostly) couplets:

> With the sun on their faces through sand
> And the polyps a-building the land . . .

And so on. Awful. Enough about that.

2

At a second stage, perhaps a trifle less superficial, I find myself thinking how very strange is the poetry of meditation musing on inwardness, where the images of the world are spells whose repetition designs to invoke — sometimes, alas, only in the poet — a state of extraordinary perceptions, of dreaming lucidities sometimes too relaxed. This poetry has not much to do with the clean-cut, muscular, metaphysical way of coming to conclusions; probably in English Wordsworth is the inventor of those landscapes most closely corresponding to certain withdrawn states of the mind, reveries, daydreams — the style that Keats, with a sarcasm in which there seems all the same a proper respect, calls the Wordsworthian, or Egotistical Sublime.

One of the qualities of such a poetry — or of Mr. Dickey's poetry, to come off the high horse — is a slight over-insistence on the mysteriousness of everything, especially itself:

> A *perfect, irrelevant* music
> In which we *profoundly* moved,
> I in the *innermost* shining

> Of my blazing, *invented* eyes,
> And he in the *total* of dark . . . .

This is the language of a willed mysticism, and it is hard to see any of the words I have italicized as performing a more than atmospheric function—the poet wants the experience to be like profound, perfect, innermost, &c., and incants accordingly.

Another quality, which I take to be related also to the tonal intention of a grave continuousness, is the often proceeding by participles, as though nothing in the world of the poem ever quite happened but just went on happening, e.g. (from the same poem):

> With my claws growing deep into wood
> And my sight going slowly out
> Inch by inch, as into a stone,
> Disclosing the rabbits running
> Beneath my bent, growing throne,
> And the foxes lighting their hair,
> And the serpent taking the shape
> Of the stream of life as it slept.

The objections of this stage have a perfectly reasonable air of being right: you describe a characteristic, and present evidence to show that this characteristic *is* in the poetry. Surely this is How To Do Literary Criticism? All the same, I am still suspicious, and even beginning to get annoyed, because by this time, in order to say what I have said, I have had to read many of the poems a number of times, and have realized that I care for some of them a good deal. In particular, "The Owl King," from which I have quoted the two passages, looks to me like a moving and thoroughly accomplished performance. Even more in particular, the two passages themselves, when read in their places, look appropriate to what is going forward. I have a residual feeling of being cantankerously right in my objection to the first passage quoted, but would incline to say now that the passage is a weak place in the poet's process, but not destructive of the poem.

3

There does come a further stage, where one begins to understand something of the poet's individuality and what it decrees for him in the way of necessities, his own way of putting together the bones and oceans of this world.

Mr. Dickey's materials have a noble simplicity, a constancy extending through many poems. Merely to catalogue them is no use; to pro-

ject in a single relation their somewhat delicate developments is perhaps impossible, but I shall have to make some more or less compromised try at it.

My impression of the process of his poetry is that it runs something
like this: water—stone—the life of animals—of children—of the
hunter, who is also the poet. It is rarely or never so simple as this, yet
the intention seems often enough this, a feeling one's way down the
chain of being, a becoming the voice which shall make dumb things
respond, sometimes to their hurt or deaths, a sensing of alien modes of
experience, mostly in darkness or in an unfamiliar light; reason accepting its animality; a poetry whose transcendences come of its
reconciliations. Salvation is this: apprehending the continuousness of
forms, the flowing of one energy through everything. There is one
other persistently dramatized relation, that of the child to his father;
and one that is more autobiographical, that of the poet to a brother who
died before he was born. And now to particularize this matter.

These are poems of darkness, darkness and a specialized light.
Practically everything in them happens at night, by moonlight, star-
light, firelight; or else in other conditions that will make ordinary day-
time perception impossible: underwater, in thick fog, in a dream—I
note especially a dream of being in a suit of armor—, inside a tent, in a
salt marsh where because of the height of the grass you "no longer
know where you are."

Another term for this situation is blindness: the blind child whose
totem, or other, is the owl king who cannot see by day but for whom,
at night, "the still wood glowed like a brain." In another poem the
owl's gaze "most slowly begins to create / Its sight from the death of
the sun." For this power of creation from within, and for being a
hunter, the owl is the magician-poet of an intellectual and "holy"
song; in "The Owl King" it is he who for the lost, blind child incar-
nates the mighty powers of sight, growth, belief, resulting in reconciliation and understanding:

> Far off, the owl king
> Sings like my father, growing
> In power. Father, I touch
> Your face. I have not seen
> My own, but it is yours.
> I come, I advance,
> I believe everything, I am here.

The power of poetry, which is to perceive all the facts of the world
as relation, belongs in these poems equally to both parties: to the

hunter and his victim; to the child and the father he is trying to become; to the father and the child he was, whom he has lost and is trying to find again. The paradoxical continuousness of all disparate forms one with another, in this generated world, is what Mr. Dickey's poems concentrate on representing, often by the traditional lore of the four elements, as in "Facing Africa," where the speaker and his son look out over the ocean from stone jetties (hence "the buttressed water"), where

> The harbor mouth opens
> Much as you might believe
> A human mouth would open
> To say that all things are a darkness.

Thence they look toward an Africa imagined to "bloom," to be "like a lamp" glowing with flashes "like glimpses of lightning," giving off through the darkness "a green and glowing light." In the crisis of the poem this serial relation of the elements is fused in the imagined perception of the other continent, the alien life:

> What life have we entered by this?
> Here, where our bodies are,
> With a green and gold light on his face,
> My staring child's hand is in mine,
> And in the stone
> Fear like a dancing of peoples.

Perhaps it is central to Mr. Dickey's vision that stone and water are one, the reflected form of one another.

Possible to continue for a long time describing these complex articulations of simple things. Very little use, though, to a reader who has not the poems to hand. Besides, it must be about time for someone to ask, "Well, is it great poetry or isn't it?" and someone else to ask, "What about objective, universal standards for judging poetry?"

About all that I shall say to the reader: If you believe you care for poetry you should read these poems with a deep attention. They may not work for you, probably they cannot work for you in just the way that they do for me, but I quite fail to see how you are going to find out by listening to me.

Probably the reviewer's job goes no further than that. Not to be thought of as malingering, though, I shall make a couple of other remarks.

I have attended to Mr. Dickey's poems, and they have brought me round from the normal resentment of any new experience, through a stage of high-literary snippishness with all its fiddle about "technique," to a condition of sympathetic interest and, largely, assent. There are some brilliant accomplishments here: among them, apart from the ones I have partly described, "Armor," "The Lifeguard," "The Summons." There are also some that sound dead, or (what is effectively the same thing) that I do not much respond to, including some that I don't understand. Where his poems fail for me, it is most often because he rises, reconciles, transcends, a touch too easily, so this his conclusions fail of being altogether decisive; that near irresistibly beautiful gesture, "I believe everything, I am here," may represent a species of resolution that comes to his aid more often than it should. Perhaps he is so much at home among the figures I sort out with such difficulty that he now and then assumes the effect is made when it isn't, quite.

There is this major virtue in Mr. Dickey's poetry, that it responds to attention; the trying to understand does actually produce harmonious resonances from the poems; it seems as though his voyage of exploration is actually going somewhere not yet filled with tourists: may he prosper on the way.

The Fascination of What's Difficult

Ben Belitt, *The Enemy Joy: New & Selected Poems.*

The author of this book is my friend; moreover, one of the new poems in it is dedicated to me. So much notice to the reader seems only fair. Yet I hope it will also be fair for me to put down some of my observations on Ben Belitt's poetry, escaping the charge of puffery simply by not puffing, only observing. My object is two-fold: first, to increase my own understanding and pleasure; second, to persuade the readers, by the way of demonstration rather than the way of exhortation, of the pleasure to be derived from the study of this poetry which is not only difficult but in other ways unfashionable as well.

A couple of things first about style, so far as this can be discussed in abstraction from its characteristic materials. Belitt receives the world more exclusively by the ear than most; he writes by a kind of radar, and a relevant sound, by the rules of his procedures, is assumed to be a relevant sense; as though the one response would naturally evoke the other. Sometimes the defect of this virtue makes him put his elements a little too close together, as when he writes "a temple's example." But more often it is this reliance on how things sound that makes possible his characteristic combination of great elaboration with great intensity, in such phrases as "the pit of a petal's serration," "the plough, on its side in the leavening cloud / And the dazzle of stubble," "the kingdom of nuance, the fiends of inhuman refinement." A menacing intensity, I was going to say, but I realize that by now he's got me doing it too.

These instances suggest another trait of the style. More than any other poet writing in English, more than Mr. Ransom or Miss Moore, Belitt plays that dangerous game of the *mot juste*, the specialized name kept for the one occasion, what he calls, in a phrase that may serve for definition and example at once, "the matched and extortionate word." This predilection for what is not only odd but also oddly right may have been nurtured in him by his many years' work at translation, that desperate double-entry bookkeeping where you get the word exactly matched at a price you hope isn't always extortionate, the momentary perfection at the risk of stopping the discourse while everyone says Ah!—

> The cinqfoil thicket laced with a pollen of poppies.

It goes with this that he very often writes poems in which the discourse is more radical than linear, in which the meaning of the poem is gained not from reading through it so much as from reading around in it, and from listening to recurrences and obsessive preoccupations in a series of poems. This kind of writing suggests something that may perhaps be true of all poetry, though less apparent in most, that the body of a poet's work supplies the attentive reader with a grammar and a lexicon which he must elicit in order to read beautifully. Trying to say this another way: a fine poem is not so much a thought as it is a mind; a much simplified model of the motions of the human mind, but all the same you have to talk with it awhile before it will say what it's about.

The attraction of a poetry somewhat deeply enciphered is, I think, that we get to know it rather as we might ideally get to know this world itself, not by moralizing instructions but by the repetition and variation of its forms; such a poetry may contain sermons no less than the plainer sort, but the sermons will be *in* the stones, and not whitewashed across their surfaces. That thought of stones, by the way, is piously appropriate to Belitt's subject matter; and the surfaces, of stone, of poem, are often to a first look unyielding of much in the way of meaning or general proposition, their effect is

> To humble the conjuror and mock the enchanter
> With the unreflective revelation of the obvious.

So when I read the first poem in this book, "The Hornet's House," one I haven't seen before, I am mostly just puzzled, though delighted moment by moment with striking surprises of the language, "a wafer of smashed candelabrum," "the Chaldean increases / Of stars in the hexagon, the bells of beneficent amber," and so on. Instead of trying at once to "solve" these difficulties, though, I read on, among poems I know and poems I don't, listening for the characteristic con-figuration of details that will compose its world, and whose varied repetitions will yield something of the meaning of that world.

It is, in the first place, a very hard world. Even those hornets are mating and making their house on the underside of a millstone, and hardness is the first fact of poem after poem: stone, bone, chitin, armor; blades of knife, sword, axe, adze; the working with hardness brings out a fierce constructive violence in the verbs, as all this "adamant" and "flint" sort of stuff is honed, splintered, blazoned. Even a lake is seen as "a burnish of water," and I suspect Belitt singles out pomegranates for special attention among fruits, not for the usual "poetic" reasons associated with romanticism and exotic tropical climes, but only because they contain granite.

The fit inhabitants of this hard world are insects: hornet, wasp, bee, turn up over and over, characterized by their stinging weapon, which may also be the constructive instrument of art ("needle," "burin") as well as having sexual meaning, and by their exoskeletal armor. In the guise of Adam naming the creation, the poet sees living things primarily as armored aggressions: "the horn of their jawbones shining," and "wing-cases breaking like clasp-knives."

But the evocation of a world of unliving obduracy, where only insects (and armored men) are at home, begets a concentration on the equal and opposite sign, of flower and fruit clutching the rock for their living: in a granite quarry he sees how "the maple sweetened the block at its root," how it was "Rigors of quartz" that "Darkened the sheaf and emptied the apple-crystal," so that "the taste of the granite followed the taste of the fruit." Confronting a mortal situation, the choice of attitude is "between sugar and granite," "and the death of a son needed granite."

The efforts of insects (or men) to endure on a stone world leads on to thoughts of architecture, and the relation may work both ways: "the bee in his ziggurat" of one poem answering in another to the Alhambra seen as "an ascending wasp's nest heaven." In this world the soft, defenseless organism must adapt the armor of the inorganic or imitate it organically; in Ucello's *Battaglia di San Romano* a warrior carries "a locust's weight of armor." And sexuality too is closely related with these thoughts of adamant security, wherein the additional distancing of art is possibly an added element: on a painted fan a shepherdess is "stilled in a spangled sierra; lace / on a whalebone pubis."

Trying to see and give some impression of the felt unity in this growing complexity of related relations is not easy, but it is fun to do. And it is fun to do only because the poetry itself beautifully responds to the effort, by reason of the musical, echoing, inter-allusive mode of its composition; wherever you touch it, some relevance appears, like answers to like, an imitation not quite exact enlarges the area of apprehended relations and one's sense of their fluent order.

I have not the power any more than the intention of exhausting the possibilities of the poet's language. But perhaps I should try to complete the present demonstration as far as I can in a little space, bringing my account to where the complex of clustered associations begins to point toward unity.

Returning to "The Hornet's House" with a little more perception of how it might constitute an emblem for the poet, who has put it at the head of his book, I read again of the insects' triumphant establishment of home and continuance on their unpromising millstone, and I come to the surprising last lines, where with the mating of the hornets the poem also

> arose like a hornet, in rabbinical blacks and siennas,
> On craters and crosses.

Taken by itself, this might be not merely hard to read but impossible to read. Put together with other evidences, though, it appears as consistently an element in the poet's reading of this life; his story of how, out of the desperate, unforgiving relation between a world of stone and the growing things that cling to it by imitating its armored ways, arises strangely the realm of articulate thought, painting, poetry, the art work considered as revelation, sacrament, and protective talisman, by its distance and its "stillness" itself a kind of armor against death and, possibly, love also. So in the Court of the Lions at the Alhambra the verse-forms of ancient poets are woven into the architectural design. In a richer example, Paolo Ucello's painting, drawn from the violence of battle, stills that violence and eternizes it in art, the painter's art first and now the poet's:

> I would fight that battle after the battle,
> Inward and naked, after the outward
> Packs like a weaver's spindle or poises like a picture
> Baroque with the ceremonious violence of the shuttle,
> The pencil, the burin, the matched and extortionate word. . . .

In the richest example of all, the lightning that once struck a house in Vermont, and that then evoked its correlative scene in the poet's childhood, leads at last to the art work seen as a sacrament:

As once in Toledo:
>   A Greek at a burial, coming nearer,
> struck at the shroud of Count Orgaz, found the eschatological greens
> in the rust of a cardinal's cape, the gold of the surplice's
> threads, rolled back the stone of his eyeballs
> in the place of the skulls, and shewed us the bread of our lives.

Struck. The same sexual and fatal word introduces the last stanza of the poem about the hornets. And I think to see how for this poet the idea of being "struck" focuses a complex of meanings indissolubly concerned with childhood, sexuality, death, and art, with the revelation of the forbidden and sacramental; that is "why" the poem arose like a hornet—because the sting in the hornet's tail, the lance of the warrior that "forces mortality's sweat drop," and the lightning that struck from heaven, are one.

Apart from its being necessarily incomplete, my demonstration is perhaps not very beautifully ordered. That may be not only on account of my incompetence, but also because the transaction between poetry and its reader may be not so much a "structural" matter, as people are fond of saying in the classroom, but rather more like an electrical figure, of accumulation and discharge, a process of which I have recorded what I could of the fleeting traces. Ideally, one could learn this poetry best with someone else who was reading it at the same time, and that is just what a review—if this is a review—cannot do. But I hope that my detailed and pedantic enthusiasm may incite some people to read Belitt's poems. Yeats, whose phrase gave me my title, spoke also about the need to set one's chisel to the hardest stone; readers, as well as writers, ought to consider it.

Everything, Preferably All at Once: Coming to Terms with Kenneth Burke

In one perhaps accidental symbolic act, Burke expressed his essence: he had some of his early books reissued by *Hermes* Publications. Hermes, originally a boundary stone, presently grew a face and a beard and went on to become the Roman god of boundaries, Terminus. Rising still further, he became Hermes Trismegistus, "the fabled author of a large number of works (called Hermetic books) most of which embody Neo-Platonic, Judaic, and Cabalistic ideas, as well as magical, astrological, and alchemical doctrines." In other words, everything, and preferably all at once.

The dictionary from which I drew this description of Burke in his aspect as Hermes identifies him with the Egyptian scribe Thoth, who above all "created by means of words," and "appears sometimes . . . as exercising this function on his own initiative, at other times as acting as the instrument of his creator." That is a doubt one may properly have about any scribe whose *oeuvre* is imposing enough to make one wonder whether he is representing the world or proposing to replace it; Milton, for instance, invoking his heavenly muse, claims to merit the instruction by reason of his "upright heart and pure"; and yet through the intended humility I have always heard a certain obstinacy in "upright," and thought of it as comparable with another Miltonic epithet, "erected." But the doubt may be peculiarly appropriate to Burke, who "above all creates by means of words" in the special sense that he creates words, terms, terminologies—the business of Hermes. And when you ask whether he does this on his own initiative or as the instrument of his creator, you get the somewhat cryptic though certainly comprehensive reply from his address to the Logos:

> For us
> Thy name a Great Synecdoche,
> Thy works a Grand Tautology.

Schopenhauer once called the world a vast dream dreamed by a single being, but in such a way that all the people in the dream are dreaming too. A lovely figure, and in its logological translation it might do for Burke's world as well: a vast dream dreamed by a single Word, but in such a way that all the words in the dream are dreaming too.

But I have just remembered that part of my title, "preferably all at once," is about Burke intensively: it comes from him. (Somewhat as when you make what seems a good pun you can never be certain it isn't waiting for you in *Finnegans Wake*.) There is a passage late in *A Rhetoric of Motives* that I had been meaning to cite somehow, as an instance of Burke's excessiveness about terms and of one's appreciation of his rightness if one would only think about it (as I. A. Richards said, a book is a machine for thinking with).

The passage is called "Rhetorical Names for God," and after some introductory talk a page-and-a-bit goes to a listing of terms you might use when appealing to the Deity. The range is indeed extensive, as is proper to the All in All, going from "ground of all possibility" around to "nothing" and taking in *en route* such things as real estate, money, sleep, excrement, and death. But now I especially note: "Center, circumference, apex, base (preferably all at once)."

By this example I mean only that when you speak of the writers you care most for, you not only speak about them—you also speak them.

Here is a sort of monkish metaphor for what Burke does: he illuminates texts. In its application to criticism the figure tells us one of the things we most expect from critics, that they should offer us particular enlightenment about particular works, showing us things we had not seen and that, once seen, compel us to acknowledge their truth and significance. In its more medieval aspect the figure suggests an independent activity integral to the other and, in Burke's criticism, identical with it: as in the illuminations of the *Book of Kells*, Burke is using the text while weaving up his own designs.

Most simply put, he can get more thoughts out of a book than anyone else can, evoking in his reader time after time a mixed attitude of
surprise, gratitude, and chagrin — "yes, of course, why couldn't I have
seen it for myself?" — while at the same time, in the same gestures,
often in the very same sentences, he is developing a method and a
terminology which the reader, if he will, can master for application
elsewhere.

For this reason, there is very little in Burke's writing of what Whitehead stigmatized as "inert knowledge." Everything is in movement,
in development; everything is always being used for all it's worth,
and sometimes maybe more.

There is an enthusiasm in all this that sometimes comes near
enough to madness: criticism as rhapsody, or *furor poeticus.* Nor do I
mean that in disparagement, though aware that some writers would;
for among the most appealing things about Burke, to my mind, is the
sense he has, the sense I get from reading him, that thought, if it is to
matter at all, must be both obsessive and obsessively thorough, that
thinking, if it is to salvage anything worth having from chaos, must
adventure into the midst of madness and build its city there. Also that
this action never really ends until the thinker does; everything is
always to be done again. Also this: that system begins in inspiration,
order in improvisation, method in heuristic. Here is one of Burke's
own and somewhat breathless descriptions:

> So we must keep trying anything and everything, improvising, borrowing
> from others, developing from others, dialectically using one text to comment
> upon another, schematizing; using the incentive to new wanderings, return-
> ing from these excursions to schematize again, being oversubtle where the
> straining seems to promise some further glimpse, and making amends by re-
> duction to very simple anecdotes.

That seems characteristic, even to "we must" — for Burke makes
many and difficult demands upon his readers — and even to "make
amends" — for he is as magnanimous as he is demanding.

Back in the days when such things mattered more to the literary community at large than perhaps they do just now, there was much debate
upon a question, raised I believe by T. S. Eliot, as to whether criticism
could be, or should be, "autotelic." Much debate, but relatively little
illumination, probably because that forbidding word "autotelic" implied the expected answer, that criticism had better humbly confine
itself to the ancillary task of digging nuggets of wisdom, or pure form,

or whatever, out of the superior materials provided by the poets and novelists, and not set up in business on its own. And indeed there was much local and practical justification for the expected answer, inasmuch as when criticism did its thing, usually under the formidable name of aesthetics, the results were often of a dullness far beyond the call of duty.

But all the same, the very fact that the question was raised indicated some anxiety about the expected answer; and the massive development of criticism as both an art and an industry around that time suggested the perhaps horrifying thought that if the critics went on as they were going there was some remote chance that some one among them might one day actually learn something about literature *in principle*, and not only about this work and that work in snips and snaps and *aperçus*.

Well, in Burke and some others (among whom I should name especially I. A. Richards and William Empson), I conceive that there began to appear ways in which criticism could be "autotelic" in such a style as not in the least to prevent its traditionally imputed function of praising and damning and qualifying the work of "creative" writers; and it appeared indeed that by its new independence criticism was able to perform its traditional function not merely better than before, producing "insights" at such a rate as for a few years almost made people believe in progress once again, but also at depths and over ranges not previously suspected to exist. Having begun with the usual critical attempt to winkle "meanings" out of literary works, Burke and the others (and a good few more than I have mentioned) were led on into quite new questions—at least for the tradition of criticism in English, and in modern times—about meaning in general, what it is and how it arises and in what ways it relates to language. In fact, the same question that had been asked about criticism now appeared about language: was it ancillary to meaning, instrumental to thoughts that somehow had an independent existence? Or was it autotelic, and capable of generating worlds, or the world, primarily by reason of its own internal arrangements, as the language of mathematics, or, more darkly, of music, seemed to suggest?

Kenneth Burke's researches in this area seem to me venturesome, enchanting, and productive. And I have sometimes thought of them as contributing to the development of a new species of epic poetry, a poetry containing its own criticism much as a dream sometimes contains its own interpretation more or less explicitly; this poetry might be that intellectual comedy which Valéry, himself an anticipator of it, said he would value more highly than either the divine or the human.

86 *Reflexions on Poetry & Poetics*

(The question whether such a poetry would have to come in verse seems entirely secondary; from the "creative" side one might cite *The Magic Mountain, Finnegans Wake,* and *Remembrance of Things Past* as works containing their own critique.) In what follows, rather than trying to describe Burke's "system" or "doctrine," which anyhow is always evolving out of and dissolving into method, I shall try a species of rhapsodic impressionism and imitation.

Putting first things first, in accordance with Burke's principle of "the temporizing of essence," the mind's first move upon the world is to assert something, to be active. The assertion will probably be suggested by the world, yet it will also have in it something both arbitrary and peremptory, and at least prospectively insane. This is what writers commonly call "having an idea," a phrase usually treated as ultimate and unquestionable, but which with Burke's help we may see a bit further into.

The essence of "having an idea" is "giving a name." Its effect is always to say to the phenomenon, "Be other than thou art." It is both prayerful and commanding, it both asks and asserts. It challenges, and upon the challenge it moves into a combat with "the world" which at its best it both wins and loses. Wins, in that a more or less large range of particular appearances is brought into patterned clarity, simultaneously articulated and integrated, by coming under the sway of the idea. Loses, in that the victory is only for a time, and more especially in that the idea of its own nature overextends itself and like a tragic hero perishes in its pride, in its triumph, in the *hubris* brought on by success. This happens from two considerations in particular: every One, in becoming many, attempts to become All and falls abroad into chaos, nothingness, the abyss. Or else: every idea, at the end of the line, loses all content and meaning other than itself; it reaches redundancy, tautology, pleonasm, and at last says, uninformatively enough: I am that I am. These two ways of losing may be regarded as the damned and redeemed forms of one single but unsayable thing.

These two ways, moreover, have to do with simple figurations that may stand for the base of all thought: the line and the circle. Nor is it accidental, I think, that line and circle, and the spiral compounded of their motion, make up our ways of thinking about time—bringing us again to the "temporizing of essence."

We do not ordinarily believe we make progress by going 'round in circles; and yet in a round world we may have no other course. Consider how it is precisely, though mysteriously, the circling of the heavens that creates time, whose even progress along a straight line is among the blandest of our metaphysical assumptions, though possibly surpassed in this respect by the one that claims we don't have meta-physics any more. Or a homelier example: almost any literary critic will affirm, if only as costing him nothing, the assertion that "Finally, what the poem means is what the poem says," a pure yet somehow heartening tautology in that he will as readily affirm from experience that our circular course from what the poem says at first to what it says at last, or as near last as we ever get, improves our knowledge in reckonable ways.

Perhaps both line and circle have damned and redeemed forms, or ways of being thought about. The circle, from antiquity a "perfect" and sacred figure, is complete, hence eternal, simple, and rounding upon itself: the mind of God, in a phrase I've heard attributed to half a dozen writers from Bonaventura to Pascal, is a circle whose center is everywhere and whose circumference is nowhere. Alternatively, the circle may stand for futility and unending repetition and the bore-dom of a bad eternity. In the same way, the line in its optimistic leap-ing forth suggests progress; but as the progress is from an unknown (or nonexistent) past to an unknown (or nonexistent or endless) future, it may likewise engender feelings of hopelessness.

Otherwise put: If a storyteller says to us, in effect, "This happened, and then that happened, and then something else happened . . ." we are bored; no matter how many things happen, we "keep waiting for something to happen." Whereas if a story were limited to the recital of its *idea*, there could be no story; for stories have to be one thing after another. So that a story *is* the compound of line and circle, as Burke indicates in a simple figure:

upon which he comments:

Any narrative form . . . in its necessary progression from one episode to the next is like the stages from A to I along the arc. But as regards the principle of internal consistency, *any* point along the arc is as though generated from center O. And the various steps from A to I can be considered as *radiating* from generative principle O, regardless of their *particular* position along the arc of the narrative sequence.*

What is said of stories holds also for philosophies, which arose out of stories and which retain, using terms for persons, the "dramatistic" cooperations and conflicts, mergers and divisions, of stories. It may hold true in a peculiarly poignant way of Burke's philosophy, a corpus of mythology relating how certain heroes or demigods, called by the family name of *terms,* incarnated themselves in the world of action where they overcame the old dragon of chaos, established order, gave laws, and so on, until at last defeated by the dragon's mother, once named by Burke as "material recalcitrance." But, happily, new generations of terms arose . . . and the story is always beginning just as it is always ending.

Burke's mind must be a fascinating but terrifying place to live in. So it would seem, anyhow, from the homeopathic experience of it in small doses that one gets from his books. Despite the order imposed by narrative, despite a grand friendliness of manner and a most beguiling disposition to admit mistakes, to begin again, to reveal not only the result of thought but much of its process as well, the chief thing I note about his mind is that it cannot stop exploding. In the early books the footnotes, like large dogs leashed to dwarfish masters, often marched along for pages under a few homeless-looking lines of text; in the later books this habit has been overcome by the expedient of relegating the footnotes into appendices (the dogs get bigger, but are kept in their own kennels); while after *A Grammar of Motives* and *A Rhetoric of Motives* (1945 and 1950 respectively) the completion of the proposed grand design has been deferred by a huge volume called *Language as Symbolic Action,* a smaller though still substantial one called *The Rhetoric of Religion,* and an unpublished though mimeographed *Poetics* of three hundred pages, not to mention numerous uncollected articles, unpublished notes, etc. (the dogs are beginning to wag their kennels?).

Once, when asked to make suggestions about a Burke essay in manuscript, I indicated a few places where it might be cut. Some weeks later a letter announced earnestly that after thoroughly considering my remarks he had rewritten the whole thing and cut it from sixty-five pages to seventy-six. And during the question period after a

---

* Kenneth Burke, "Dramatic Form—And: Tracking Down Implications," *Tulane Drama Review* (T 32), Vol. 10, No. 4 (Summer 1966), pages 59–60.

recent lecture in which he had been talking about the cycle of terms
and the generative power of any dialectical term to spawn a terminology, I heard Burke tell the class: "Any term will lead you to the
others. There's no place to start." Ah, I thought, that means there's no
place to stop, either. And I wondered: which half of Burke's mind will
win? The linear, progressive, orderly half that proposes to itself systematic philosophy and sequential argument from beginning to end?
or the radical, explosive half, the lyric and rhapsodic philosopher
whose entire effort is to make every poor part contain the glorious,
impossible whole, as in the Ptolemaic cosmology the Primum Mobile
goes racing 'round at enormous speeds only in order that every place
may catch up with every place and be at rest in the peace of the Em-
pyrean? For, certainly and a little remarkably, I still have scarcely any
idea of what the proposed third canticle, *A Symbolic of Motives*, may
contain, no matter what anticipations of it must inevitably have come
up in the story so far. Surely a place where any writer might beseech
Apollo for both peaks of Parnassus, where either one had served
before.

I mention this because it belongs to the figures of line and circle
which I seem to have got stuck with, and because it is at the heart of
that cooperative conflict between narrative and essence, image and
concept, myth and philosophy, that Burke calls "the temporizing of
essence."

Language, for Burke, not merely mirrors the world it seems to see,
but also generates it. This is the sticking point at which over and over
he divides from all philosophies proposing to base on scientific
models; and not only divides from, but undercuts and gets beyond,
seeing the human hope precisely in the rich polyvalence of terms, the
Shakespearean equivocations, which those philosophies propose to
exclude.

That language in any sense makes the world is a thought intolerable
to those who view the world, implicitly or otherwise, as a solid exist-
ent (like Descartes's *res extensa*) which the mind passively records as
a camera does in univocal concepts which it may then manipulate as a
computer does.

For Burke, language is literally making, constitutive, or *poetic* of
"reality." To the extent that its terms are not only positive ones, such
as "house," but dialectic ones, such as "good" or "high" or "sinful,"
capable of division into and merger with other terms, it is language
itself that makes the symbolic world. This is the distinctively human
world in which we struggle along on the guidance of phantasy, the
world of human action as over against the world of sheerly physical

motion described by physics according to models that positivist philosophers constantly claim to emulate by various "reductionist" schemes according to which human motives are viewed as mechanisms, and according to which "God," "soul," and "spirit" are progressively read out of the act until at last, by a miracle comparable with the stomach's digesting itself and emitting a satisfied belch, "mind" too is read out of the act by the very mind that claims to be doing the reading.

Yet there is an important way in which Burke, while at odds with "scientistic" philosophers if not with science itself, is adventured on somewhat the same quest as that of physics: he would bring the world of human action, as it would the world of physical motion, under the dominion of few, simple, and elegant laws. It is tempting to wonder what would happen if his discoveries in this line educed the kind of cooperation among the learned that routinely goes on in physics; but they do not. And besides, this kind of thought may be peculiarly related to its thinker; as I have heard it observed of another original and self-made philosopher, Rudolf Steiner, that he was everywhere and his disciples nowhere.

The sense in which the internal resources of language themselves generate views of the world formed the subject of *A Grammar of Motives;* whereas *A Rhetoric of Motives* studied the ways in which these same resources might be wilfully manipulated for conflicting purposes. Between the two there was already noticeable a considerable area of overlap, which will perhaps extend also to *A Symbolic of Motives* in its presumable "transcendence" of the area of competitive identifications—the marketplace, the human barnyard, as Burke says—by considering the forms and methods of literature as "timeless" patterns.

So we have a triad, and the progression through it, something like Inferno-Purgatorio-Paradiso, and something like the equally celebrated id-ego-superego. Something like, at least, in the important respect that the outer terms are represented as eternal fixities while the middle one is the scene of conflict, development, and playing-out in time and history of the patterns beneath and above. As if, to adapt one of Burke's analogies, the grammar is a chord which the rhetoric breaks into linear form as an arpeggio, while the symbolic, the chord again and newly understood in relation to its constituent notes, will be but a moment in time, the ear of corn reaped in silence before the initiates at Eleusis, whose trials had brought them to that wordless understanding upon which even Plato and Aristotle agree.

That seems a good place to stop, a high note to sustain so that we know this particular aria is over. Of the much more that might be said, I will bring us down to the ground by only one further reflection.

It was during the normal confusions of sophomore year that a friend gave me a copy of *Attitudes toward History*—"two mouse-grey volumes," he said, "containing all knowledge." And I could see what he meant. The two things in especial that Burke said to a young man of eighteen were "Everything is interesting" and "Everything is a language." The sense in which those two things are one might well take thirty years or more to put together, but I'll try to put my results into a small anecdote and an emblem.

Most of one's education in those days was not only liberal education but self-education, and permissive extremely. The Great Books were the ones we thought our teachers had never read; at least, they were never mentioned in lectures. Still, I once confided in an admired professor that I'd been reading Kenneth Burke. "Ah," he said, and there came upon his face an expression of solemnity which ever since I've identified with Harvard Square—when you meet it elsewhere it's derivative—as he said: "Brilliant; brilliant, yes. But hardly solid."

I have sometimes unworthily thought—for that professor was admirable at teaching—that some people found solidity so universal a value they even wanted it between the ears. But thirty years later I found my emblem in an invention that was new when the world—the symbolic real one, of course—was new:

Rounding upon itself, it became a perfect sphere when closed. It was made mostly of nothing, its critics pointed out that it was full of holes; besides, they said, it obviously leaks. Philosophers added that it was vain to suppose you could encompass the Void with bits of string, and as a final blow they said it was a tautology.

All the same, it caught fish.

Conrad Aiken

Conrad Aiken, *Ushant.*

Ushant is a strange, deep, mysterious book. It is written in prose, but the kind to which it belongs is epic poetry, poetry according to that tersest of adequate definitions given by Valéry: It is what it says. It illuminates, as in turn it is illuminated by, the succession of Conrad Aiken's poems, novels and stories. And it puts the world together in more ways than I will be able to describe, though I will have a try; first, though, a few general observations.

If one had to elect a single motif that more than any other characterizes the modern thing, it would be this: art becoming conscious of itself, and with that, though often heroically, doubtful of itself. The change marked in the present work is from "the autobiographical novel" to autobiography given the distance and formal properties of fiction. Instead of *ars celare artem,* what Aiken seeks, along with other modern masters, is the art to see through art — if possible without destroying it, but if not possible, well, that too was included in the bargain from the start. A peculiarly fruitful theme in the present century, though one sees it beginning, in however tentative and reticent a way, with *The Prelude.*

Ushant is the autobiography of a writer, but its convention is not the usual one putting foremost and in the order of their occurrence the childhood, the education, the influences, the books written and read, the literary acquaintances, the career, prizes, honors. . . . Its convention, rather, is fictive and poetic, belonging to memory (for which all the accessible past is equidistant), subjected less to the Chaldean conveniences of calendar and clock than to the perpetually weaving and raveling web of associations, so apparently arbitrary at the start, yet in retrospect so inevitably productive of destiny in the life and of law in the matter of composition, architecture, style. The method is reflective, and also reflexive: the book comes to be about itself.

For Aiken in his poetry as well as here in his autobiographical essay, the question of method concerns not so much what one knows as how one came to know it; and this has a transforming effect on the knowledge itself. The distinction was given form by Coleridge: The ideas one thinks of are of altogether less importance than the ideas one thinks with. Aiken's book is, or should become, one of the ideas we think with; and its premise is a humbling of the self and a charity of the imagination before experience; for once the author chooses to abandon the framework of chronological sequence that will suffice for the entry in *Who's Who,* he has to begin, and we have to begin with him, in chaos itself, listening for the resonances that alone will establish pattern and the prospect, however far off, of meaning.

The traditional image for chaos is the sea, and for life a sea voyage. *Ushant* begins aboard ship in the Atlantic: a man lies in his berth, remembering, reflecting, dreaming. . . . And in fact, however far his meditation ranges in time and place, its literal scene is always this one sea voyage, which gradually, by the introduction of details more or less randomly and cryptically disposed, gets a local habitation and a name: the narrator, D.,—perhaps Demarest the protagonist of *Blue Voyage,* a novel by Conrad Aiken here disguised with a deliberate thinness as *Purple Passage*—is going to England, there to join his third wife; the time is 1945, just after the end of the European part of the War; the ship, *The Grey Empress,* has until recently been used as a troopship, and its teakwood deckrails are "scrolled, chased, hieroglyphically carved and filigreed with the innumerable initials of heroes. . . ." The voyage, beyond its literal sense, has resonances of myth and destiny: "For that which goes forth, comes back changed or dead."

So the voyage forms one thematic center for the book, as for the life (how many of Aiken's works are about it!)—or else it is one possible place the reader may begin with, but by no means the only one, for several other motifs have equally great powers of symbolic radiation and reach: the house, the dreams, bells, writing, translating, the name Ushant, and so on. But one of the fascinations to reading this book is in following out the expansions of one of these epicenters until it reaches the others. And at the center of them all? Well, maybe one never does reach that silent place. But the web around it is spun somewhat as follows.

The present voyage flows into and elides with other voyages, the war just past with the earlier war, with the lives changed and broken

by "the giant footstep of interference." The "continuum of shimmer"
spread by the narrator's reverie begins to be punctuated by events in
the external world: by the conversation of his present shipmates, by
memories of places and memories of people, some of whom are remembered as giving magnificent set speeches, like arias, about D.,
his life, conduct, probable future; as terse and telling, these, as the
speeches in Tacitus, and as severe with their subject as he with his,
for D.'s view of his own life is not a complacent one. And in the course
of all this there emerges, guaranteed and given its truth by a hundred
detailed remembrances I haven't space to illustrate, the early identification of ship with house, especially though not only the childhood
house in Savannah. And from this central constant of identity between
house and ship there begins to exfoliate a marvelous world of perception and pattern, individuation and inheritance, wherein the tragic
drama and the funny story, the minute impression and the whole
development of a human life between eros and art, unfold themselves
lucidly and in seeming simultaneity. From the house, for instance,
we are led through one of D.'s many projects, that of interpreting himself in terms of rooms, streets, houses, of "that amazing house that
was oneself"—leading, in turn, to the poetry, one of whose earliest
heroes, Senlin, had said as far back as 1918, "I am a room, a house, a
street, a town."

The pattern is one of place, a kind of cross formed North and South
by New England and Savannah, East and West by England, or Ariel's
Island, and America, "the shadow of the Old Country falling with a
disturbing and revealing suggestiveness on the simple planes of the
new." But the pattern is in time as well, and might again be thought
of in the form of a cross: longitudinally, we have the child D. on the
floor in a room in the house in Savannah reading a couple of sayings
in a book, the memory of which was to send, years later, the young
man D. to England and make him into a writer; and then the same D.
in middle age, a writer who is doing the reflecting on this series of
which he is the latest manifestation; while laterally we have to consider the relationship between this D. and Conrad Aiken. He must be
Aiken, for the events of his life—and there is no attempt to conceal
this—are those of Aiken's life, though the names have been changed
to protect the guilty; at the same time, he cannot be Aiken, because
Aiken is sitting somewhere else, outside D. and outside the book
Ushant, writing both him and it. Writing, too, of D.'s artistic and
erotic lives, and of how these did or did not develop, or transform
themselves, into certain fictions whose titles—*Purple Passage*, for
instance—relate to certain fictions by Conrad Aiken—*Blue Voyage*,
for instance—in which someone rather like D. is a character.

But there is more to the weaving than that. For the voyage is also a dream, or two dreams, and both of them are about writing, both of them also reflexive. One is about four people doing into English a novella in which they also, as it happens, are characters, and in which one of them—or perhaps all four? the dream wavers about this—is moving toward some nameless disaster in the little town to which they are traveling without quite ever getting there. The other, first dreamed during a voyage many years before this one, and in the waking life taken up, annotated, discussed with friends, and often laid aside, is about a literary project called *Ushant, or Reading a Book*, which by magical transformations and translations becomes *Ushant*, the book we are reading now.

The title, in addition to meaning "You shan't" as an epitome for those commandments another writer called "ten heavenly don'ts," is the English for the Île d'Ouessant off the Brittany coast. It stands as a kind of dream emblem, promising and threatening, for D.'s approach to Ariel's Island, but its resonances make a further appeal than this, as it stands for the place of the dead, hence for the autobiographical adventure itself in which D. returns to the past to make his peace with the ancestors and become reconciled with the only true inheritance from them, himself, his genetic and cultural variation on their theme, their communication to the future:

And Ushant—there was *that* element, and in its way the most important, to be got in, too: that name had dominated the germinal dream, and therefore the theme of the imagined book; for, like that timelessly unfalling wave, in the shadow of which the four people seemed to be waiting, so the vaster shadow of Ushant, the Île d'Ouessant, and its rocks and reefs and shoals, toward which the ship bore the voyager and his dream, overhung, with promise of landfall or menace of shipwreck, both voyager and ship. *Enez Eussa:* so the Bretons called it: to the ancients . . . it had been known as the end of the world, and as the last resting-place of the souls of the departed—on their way whither? On their way to the West?—*"Qui voit Ouessant, voit son sang;"* and again and again that had been true. . . .

So the autobiography, mediated to us as by a series of receding planes, emerges from hints and foreshadowings, turns and returns, in lucid order after all, improbable as such a result might have seemed at the beginning—but somewhat as we might come to know a complicated terrain by circling over it many times at various heights, until contour and detail found their most perspicuous relation, until picture and map phased into each other and became one thing.

Ushant helps us to see to what a great extent Aiken's entire work has been about the agon between rebellion and piety, the search for

reconciliation in understanding—but always and only such understanding as is possible for *human* beings; the kind of humane reverence Montaigne had for Socrates, Aiken has too, and adds Freud as a
second exemplar; while it is without animus, but only with regret, that
he views his friend Eliot's conversion:

That the achievement was unique and astounding, and attended, too, by
rainbows of creative splendor, there could be no doubt. Indeed it was in the
nature of a miracle, a transformation. But was it not to have been, also, a
surrender, and perhaps the saddest known to D. in his life?

In D.'s own life, too, the progression is through the father and the
mother and the tragic agony of their suicide, to the grandfather with
his serene acceptance whose emblems are the ship subduing to her
purpose "the confused power of ocean, the diffused power of wind, /
translating them swiftly to beauty," and the dream of a worship
"purified of myth and of dogma," the grandfather whose communion
service with the child D. takes the form of an elfin tea party where the
cups and saucers are made out of acorns. (These illustrations are
drawn from the marvelous poem "Halloween," late in the second edition of the *Collected Poems*, 1970; though the last of them appears
also in *Ushant*.)

What Aiken has written is autobiography blessedly not of the self-
congratulating kind, but full of confession, repentance, rueful humor,
the learning on one's front teeth the truth of "the only religion . . .
any longer tenable," Know Thyself: "Freud had merely picked up the
magic words where Socrates, prototype of highest man, had let them
fall." *Ushant* is the artistic reflexion of a life truly and fully and with
difficulty lived, of a mind and conscience examined. Even its working
out at 365 pages has a mythological appropriateness in this writer
whose pious awareness of the cosmos is present even in domestic
and daily doings; the Great Circle which he chose as the title of one
of his novels being not only the path followed by Atlantic liners but
also the circle of the year.

One more thing, a somewhat surprising result of reading *Ushant*
again. For several days since, I've found that most any narrative I've
picked up, by anyone at all, began to get itself woven into the fabric
and symbolism of this one—an unexpected result of the echoing,
musical method of composition, whereby Aiken may yet become the
hidden author of a large part of our literature. All authors try to write
the world, but only a very few succeed in teaching us how to read it.

Randall Jarrell
(A Myth about Poetry)

Randall Jarrell, *The Complete Poems.*

Language is a great magic. The young poet turns it on and it begins to tell him wonderful things, so many wonderful things he can scarcely believe, at times, that this instrument that the mouth of man has been playing the tunes of for hundreds of years and for thousands of years should yet have reserved to himself so many fresh inventions, marvelous cadences, new sayings of oldest thoughts; and all done by sending out on the indefinitely accommodating carrier wave of the sentence the huge and fathomless words of power: night, cold, sky, life, love, water, bread, grief, fire, death. . . . It is the world over again, the world made new. His favorite poet has said it: *"Im dunkeln Dichter wieder-holt sich still | ein jedes Ding: ein Stern, ein Haus, ein Wald."*

A star, a house, a wood, that's how it goes, simple and miraculous. And to be a poet, a *dark* poet, in whom as in his favorite poet's favorite figure of pool or lake the world reflects itself again, how fine that is!

The poet works, of course he works; he scribbles and revises and thinks: There! that's a bit better. But it is not so much like work as it is like watching; he has to be there to watch — that is the condition of its doing itself under his hand, under his eye; but he has no doubt that it does itself. He is only the sorcerer's apprentice, who has turned on the broomstick; a fateful comparison, which we should prefer not to have made, did it not force itself upon us. For great magic is always dangerous to the magicker.

The language that tells the poet wonderful things is in this way an embarrassment and then a danger, that it won't stop telling him wonderful things. More than that, as the wonderful things accumulate they also tend to integrate and form coherencies willy-nilly; they bind up into a story that the poet is not only telling but also being told; they may even insist, finally, on telling him the truth, which is no less true and no less perilous for being true not of some merely objective world but of that peculiar universal, the world with himself in it, or, as literary people like to say, *his* world.

That is something he need not consider at first, for at first what he hears is not *a* story, it is many stories, each one different from the others, and they well up in all their rich particularity and selfness as from a source that ever supplies itself again. Only after many years, maybe, does the outline of the poet's own and unique story begin to emerge among the multitude of stories he has told; a very mysterious course of development, in which his preoccupations, or even his obsessions, go out into the world and shape it slowly in their own image, until by an unreckonable reversal that world returns upon him to flood his consciousness with his own obsessions. It is perhaps this that makes poets, as they grow old, fall silent or else repeat themselves: having made their reality, they have to lie in it.

Something else happens, too. The world goes on, and the poet's life outside the poems goes on, in the inextricably double and mutually concealing motion of its history and his biography, so that change in the one and change in the other, recognition and reversal, increase of anguish in the world and increased consciousness of anguish in the self, can never be quite distinguished one from the other, much less kept separate. And the marvelous sayings that language has said? Language goes on saying them, with an undiminished energy in which there is something impersonal, overpowering, indifferent. Moreover, without the poet's being able to do anything to stop them, the sayings begin to appear as true in application to the world outside the poems that earlier had encompassed them and kept them in their fictive world, the only world in which such sayings may be safely said. The poet had always wanted to reach reality, hadn't he? His elders had always said reality was the object. And there he is at last. His story phases with the world and becomes the world; with its great power of patterning and formulating and recasting every material in its own image, it cannot do otherwise.

In some such way do poets come into the desolation of reality, or wither into truth. There are many expressions for this condition; many modern artists rather rashly seek it out, optimistically calling it "the breakthrough." Fashionable people a few years ago called it "The Existential Level," unconsciously and not wrongly suggesting it was more like falling through than breaking through. Blake thought of it as a dumb Despair always existing beneath "the rough basement" of language. A semanticist called it "the objective unspeakable level," and our poet, in that novel of his where the characters' clichés are wittier than most writers' epigrams, named it "definition by ostentation." How do you do it? "You simply point." And he seems to define it, a few lines later, as the condition in which one sees the world as "one of those stupid riddles whose only point is that they have no point."

That is one side of it, of which Wordsworth said: "We poets in our youth begin in gladness, / But thereof come in the end despondency and madness." And Eliot said:

> That is the way things happen.
> Everything is true in a different sense,
> A sense that would have seemed meaningless before. . . .
>
> And in the end
> That is the completion which at the beginning
> Would have seemed the ruin.

And the other side? The other side is, I think, more personally the poet's own, and to it belong the wit, the charm, the gaiety, the energy, and the courage that for many years and many poems sustain the life, sustain the work, above the gulf—demonic, divine, or void— where all things lose their names.

The foregoing is a myth about poets and poetry. I do not know whether it is true, or whether it is applicable. It came to mind from reading Randall Jarrell's *Complete Poems,* and from reading over also much else that he wrote, and from reading much that was written of him by friends, colleagues, acquaintances, and by his wife in the collection bearing his name edited by Robert Lowell, Peter Taylor, and Robert Penn Warren (1967).

A myth is not a review. Randall Jarrell and I reviewed one another amply during his life—perhaps as many as three times each; we said, both of us, some harsh things, some funny things, some kindly things, and altogether were nothing if not critical. I should feel sorry to write, from ignoble security, literary criticism that is unable to evoke, indeed provoke, his answering voice.

III

Two Ways of the Imagination:
Blake & Wordsworth

I

The poetry I wish to talk about may be considered as meditation upon analogy by means of analogy, or as perceptions regarded from the point of view of what they tell us about the nature of perception, or as the making of equations between the inside of things and the outside of things. These are hard sayings, and worse are to follow. Here, for instance, are some sentences of the largest obtainable generality. You need not quite believe them, only entertain them speculatively for a time; and grains of salt will be handed out by the ushers. Anyhow, as Augustine said, "These things are true in a way because they are false in a way."

1. The subject of poetry is the relation of soul and body, mind and world.

2. The poetry in English during the whole of the "modern" period — since Shakespeare — has had increasingly to define itself in relation to the conventional worldly view of this relation, the view named by Alfred North Whitehead as "scientific materialism": "the fixed scientific cosmology which presupposes the ultimate fact of an irreducible brute matter, or material, spread throughout space in a flux of configurations. In itself such a material is senseless, valueless, purposeless." [1]

3. The so-called alienation of poetry from society is a function of this self-definition, and so, too, is an observable tendency for poetry to become the subject of itself.

[1] Alfred North Whitehead, *Science and the Modern World* (New York: The Macmillan Company, 1925), p. 25.

These are simplicities, and that is what makes them difficult. An appropriate gloss upon the problem they present might be the following passage from Whitehead; he is writing of the same period, roughly from the beginning of the seventeenth century:

The enormous success of the scientific abstractions, yielding on the one hand *matter* with its *simple location* in space and time, on the other hand *mind,* perceiving, suffering, reasoning, but not interfering, has foisted onto philosophy the task of accepting them as the most concrete rendering of fact.

Thereby, modern philosophy has been ruined. It has oscillated in a complex manner between three extremes. There are the dualists, who accept matter and mind as on an equal basis, and the two varieties of monists, those who put mind inside matter, and those who put matter inside mind.[2]

It is the charm of that last statement, that it gives to the amateur at thought a master's assurance that his problem is simple even while it is also impossible.

I am not to attempt a history of this development as it reveals itself in poetry, but hope rather to elucidate my sentences by means of a comparison between two poets, Blake and Wordsworth, whose major writings offer evidence that a problem exists in the mind's relation with the world, and who represent two approaches to its resolution. First, however, I should like to consider very briefly something about the simplicities of Shakespeare, for whom all this, though a mystery, seems not to have been a problem at all.

Shakespeare's tragedies seem to work on the belief, deep enough to require no justification, that there exist several distinct realms of being, which for all their apparent distinctness respond immediately and decisively to one another. There is the realm of the soul, the mind, the secret wish, or dream, or thought. There is the realm of human community, in itself a complex of several related relations: the lovers, the brothers, the body politic, the nation which is at the same time the family. There is the realm of sublunary nature, ranging, say, from the primrose to the storm at sea. There is the realm of the ancestral dead, shaken from their sleep and appearing ambiguously as portents or symptoms of great mischief. There is the realm of the astronomical and astrological heavens, and there is the realm of supernatural solicitings, which in themselves "cannot be ill, cannot be good." And there is the realm of the gods, or of god.

All these mutually reflect one another. You cannot disturb the balance of one mind, or of one king's court, without the seismic registration of that disturbance in the near and remotest regions of the cosmos:

[2] *Ibid.,* pp. 81–82.

an error of judgment will strike flat the thick rotundity of the world; a wicked thought will tumble together the treasure of nature's germens even till destruction sicken. The result is a world of dreadful splendors, but every piece of it is rhythmically articulated with every piece; and the realms which have priority in initiating the great releases of energy are ambiguously psychological and supernatural at once, but unequivocally the realms of spirit, will, mind. All life, and all the scene of life, the not-living around and beneath and above, poise in a trembling balance which is complete, self-moving, extensive in detail through the four elements, from "Let Rome in Tiber melt" and "kingdoms are clay" to "I am fire and air" and "O eastern star!" This, then, is the sublime and terrible treasure which afterwards was lost. Our theme is the attempt of the poets to find it again, and of two poets in particular.

William Blake (1757–1827) and William Wordsworth (1770–1850) are poetically about as unlike one another as they could be. But what makes the unlikeness significant and the comparison possibly illuminating is the fact that it arises out of numerous and rather particular resemblances between them.

Although they are by thirteen years not of an age, the substantial overlap includes for both men the period of their greatest and most significant production. This was the period of the French Revolution and of Napoleon, time of radical hopes, radical despairs, amounting to a dramatically sudden overthrow of ancient ways of looking at the world, and the overthrow, as dramatic and sudden, of the new way which was to have replaced these. Both poets approached the French Revolution as radicals, to a certain extent even as "subversives," "English Jacobins," strongly opposed to the English war with France. For both poets the events of the period had disastrous repercussions on the personal life—for Wordsworth, his immediate experience of revolution and the Terror, and his liaison with Annette Vallon; for Blake, his trial on a false and malicious charge of sedition—and for both the Revolution became the subject of a poetic analysis which made of the political and social events a myth about human motive. Both, in their very different ways, began poetical revolutions against the canons of the eighteenth century, and these revolutions, however they may seem to have begun with technical questions such as the reform of diction, involved their authors in a deeper examination of the premises of perception, the question of the relation between thoughts and things. Out of their poetical inquiries came radically different though related assertions concerning world and mind, or soul.

For both Blake and Wordsworth, poetry has a crucial connection with childhood, and this connection too, however differently they handled it, is revolutionary, a new and independent discovery made by each alone. (Some hints may have been got from Vaughan, but Traherne's work, lost after his death, was not recovered and published till much later.) And both poets, after achieving reckonable success with brief lyrics, turned to the largest possible form of epical and prophetical writings, with the double object of system and vision — oddly, as these two traits may appear to go together.

Finally, both Blake and Wordsworth wrote poems which were in a decisive way about writing poems. They attempted, that is, to imagine the imagination, Wordsworth in *The Prelude* especially, and Blake in many places, but especially in *Jerusalem*.

This seems to me a very strange and fascinating circumstance, because the concern of poetry with itself in this decisive way had really not happened before in English, where the self-reference, or reflexive character, of poems had been largely conventional and as it were by the way: assertions of immortality in and by means of verse, invocations to the Muse, or jokes — "I am two fools, I know, / For loving and for saying so / In whining poetry." [3]

So we may say that in writing works whose subject included and largely was the question of what it means to write works, these two poets introduced into poetry something substantively modern, that is, a doubt which led them to view their own vocations as problematic and subject to investigation. For neither does this mean any diminution of the claims of the imagination; rather the reverse. Imagination now becomes central to the universe and the most important thing to understand about the universe; but becomes this precisely because it has become problematic and doubtful. I should add that this characteristic of the imagination reveals itself no less in Blake's fierce intellectual anger, the appearance he gives of absolute intolerant certainty, than in Wordsworth's more hesitant and tentative balancings, his quieter confidence going over occasionally into a religiose smugness.

II

The Prelude, William Wordsworth's creation myth about himself, is in the first place an autobiographical work — it is, said the author, "a thing unprecedented in literary history that a man should talk so much about himself." His observation is in error, for we think at once

[3] We must make one grand exception for Alexander Pope, whose *Dunciad* ought ideally — given enough time — to be studied in connection with our theme.

of Pepys or Evelyn, but the error is a useful one, directing our attention to a striking trait of this autobiography, subtitled "The Growth of
a Poet's Mind," which is, that it does not at all consist of the daily
life, the record of events such as usually occupies journal or diary.
From the very beginning the biography is idealized, mythified, made
into fiction, and regarded from a lofty distance, whence it gains its
form. Gains, in fact, two forms, both of them perceptible: the intended
one, and the one that actually resulted.

The intended form of this early portrait of the artist is a pilgrimage,
or journey to salvation. It is a Comedy, in the sense that, although it
tells sometimes of lamentable things, it ends happily, with a grave and
dedicated happiness. It is also, as I have said, a myth. The stages of
the journey are the stages of initiation, wherein the hero, a child especially favored by a divinity, in this instance Nature the Great
Mother, enters the world in blessedness, falls into alienation through
knowledge, endures certain trials associated with terror, death, the
loss of identity, and is reborn "on a higher plane" in such a way as to
redeem his early promise and assert more fully the theme of his original divinity.

In this respect *The Prelude* resembles the story told by Dante, the
story told by Bunyan; it resembles those modern stories of Stephen
Dedalus, Paul Morel, Marcel, Adrian Leverkühn, wherein the young
artist, passing through worldiness and suffering, including especially
sexual suffering, achieves, or fails to achieve, wholeness, dedication,
strength. And the poem is reflexive, like Proust's novel, telling how it
came to be, and having for subject that life which prepared the way to
its composition.

So much for the form which appears as the intention. A man writes
a poem telling how he got to be a poet. Toward the end of this poem,
he announces that he is a poet, and offers the poem itself as interim
evidence of the fact, to suffice until he does something still greater,
or anyhow (as it turned out) still bigger.

But there is something else, amounting toward the end to a quite
different form for the poem. For surely many readers of this immense
and beautiful work find that somehow it fails of the planned completion, that the promised rebirth, confidently proclaimed to have happened, either did not happen at all, or not to the degree asserted, or
else went by us unremarked. Perhaps this has to do with the unwritten
but powerful law which forbids a man from describing his own success: even in speaking of one's own humility a tone of pride sneaks in,
even in ascribing the victory to God, Nature, or Reason, there may appear a flat noise of self-gratulation:

Long time in search of knowledge did I range
The field of human life, in heart and mind
Benighted; but, the dawn beginning now
To reappear, it was proved that not in vain
I had been taught to reverence a Power
That is the visible quality and shape
And image of right reason; that matures
Her processes by steadfast laws; gives birth
To no impatient or fallacious hopes,
No heat of passion or excessive zeal,
No vain conceits; provokes to no quick turns
Of self-applauding intellect; but trains
By meekness, and exalts by humble faith . . .

Yet in somewhat failing thus, if it does, the poem achieves a sort of
grandeur other than that intended: not quite a tragedy, perhaps, yet
not without elements of the tragic, it has a solemn pathos attendant
upon the spectacle of a human failure, which commands sympathy because we all must fail, but it has also a certain grim and moralizing
humor because of the poet's resolute refusal to allow for what may
have happened, or failed to happen. He goes on proclaiming praise to
the end, whereas we might see rather a sad parody of what is claimed
in the titles of Books XII and XIII: Imagination and Taste, How Im-
paired and Not Quite Restored.

A reason for this failure, less personal than the one already suggested, is built into the formal problem of a reflexive poem, a poem
about poetry. For poetry may be a subject like time, of which Augustine
said, "I understand what it is until I try to tell you." There may be a
necessary anticlimax in the poet's announcement that he has just now
achieved what we have seen him doing extremely well for a dozen
books and more. We may see from many modern examples that for a
poem to be about poetry is no guarantee of its being a good poem, if
only because a poet in doubts or difficulties about the meaning of
what he is doing is always liable to appeal to this apparently easy way
out and end with a vision of himself standing there with his mouth
open, in lines which are the equivalent of the fighter pilot's "There
I was at five thousand feet with no oil pressure."

To put this in another way, I read in the operating instructions for
a sewing machine, "The machine will sew its own thread in crossing
from one piece of material to another, but it is not advisable to let it
do this for long." O well, I thought, that's true of any Singer.

So Wordsworth's problem at the end of *The Prelude* is a vexing one,
and his solution for it is in the main assertion that the miracle has

happened, prayerful pleas for belief that it has happened, and expla-
nations of what it is that is said to have happened. There are, to be
sure, several visions—of the girl on the hill, of the Druids at Stone-
henge, the revelation from the top of Snowdon—yet these revelations
are curiously reluctant to reveal, they do not always reveal exactly
what they are announced as revealing, and the insistent work of assertion resumes once more.

Another reason for this failure is more difficult to present because
it demands knowledge not given in the poem—indeed, specifically
withheld by the poet. Without the researches of Emile Legouis and
George McLean Harper we should not be able to see that the brief
sketch of two lovers at the end of Book IX was Wordsworth's attempt
to deal with—or avoid dealing with—his love, his illegitimate daughter, his betrayal (whether or no he could have done otherwise) of
Annette Vallon, which amounted at the same time to a political conversion to a conservative point of view.

Poetically—which is to say, somewhat ruthlessly—this crisis might
have been divinely appointed for the crisis of this poem, for in it the
personal and the political become subject to one decision, a parallel
in the true Shakespearean style, hence the opportunity of a dramatic
rather than a hortatory ending. But the poet was somehow under the
necessity of avoiding it. We are not to judge of this necessity, nor to
tell that well-known story again, but rather to make some observations
about *The Prelude* which can now be made independently of the
story, even though the story is what started us thinking about the
poem in a new way.

A striking thing about Wordsworth's vision is that it contains almost
no natural evil. Such natural evil as it does contain tends to be majestic
and awesome and soothingly remote; all grandeur and no poison ivy.
Aldous Huxley put the point neatly in an essay called "Wordsworth in
the Tropics," saying that the Nature Wordsworth wrote about was
already humanized, civilized, not to say Anglicanized, and that a few
weeks in the equatorial rain forests might have cured the poet of "the
cozy sublimities of the Lake District." Of course, Huxley saw quite
well that the problem is not to be solved by a simple change of venue,
for it is a problem of imagination, or primary belief, without which no
"Nature" is thinkable. We may confirm this by noticing that Blake, at
about the same time and also from England's green and pleasant land,
was viewing Nature as "a devouring worm," as

> a wat'ry flame revolving every way,
> And as dark roots and stems, a Forest of afflictions, growing
> In seas of sorrow.

The difference is accountable to the fact that Blake reads Nature as illusion (Vala, the veil) resulting from the shrunken senses of the divided man; resulting, that is, from the Fall. But for Wordsworth Nature is herself divine, and the Fall a rather limited, almost parochial phenomenon having to do with his fastidious or even fearful reprehension of cities, human beings, love, and accordingly he approaches the crisis of his poem, the second journey to France, by seeing himself Miltonically as Adam

> yet in Paradise
> Though fallen from bliss, when in the East he saw
> Darkness ere day's midcourse, and morning light
> More orient in the western cloud, that drew
> O'er the blue firmament a radiant white,
> Descending slow with something heavenly fraught.

If I pursue the question a little further, asking what is the evil which is missing from the Wordsworthian Nature, I remember the definitions offered by the psychoanalyst Ella Freeman Sharpe, to the effect that, for the superego, good is whatever has nothing to do with sex, and evil is whatever has anything to do with sex. It is true, and rather remarkable, that *The Prelude*'s great meditation on how things come to be and on the sources of our being is just about entirely silent on the subject of carnal generation. Even in the lines about the two lovers, Wordsworth contrives to avoid the mention of sex and birth entirely by referring the reader to his poem about Vaudracour and Julia (originally composed for this place in *The Prelude*, but withdrawn) instead of telling their story.

Amateur psychoanalysis is not to the purpose, even though an autobiographical poem might be supposed to be self-revealing. But, continuing to speak only of the poem, the absence of any account of natural generation suggests another observation, on what might be thought of as the absolute segregation of the sexes in Wordsworth's view of life. It is a very slight exaggeration to say that Wordsworth, like some primitive people, does not know about the role played by the father in the getting of children. Certainly he never acknowledges it. The world of *The Prelude* is very largely the world of mother and child in the first place; and it is right, I think, to say that every male figure entering the poem is a solitary: the veteran met on the road at night, the Bedouin of the dream who is also Don Quixote, the Blind Beggar seen in London, the Shepherd (portrait of the poet's ideal type among men), the French officer modeled on his friend Beaupuy ("A patriot, thence rejected by the rest"), and finally, of course, more than the rest, Wordsworth himself. His mother receives an elegy of some fifty lines — beginning, I am afraid, "Behold the parent hen amid her brood!" — but his father is mentioned only once, to say that he died, and that certain related circumstances made the event appear "a chastisement."

It is perhaps not this avoidance alone which impairs the poem as an account of creative mind, but certain parallel avoidances implied in it and made necessary by it. The omission of fatherhood in the natural sense somewhat weakens and limits the account of a process which may be not so natural as to a thoughtless eye it may at first appear, the process of the imagination's dealing with the world, and this poet cannot say, as Shakespeare does, "My brain I'll prove the female to my soul, / My soul the father," or speak so energetically as Shakespeare does of "the quick forge and working-house of thought." His "wise passivity" seems sometimes a touch too passive, too receptive, and of his attempt to hold, as at his best he does, a monist and interpenetrating balance between the mind and nature, we might say, as I suspect Blake is saying in certain passages we shall soon consider — if you don't beat nature, nature will beat you; there is no middle ground.

How this works in *The Prelude* may be seen from the poet's unconscious use of that tradition of natural symbolism, the initiatory ascent from earth through water and air to fire, which all poets come into some relation with whether knowing or unknowing. Seen in one way, *The Prelude* is a series of mountain climbs, with visions at the top of each mountain, climaxed by the grand vision from Mount Snowdon; that is, each time he attains the Earthly Paradise, the most refined earthly element of air, traditionally feminine (Blake calls it the region of Beulah) and traditionally representing the achievement of a purified natural reason. Further than this, the point at which Dante takes leave of Virgil and flies beyond the sun and stars, Wordsworth does not go: the sun, the fire, the father, remain unknown to him; his poem belongs to earth, water, air, to Nature as protecting mother, it is written under the auspices of the powers of the air, and its highest moment of vision — universal mind, "a majestic intellect" imaged by clouds imitating the forms of earth and sea — takes place not in the fiery sun but by the light of the full moon.

One excerpt may serve to sum up the poet's approach to and withdrawal from the complex of feeling I have tried to outline. It comes in Book XII, just before the mention of his father's death, to which in scene-setting it is explicitly a parallel.

He remembers how as a child he strayed into a valley "where in former times / A murderer had been hung in iron chains." Though gibbet and bones were gone, there remained on the turf the murderer's name, carved in "monumental letters" annually cleared of grass "by superstition of the neighborhood." Fleeing in fear from this gloomy scene he climbed a hill and saw

> A naked pool that lay beneath the hills,
> The beacon on the summit, and, more near,
> A girl, who bore a pitcher on her head,
> And seemed with difficult steps to force her way
> Against the blowing wind.

It is for him an "ordinary sight," yet full of "visionary dreariness," and fascinating enough for him to speak again of

> moorland waste and naked pool,
> The beacon crowning the lone eminence,
> The female and her garments vexed and tossed
> By the strong wind,

and to remember that the same scene, when he was in love, appeared pleasurable.

This is his closest and clearest approach to the mystery of generation, composed in the sign of crime, punishment, and superstition, the murderer's name spoken as by the earth itself. He views the landscape exclusively in genital and sexual terms: hill and naked pool its natural symbols, beacon and pitcher its emblems in the realm of human artifice. The girl with the pitcher walking against the wind, her garments "vexed and tossed," glancingly allusive to legends of virgins impregnated by the wind—he sees that all this is somehow about love. But it puzzles him, and he retires on a somewhat general moral, which the passage itself only in very general terms will support, and delivers a sadly accurate prophecy of the future as a falling back, a return to the past:

> So feeling comes in aid
> Of feeling, and diversity of strength
> Attends us, if but once we have been strong.
> Oh! mystery of man, from what a depth
> Proceed thy honours. I am lost, but see
> In simple childhood something of the base
> On which thy greatness stands; but this I feel,
> That from thyself it comes, that thou must give,
> Else never canst receive. The days gone by

> Return upon me almost from the dawn
> Of life: the hiding places of man's power
> Open; I would approach them, but they close.
> I see by glimpses now; when age comes on,
> May scarcely see at all. . . .

Those hiding places of man's power are indeed associated with vision, though sometimes negatively and dreadfully, as in Edgar's saying to Edmund about their father, "The dark and vicious place where thee he got / Cost him his eyes." But for Wordsworth, what Nature generates, over and over again, is thought, and thought alone.

Much might be said in defense of the poet; for surely the times were out of joint, they always are. But after it is said there will remain something about this wonderful poem sad, guilty, and unachieved. There is a marvelous moment just about at the middle of *The Prelude*, when the poet sees something about the human condition, and sees it clearly. In a London street, "lost Amid the moving pageant," he sees a blind Beggar,

> who, with upright face,
> Stood, propped against a wall, upon his chest
> Wearing a written paper, to explain
> His story, whence he came, and who he was.
> Caught by the spectacle my mind turned round
> As with the might of waters; an apt type
> This label seemed of the utmost we can know,
> Both of ourselves and of the universe;
> And, on the shape of that unmoving man,
> His steadfast face and sightless eyes, I gazed,
> As if admonished from another world.

"My mind turned round as with the might of waters." Or, as Blake says, "in Time's ocean falling drown'd." For that written paper includes all the poems ever written or to be written. But from this dire vision of blindness Wordsworth retreats, as we all do every day, as only the very greatest now and then do not.

Wordsworth and Blake were not acquainted, though Wordsworth read some Blake poems in manuscript sent for his inspection by Henry Crabb Robinson, and was "interested" — as well he might be, writes Robinson, for there is an affinity between them "as there is between the regulated imagination of a wise poet and the incoherent outpourings of a dreamer."[4] Blake, on the other hand, thought

---

[4] George McLean Harper, *William Wordsworth, His Life, Works, and Influence*, II (New York: C. Scribner's Sons, 1916), p. 342.

Wordsworth the greatest poet of the age, but sometimes feared he
might be an Atheist. For Blake, as Robinson correctly reports, "Athe-
ism consists in worshipping the natural world, which same natural
world, properly speaking, is nothing real, but a mere illusion produced by Satan." Robinson also preserved for us Blake's marginal
annotations in a copy of Wordsworth's poems, and some of these may
exhibit strikingly the difference which is our subject.

For Wordsworth at his best the mind's relation with Nature is mu-
tual, a matter of the finest, most hypnotic transactions flowing between substance and sense, whereby the world becomes what Yeats
calls "a superhuman mirror-resembling dream." But for Blake the
point of art becomes increasingly as he goes on the rejection of nature altogether as a wicked enchantment. Of Wordsworth's famous
"natural piety" — epithet as celebrated in its time as "artifice of eternity" in ours — Blake writes in the most unequivocal manner: "There
is no such Thing as Natural Piety because the Natural Man is at En-
mity with God." Similarly, if Wordsworth regards Natural Objects as
strengthening the imagination, Blake's response has the sound of immediate violence: "Natural Objects always did and now do weaken,
deaden and obliterate imagination in Me. Wordsworth must know that
what he Writes Valuable is not to be found in Nature." And, later on,
"Imagination is the Divine Vision. . . . Imagination has nothing to do
with Memory." Wordsworth writes in *The Excursion* of how exquisitely the mind is fitted to the external world, and how exquisitely,
too, the external world is fitted to the mind; Blake writes in the mar-
gin: "You shall not bring me down to believe such fitting and fitted. I
know better and please your Lordship."

These too are hard sayings, and it should go with them that Blake
said, about a proposed meeting with Wordsworth: "You do me honour.
Mr. Wordsworth is a great man. Besides, he may convince me I am
wrong about him; I have been wrong before now."

Blake's views of Nature and the Imagination are not easy for us to
understand or give a full assent to. Yet it remains true at the very
least, as Professor Harper writes, that "the convictions, however
singular, of this rare spirit demand our entire respect, and are of value
to us in proportion as they conflict with all our ways of thinking."

Jerusalem is a huge poem, in many details extremely obscure, and
in any event scarcely compassable in only part of one essay. But it is
also a very reckonable poem, whose incoherencies are largely periph-
eral (I sometimes think that some of its incidental impossibilities,
such as huge compounds of geographical, historical, and mythical
names, are there *because* similar things happen in the Bible). As its
center the poem is coherent for all its strangeness, and our difficulties

with it might well be resistances masquerading as criticism. Blake is really writing prophecy, that is to say, a very ancient thought lost sight of by his contemporaries yet about to become, in part by his instrumentality, a very modern thought; no wonder if the expression of it was full of difficulty.

Jerusalem is a vision of the Fall of Man—of the giant Albion, who is like the primal man of light, the Adam Qadmon, of The Cabbalah— and its consequence in his enslavement to space, or Nature, and time, or History. The piece ends with the redemption of Albion by the fiery work of Los (Sol?), the poet, poetry being seen as the type of man's proper work; but the plot moves rather by repetition and development than in linear sequence, and might be thought of as having the form of a theme, variations, and finale. It views the events as *always happening;* one of the substantive claims of the poem is that the process described in it is psychological and metaphysical in a primary way, and historical only secondarily:

> All things acted on Earth are seen in the bright Sculptures of
> Los's Halls, & every Age renews its powers from these Works
> With every pathetic story possible to happen from Hate or
> Wayward Love; & every sorrow & distress is carved here,
> Every affinity of Parents, Marriages & Friendships are here
> In all their various combinations wrought with wondrous Art,
> All that can happen to Man in his pilgrimage of seventy years.

The key to this poem, its metaphorical or mythical or religious premise, is that the spiritual is primary and substantive, the material world its phantasied derivative. The failure to see this *is* the Fall, dividing man against himself and creating the world of Nature, that is, of sexual generation and death. For because imagination is primary, the universe is in the first place human, its truth a human truth. Imagination, Blake says, is Jesus Christ, meaning at the very least that imaginative sympathy is the power of forgiveness of sin.

What initiates Albion's fall we are not told at once; in the very beginning of the poem he is already the "perturb'd Man" who turns away down "valleys dark," and the overwhelming of the imagination is signified by a Flood:

> In all the dark Atlantic vale down from the hills of Surrey
> A black water accumulates.

In successive episodes this fall is related variously with Pride, Fear, & Lust, and held responsible for creating the body, the world, extension in time and space. But its primary form is the separation of the abstract reasoning power from the rest of man's faculties, and its attempt to create and impose on the creation the tyranny of an abstract, rational, and ultimately punitive world whose God is both invisible and merciless. This is the world of human institutions, religious, political, educational, and scientific equally, an insane, meaningless mechanism devoted to suffering, repression, and death:

> I turn my eyes to the Schools & Universities of Europe
> And there behold the Loom of Locke, whose Woof rages dire,
> Wash'd by the Water-wheels of Newton: black the cloth
> In heavy wreathes folds over every Nation: cruel Works
> Of many Wheels I view, wheel without wheel, with cogs tyrannic
> Moving by compulsion each other. . . .

These wheels are the cold wheels also of the astronomical heavens, with their inhuman order, and they relate to Whitehead's vision of the "irreducible brute matter," which "just does what it does do, following a fixed routine imposed by external relations which do not spring from the nature of its being."

The Fall of Albion creates the vegetative world of generation, suffering, and human sacrifice:

> Hertfordshire glows with fierce Vegetation; in the Forests
> The Oak frowns terrible, the Beech & Ash & Elm enroot
> Among the Spiritual fires; loud the Corn-fields thunder along,
> The Soldier's fife, the Harlot's shriek, the Virgin's dismal groan,
> The Parent's fear, the Brother's jealousy, the Sister's curse. . . .

It is strange to consider that such a phrase as "the Corn-fields thunder along" will be regarded as wild, meaningless excess by people who view the statement that "an army marches on its stomach" as the plainest sense.

Now this fall consists for Blake in the false perception of this world as another, as other than human: this false perception is what at every moment creates an unreckonably large part, perhaps all, of the world of sin, pain, and death, at least all death inflicted by human beings on human beings. Since, in the refrain of the poem, you become what you behold, the consequence of man's viewing the world as other, as over against, is that he imitates in his history and institutions this phantasy of a something other, an external something mighty and imposing and ultimately immortal because inhuman: the State, and the State Religion, deemed by Reason to be the right true and deserved consequence of an alienated Nature to be appeased by Moral Virtue, punishment, human sacrifice, according to the "demonstrations" of a materialist science. Art itself, under the domination of this phantasy, becomes Memory, the mere copying from nature, and it is this that Blake means when he says that Imagination has nothing to do with Memory. Mathematic form, machines, warfare are all seen as consequences of man's pursuing an ideal other than his own being. This tyranny, under which we all live, is regarded as feminine, not because Blake is a misogynist—"the lust of the goat is the bounty of God . . . the nakedness of woman is the work of God"—but because Nature considered as thing-in-itself, rather than as an Emanation of the divine-human, is traditionally thought of as a woman (Mother Nature, Mother Earth), and the bondage to this Nature is a sexual, generative, and mortal bondage:

> If Perceptive Organs vary, Objects of Perception seem to vary:
> If the Perceptive Organs close, their Objects seem to close also.
> "Consider this, O Mortal Man, O worm of sixty winters," said Los,
> "Consider Sexual Organization & hide thee in the dust."

In *Jerusalem,* as elsewhere in Blake, this woman is called Vala, her name is sometimes associated with the word "veil" because in her separation from Albion she is Maya, the veil of illusion, and in this character she invites Albion to sexual knowledge:

> "Know me now Albion: look upon me. I alone am Beauty.
> "The Imaginative Human Form is but a breathing of Vala:
> "I breathe him forth into the Heaven from my secret Cave,
> "Born of the Woman, to obey the Woman, O Albion the mighty,
> "For the Divine appearance is Brotherhood, but I am Love
> "Elevate into the Region of Brotherhood with my red fires."

Albion's answer is sublime poetry; perhaps no poet has ever been more terrifying and majestic than Blake here in the simple statement of these relations, the devastating identification of sexuality, under the traditional image of the plow, with plowing the earth for food and plowing men under in war:

> "Art thou Vala?" replied Albion, "image of my repose!
> "O how I tremble! how my members pour down milky fear!
> "A dewy garment covers me all over, all manhood is gone!
> "At thy word & at thy look, death enrobes me about
> "From head to feet, a garment of death & eternal fear.
> "Is not that Sun thy husband & that Moon thy glimmering Veil?

"Are not the Stars of heaven thy children? art thou not Babylon?
"Art thou Nature, Mother of all? Is Jerusalem thy Daughter?
"Why have thou elevate inward, O dweller of outward chambers,
"From grot & cave beneath the Moon, dim region of death
"Where I laid my Plow in the hot noon, where my hot team fed,
"Where implements of War are forged, the Plow to go over the Nations
"In pain girding me round like a rib of iron in heaven?"

Blake's poem is, as he says elsewhere, "Allegory addressed to the Intellectual powers, while it is altogether hidden from the Corporeal
Understanding." Its language therefore is often strange to us, because in order to address the intellectual powers rather than the
corporeal understanding it is convenient and perhaps necessary to
speak of relations by giving strange and not traditional names to what
things are to be related. It was in just this sense that Aristotle said
human actions could not be depicted except by the use of human ac-
tors; and Blake's way of putting this, in the preface to *Jerusalem*, is to
say: "We who dwell on Earth can do nothing of ourselves; everything
is conducted by Spirits, no less than digestion or sleep."
    That is a hard saying, too. And yet I think we have come to under-
stand it quite well. In the seventeenth century, according to Molière's
mockery, sleep was said to be produced by *virtus dormitivus*. Another
two centuries, according to D'Arcy Wentworth Thompson, saw a great
advance in knowledge, so that sleep was said to be produced by a substance of unknown properties called "dormitin." We may translate
generally thus: in abstract discourse, in discourse having to do with
invisible things, or relations, every substantive is a Spirit, and only by
becoming a Spirit gains the potential of becoming allegory addressed
to the intellectual powers. So when Blake proclaims the fourfold
wholeness of the truly human, and names its divisions as Urizen, Luvah, Tharmas, & Urthona, the sense of these names may be teasing to
us (though not without the possibility of being interpreted even so),
but we are merely deluded if we think that the abstract names given
to forces and influences in ordinary discourse are less mythological on
account of their supposed familiarity, when in fact these nouns exist
only to stopper up the abyss which opens at both ends of a sentence.
Here for example is a contemporary account of something like what
Blake is talking of when he describes the Fall: "Possessive mastery
over nature and rigorously economical thinking are partial elements
in the human being (the human body) which in modern civilization
have become tyrant organizers of the whole of human life; abstraction
from the reality of the whole body and substitution of the abstracted

impulse for the whole reality are inherent in *Homo economicus.*" [5]

In effect, one thing that Blake is saying is that when the intellect breaks up any wholeness into parts for "purposes of discussion" (to discus = to break apart) the separate parts may become imbued with lives and purposes of their own, inimical to the wholeness from which they came. Naive believers will always be found who will take these names as realities, or gods, and defend their mysterious purposes with fire and the sword. The contemporary I have quoted is telling a very similar story: "possessive mastery over nature" and "rigorously economical thinking" regarded as "tyrant organizers" come close to being, and are no less mythological than, Blake's "Urizen," his "priestcraft" and "Druids," his skygod whom he calls "Nobodaddy."

It will be fair, by way of summary, to translate rather freely. The Fall, for Blake, begins when man, identifying his humanity with his power of abstract reasoning, turns against his bodily or animal self, the way he had of being at home in the world, and creates abstract time and space out of his new feeling of being lost; having rejected himself, he experiences himself as an other, and this other both loves and hates him. Unable to accept himself, then, he cannot accept the other human beings for whom he himself is an other; he cannot believe in the community without giving it the phantasied form of a most powerful other coming over against him from outside, a father, a mother, an abstract god who in the name of forgiveness of sins exacts obedience in the form of religious, moral, and legal codes, human sacrifice in the form of slavery, punishment, and war.

The key word in Blake's account is "division." Two divisions are especially to be remarked. Man's reasoning power divides from the rest of him and holds in subjection the other qualities which might roughly be thought of as passion, sense, and spirit; and man divides from woman, rejecting the feminine in himself (as Freud said, every love affair takes place between four people). Hence sexuality is viewed as domination and submission. For the male, it becomes a military exploit to "invade" and "possess"—setting up in this way a dialectical relation wherein the female, precisely because viewed as an other, an enemy, is by definition eternally unpossessable, the image of a cruelly smiling Nature who beckons to destruction by love and war. It is thus that Nature herself divides: Vala in eternity, in time she becomes ambiguously Rahab and Tirzah, Tirzah being prudery and sexual hypocrisy, Rahab—the harlot who saved her life by betraying the city—

---

[5] Norman O. Brown, *Life Against Death* (Middletown, Conn.: Wesleyan University Press, 1960), p. 236.

whoredom and sexual license. The separation of the Spectre, or
reasoning power, on one side, and the Emanation, or sexual love, on
the other, leaves Los "the victim of their love & hate," and the Spectre, mocking, says of Man and Woman, "I will make their places of joy
and love excrementitious."

Blake sees these and other, consequent divisions as responsible also
for the mad dream called History, that record of the relation of suffering and knowledge which, speaking plainly, appears very often to
have the purpose of propitiating the god of any given time, whatever
his name, with human sacrifices. In the following passage Luvah, one
of the four Zoas, or primary qualities of the human, may be thought of
roughly as Passion, set free from the original balance and growing
cancerously in freedom:

> Luvah tore forth from Albion's loins in fibrous veins, in rivers
> Of blood over Europe: a Vegetating Root, in grinding pain
> Animating the Dragon Temples, soon to become that Holy Fiend
> The Wicker Man of Scandinavia, in which, cruelly consumed,
> The Captives rear'd to heaven howl in flames among the stars.
> Loud the cries of War on the Rhine & Danube with Albion's Sons:
> Away from Beulah's hills & vales break forth the Souls of the Dead,
> With cymbal, trumpet, clarion & the scythed chariots of Britain.

> And the Veil of Vala is composed of the Spectres of the Dead.

Wordsworth too has a vision of that Wicker Man, a sort of cage in
which victims were hung over the flames, and a comparison of the two
passages is of interest.

In one of the greatest moments of *The Prelude*, the poet, on Salis-
bury Plain at night, sees "Our dim ancestral Past in vision clear." It is
a vision of dark horror, warfare, death, and "barbaric majesty," and
chief among its elements is

> the sacrificial altar, fed
> With living men — how deep the groans! the voice
> Of those that crowd the giant wicker thrills
> The monumental hillocks, and the pomp
> Is for both worlds, the living and the dead.

But this contemplation leads him on to consider the Druids and their
astronomical knowledge, until he is charmed to see, "with believing
eyes,"

> long-bearded teachers, with white wands
> Uplifted, pointing to the starry sky,
> Alternately, and plain below, while breath
> Of music swayed their motions, and the waste
> Rejoiced with them and me in their sweet sounds.

Here we may see one more extension of the theme, which says that the imagination of nature is an imagination of history also. Wordsworth sees human history as somehow reconciling despite its cruelty: the pomp, he says touchingly, is for both worlds, the living and the dead. In that marvelous line he sees something of the tragic relation between suffering and civilization, and the fearful fascination with death on which both are based; so that the poetry of human sacrifice is somehow at one with "geometric truth," though at a terrible price. In this, perhaps, he sees more deeply than Blake, who, abominating geometric truth as an example of the reasoning power abstracted from the human, intransigently holds to it that human history is evil and an offense against imagination and, finally, not necessary.

So the question of the two natures, that independent nature which is perceived and that other which is created by the imagination of man, may be seen as having to do with the question of how to handle the past; one's own and that of the race. For it may be said, and perhaps ought to be said, that poetry has always lived on wickedness, great cruelty, man's inhumanity to man, and, moreover, been richly at home in that realm; so that, morally speaking, poetry may be accused of cosmeticizing the cosmos, and bringing most reprehensible things under the dominion of beauty.

It seems to me that I am not in this to settle the rights of the matter, deciding for one poet and against the other; life is hard enough without that. But here are what might paradoxically be called some final balancings.

Wordsworth, who began by viewing nature and imagination as in fruitful tension, seems to have finished with reason: there was the world, the mind was somehow in it, and so, consequently, were the mind's institutions, state and church, the laws, modes, manners of the society of which he was a most distinguished ornament; it is true however that the imagination closed down on him.

Blake remained all his life a radical who held the imagination to be primary, and took literally its one instruction: forgiveness of sins. He held that intellectual fight could and ought to be substituted for warfare. To him, nature was a dream, history its aggravation into nightmare, and the institutions of human society could not be tolerated on the foolish, insubstantial ground that they appeared to exist. Regarded as at best a dreamer, at worst as mad, he persisted in his folly, and even some of the wise who thought him insane also thought him a saint.

But, alas, this clear division is also mythological, for we cannot say that either man was as he was because he wrote as he did. In any event, it is perhaps fortunate that the choice offered is offered in poetry, for it is an impossible choice, between a grimly reasonable despair and an exuberant, gay madness. But what is poetry if it is not the place where the impossible, and perhaps the impossible alone, is true?

It will be well to allow, here at the end, that what we have is a comparison, not a competition. *The Prelude* and *Jerusalem* are individual expressions, they are not methods or recipes. In one way *The Prelude* has had a great advantage: it seems to belong to the tradition of English poetry as *Jerusalem* does not, hence it appears technically more accomplished. But such an advantage can turn into its equivalent disadvantage almost overnight, and a "tradition" of a hundred and fifty years' solid dominance come to seem a mere parochial divagation from the true or real tradition. So subject are we to the rule of fashion, our modern name for the goddess Fortuna.

In a considerable degree, the rightness of a poem depends on our familiarity with it. That statement initiates, or takes up, a circular argument, for becoming familiar with a poem depends on interest, or love, which presumes a certain rightness even to what we do not perfectly understand. Yet within limits not clearly to be discerned the phrases of a poem gain a magic by many repetitions in many minds; and by the same means lose this magic betimes. So in the present age some few poems widely understood and agreed upon twenty years ago as sacred books now begin to appear to some of us who are older though not wiser as, to say the least of it, mistakes. We shed certain of our symbolic illusions not necessarily to reach reality, but, far more often, to pick up other symbolic illusions.

The recent renewal of scholarly and critical interest in these great lost books of Blake is probably not a mere momentary upset in a stable situation. More likely it is the symptom of a deep change in the mind of the world. If so, it is probable that Blake's prophetic phantasies will progressively lose some of their strangeness, some of their obstinacy of phrasing, and assimilate with the general character of thought, responding to intelligence, so it will seem, in the measure that intelligence has responded to them. Our symbolic world will then reverberate to Blake's language more than to Wordsworth's, and that language, or the language we derive from it, will by ironic paradox come to seem "natural" to us. For language, which Blake calls "the rough basement," is the symbolic intervention of imaginative mercy between ourselves and a further Fall into a dark and silent abyss; it was on this account, he says, that

> Los built the stubborn structure of the Language, acting against
> Albion's melancholy, who must else have been a Dumb despair.

IV Epitomes (2)

The Language of Praise: A Review of Some of Our Most Distinguished Recent Blurbs

Books of poetry are written, published, reviewed, forgotten, that's how it goes. Probably the first two steps in the process could be omitted without making any significant change in this highly ritualized situation, in what we may fancily call the "status in reality" of books of poetry. On their way to oblivion the books pass through the hands of the reviewer, sometimes through his mind, and it may happen that he blows into them a brief and puffy little life, so that they live a little. For it is well-known that existence, among us, is conferred only by public acknowledgment, and for many a poem it would be a greater tragedy not to be reviewed than not to be written.

Or if that is too cryptic, let us try a parable of sorts. I remember as one of many uninteresting experiences dining out with two ladies trained in French cookery. We were all eating pieces of leatherette chicken fried in floor-wax, but it reminded them of a chicken they had once shared at a little *auberge* in the Dordogne, and they got so fascinated with the comparison of recipes that they absolutely cleaned up their plates, even the bones. Whereas I. . . .

Dearly beloved, the leatherette chicken is the poetry of this world, the poetry actually put before you. The two ladies are the public voices of poets, critics, writing blurbs, ads, flap copy, and the recipes of the *haute cuisine* go as follows:

"Very distinguished writing."

" . . . the work of a distinguished American poet."

" . . . a poet of distinction.

" . . . one of our most serious, able, and distinguishable voices."

I suppose you can't make a man sore by telling him he is distinguished, though "distinguishable" seems rather to hedge on the full
commitment, achieving a subtlety not far from cowardice. But the
formula does raise a problem: if nine of ten anythings are distinguished, what is the tenth? On with our examples.

"——— is, in my opinion, the best poet under forty now writing. He
is also the most *conserving* poet I know; he wastes nothing." This
seems to mean, so far as meaning is among its intentions, that ———
has printed everything; an impression which the perusal of his book
does not dispel.

"Confirms ———'s early promise. . . . Can be read with complete
pleasure." This is a more straightforwardly generous offer than one
usually gets, suggesting a salami which can be eaten with complete
pleasure or the remainder returned for complete refund. But the idea
that our pleasure in a collection of verses ought to be complete, total,
without exception, is a very popular one:

"This is a completely engrossing, completely moving book."

" . . . his poems are everywhere solid, sensitive, and deeply realized."

"———'s poems are always interesting."

" . . . anyone ought to be glad to read all the poems in this collection."

Most of these and many similar statements are signed by what we
may call, with no more than unavoidable irony, distinguished names
in the poetry business, the names of persons who on other occasions
have been known to deplore the inflation of our language, the pretensions of book reviewers, the vulgarity of advertising, &c.

Now I suppose that if you saw it written: "Mr. Spenser's *Amoretti*
are everywhere solid, sensitive, deeply realized, always interesting,
and can be read by anyone with complete pleasure," you might conclude charitably that the writer had not read the *Amoretti*, but was
somehow trapped in a social situation such that he didn't want to
admit it. Less charitably, that he did not much like the *Amoretti* at all,
but that his old friend Gabe Harvey had asked him if he wouldn't say
something nice. Or you might decide that he had never in his life read
anything more complex or problematic than a menu, which is one sort
of document you might under some circumstances read with complete
pleasure. And yet the *Amoretti* does contain a number of remarkable
poems. The moral of that is that some things are better than others.

Perhaps many people share the feeble and passive delusion that
these procedures sell books; for indeed the few Americans who are at
any time willing to put down a few dollars for poetry absolutely re-

quire (and may even deserve) an assurance that what they are getting is the real stuff throughout. But probably this assurance is even more necessary to the owner than to the prospective purchaser, and the species of writing we have been considering really belongs to the class of "advertising after the fact," that grand sustainer of the economy which guarantees to the buyer of any product costing more than a dollar-fifty a certain quantity of self-esteem, conveyable by literary means: that he has shown good taste, made a wise choice, identified himself with the elite, etc. It is by these things that we live.

But it is an effect of our so living to raise up a small Moloch called Poetry, to be trotted through the streets on state occasions, borne on the shoulders of a few stainless prefabricated reputations, and utterly indifferent to the existence of poems. For if you consider the other side of this coin, the very people most assiduous in issuing blanket endorsements of the sort I have cited are found in other contexts lamenting that Poetry is in a bad way (which it always is, I guess), and even berating the tired old Modern World for not producing Great Poets in sufficiently large numbers. Both kinds of statement manifest about equally cynicism, fatigue, impatience, or indifference.

It is merely a matter of common sense to allow that many of the poems covered by those encomia not only empirically are, but in principle had to be, were destined in the moment of their conception to be, made up of insupportable pretension and unreadable guff in roughly equal parts. Which is not to say that all poetry is dreadful, that the present time is conspicuously failing in an obligation (!) to excellence, or even to say that all the poetry of the present is *either* academically glib *or* written by hairy illiterates. It is to say only this, that poetry, that odd beast, exists in such and such a manner, as one poem and then another poem, and then another poem after that.

While the poet is alive and writing, it is not only fair but a necessity for him to believe that he will surpass in excellence Homer, Dante, and Shakespeare. At the very best of the reality, in the result, he will probably have to settle for a good deal less (it is ominous even for the name of Settle to obtrude itself in this discussion). To understate the point, it would be no dishonor for him to achieve what Marvell achieved, and exist in the immortality of his literature as Marvell does in his.

Andrew Marvell, a minor poet of the first rank, left poems to the number roughly of fifty, a few of these in Latin. To the majority of those who care for him as a great poet he is remembered by one poem, "To His Coy Mistress," and perhaps one more, "The Garden." Readers who love poetry will have read a few others, still anthology pieces:

"On a Drop of Dew," "The Mower to the Glo-Worms," "Bermudas," one or two of the "Dialogues," "An Horatian Ode upon Cromwell's Return from Ireland." Beyond that, it is left for poets and "specialists in the period" to discover beauties and grandeurs undisclosed to a public view, as in "Upon Appleton House" or "The Last Instructions to a Painter"; together with, of course, a deal of inferior, minor, or occasional work.

And the moral of that is, I suppose, whatever you care to make it. For one thing, when and if you buy a book of poetry, you will be decently rewarded with the discovery of one or two poems, or three or four, that mean something to you and matter to you. These few pieces may or may not lead you on to find that the poet's decisions are right decisions in other of his poems as well; maybe he was only lucky a couple of times. But it takes an affectionate, or at least a candid, study to get to where you can make up your mind; and above all it is not done the other way round, by avowing that X is a great poet and then trying to read his poems on that basis. Nor is it done by thinking about something called Poetry as though that existed independently of one poem and another, or something called Greatness as though that were arrived at immediately, by fiat; for these things are in the first instance ritual dramas played by Time for the malefit of the vulgar. As it was said by the ancient Chinese poet No Mo:

> If you leave off being invidious
> And cease defensively simplifying
> You learn from ten thousand examples
> What beauty is.

Instant Opinions of Poetry

The Concise Encyclopedia of English and American Poets and Poetry,
compiled and edited by Stephen Spender and Donald Hall.

In English railway stations during the War there used to be posters
asking "Is Your Journey Really Necessary?" a splendid idea someone
thought up to save the rolling-stock for the war effort. Unfortunately
you didn't see these posters until you had already shlepped your kit
and caboodle through the blackout to a station, and by that time the
answer, maybe a bit embarrassed, had to be "Yes." In the same way,
it will do no good for the reviewer to ask the editors if their encyclopedia is really necessary, because they have already gone to the
trouble of putting it together, and here it is, a large volume bound in a
blue of low brilliance with the title stamped in gold giving an appearance of unassertive authority.

The editors' authority is similarly quiet in the Introduction, where
they are at pains to disclaim any immodest ambition: "we have tried
to collect information necessary to the student of poetry, and to represent the best contemporary critical opinion. . . . In order to be *Concise* we have found it necessary to put a brutal limit on the number of
words for each article. Our contributors sometimes felt that they were
asked to condense the Holy Writ into a single sentence." The editors
regret the omission of poets "many of whom we would prefer to have
included," and imply that the omissions resulted from the advice of
critics and scholars, some of whom "expressed violent disagreement."
Finally, "We look forward to more controversy."

This reviewer feels disadvantaged. His dominant response to the
Concise Encyclopedia was to be depressed by it, but will it not be
churlish to say so in the face of such disarming acknowledgments?

What can he say, indeed, that will not be the mere setting of his opinion against the opinion of others at least equally qualified?

A good deal.

"You there in the corner, you're a student of poetry. Go to the *Concise Encyclopedia* and bring me back the best contemporary critical opinion of Stanley Kunitz."

"Kunitz, Stanley (1905–   ), was awarded the Pulitzer Prize—"

"Never mind the information now, just read the critical opinion."

"It says here: Robert Lowell praises Kunitz's 'savage, symbolic drive.'"

"Is that all it says? Hmm. What about Wyndham Lewis?"

"It says he wrote a book of poems, *One Way Song*, which was praised by T. S. Eliot."

"One to praise, and very few to love, eh? Try Phyllis McGinley."

"It says, 'An admirer of hers is W. H. Auden.'"

"You mean an admirer of her work, of course."

"Well, it just says 'an admirer of hers is W. H. Auden, who wrote an introduction to her collected poems.' But you said you didn't want information, only criticism."

"Quite. Edgar Lee Masters?"

"There is no critical opinion of Masters. It just lists his books and says 'see also American Poetry.'"

Research under that heading yielded the following: "To these major figures we may add the native qualities of Sandburg, Lindsay, and Edgar Lee Masters speaking the speech of the Middle West. . . ."

If these examples were not chosen at random, they could nevertheless be matched by a good many others. It is natural for contributors given more space to shed more light, but even here concision gets in its knife, as in this example: "He is the master of *terza rima* and the radio and TV play," as well as others I shall be attending to presently.

If we seek information rather than criticism, the position is not necessarily better. There is a bibliography, with a note advising that some poets whose works are listed in the text are not included, but a few moments' perusal discovers poets whose works are listed in neither, poets whose bibliography is followed only up to seven or eight years ago while others are complete to 1962, and other evidences of editorial remissness whether owing to laxness or caprice.

Because poetry is discussed where possible under the name of the poet, works of unknown authorship tend to get left out or to turn up only by the way: *Sir Gawayne and the Grene Knight* is mentioned once, under Langland (it is "the only other masterpiece in the alliterative style"), and the Ballads appear under Popular Poetry, where they get about as much attention as the combined efforts of Guest, Tupper, Hemans, and Longfellow.

There are thirty-two general essays, very various in character and quality; I shall comment on only a few. The Empire, or its dissolution, gets a number of entries: Australian, Canadian, New Zealand Poetry are separately discussed; English Poetry in Africa is one subject, while South African Poetry in English is another; saddest of all these, Indian Poetry in English is "a blind alley, lined with curio shops, leading nowhere." The indigestible mass of the past is treated in such other entries as Anglo-Saxon Poetry, Middle English Lyric, Religion and Poetry, etc. Since there is so much more English than American past it is natural and right for the *Encyclopedia* to be more English than American; still, a certain insularity is observable, as in this non-sentence under Foreign Influences on English Poetry: "Apollinaire, Lorca, Pasternak, and a number of American poets — Wallace Stevens, Robert Frost, and Robert Lowell, in particular — the poets of modern Greece, the German Expressionists, and the French Surrealists have been accepted with interest and enthusiasm, yet direct imitation of them has rarely been attempted." Whatever that means, it is clear that American poetry is a Foreign Influence. The point is perhaps a little clarified by a similar rash of hurriedly dropped names in an article about Imagery by Hugh Kenner (otherwise one of the few really fine pieces in this book): "In recent years transatlantic cross-fertilization has been especially rapid, so that an English poet like Charles Tomlinson has been assisted by the example of Williams, Moore, and Pound to make fecund derivations from Wordsworth." Such bits of "concise" writing turn up fairly often; what the student of poetry will make of them is a question; if he knows more he may also know better (e.g. that the real agent in all that pollenizing is Wallace Stevens), but if he is a beginner I see no hope.

The essay on American Poetry is given to E. N. W. Mottram, who teaches the subject at King's College, London University, and has a clear though not necessarily accurate idea of how things are: "the epic urge produced distinctive twentieth-century structures, unique in modern literature"; being, one supposes, stuck for a sufficiently impressive list of examples to go with *The Cantos* and *The Waste Land,* he adds among other things *The People, Yes* and "perhaps" *Conquistador* and *Howl,* in order to say: "Here is a real American poetic achievement," etc. In the same writer's entries on MacLeish and Sandburg, however, the products of their epic urge receive only

the barest and most toneless mention, while Ginsberg has not got a
separate entry in the *Concise Encyclopedia*. Mottram's peroration on
American Poetry is worth having almost entire:

> There are signs that the youngest poets—Ginsberg, Corso, McClure,
> O'Hara, Ashbery, Levertov—taking their cues from Whitman, Williams,
> Pound, and their recent disciple, Charles Olson, and also acknowledging the
> wider achievement of Lorca and Neruda, Mayakovsky and Apollinaire, are
> releasing themselves from an exhausted tradition of forms. Their work con-
> tains the sense of that international world where poems are desperate acts
> committed under the shadow of recurrent disaster.

There are signs in that remarkable passage that Mottram has been
reading Ian Fleming.

A certain provincial spirit appears also in Science and Poetry,
Charles Madge is adequate to the historical past of his subject, but to
the fascinating possibilities of the theme at present he seems indifferent. It was perhaps not part of the subject to consider the scientist
as poet in his proper work, e.g. the visions (for so they are) of Darcy
Thompson or Charles Sherrington. But surely even a concise account
should show an awareness of the investigations of Kenneth Burke, of
Scott Buchanan (*Poetry and Mathematics*), T. R. Henn (*The Apple and
the Spectroscope*), Herbert J. Muller (*Science and Criticism*), Stanley
Edgar Hyman (*The Tangled Bank*), to mention only a few.

For one last oddity, the discussion of Symbolism is given to a
French writer, Yves Bonnefoy; naturally enough, despite the mention
of Poe, Blake, Shelley, Coleridge, it is chiefly an account of the sym-
bolist movement in France, with Eliot and Yeats appearing as brief
afterthoughts in the final paragraph.

To sum up. Of course there are better things in this compilation
than those I have chiefly noticed. Nevill Coghill writes well of Langland. Kathleen Raine writes finely of Blake. The student of poetry, of
course, will prefer to read her long essay on "Blake's Debt to Antiquity" in the current *Sewanee Review* (Summer, 1963).

I fear that brings me to the point of judgment. The convenience of
having remarks about so many poets in one handy volume, where flap
copy turns into history before our eyes, cannot make up for the false
assertion implicit in the whole enterprise of *The Concise Encyclopedia* that poetry is a subject to be studied in this way. The apparatus
which makes possible the study of poetry is so immense and so immediately available that its presence in libraries cannot escape the

notice of the dullest beginner. Encyclopedias, handbooks, biographies, critiques, histories, surveys, periodicals, and anthologies of criticism come to mind in overwhelming numbers, and many of them are not compromised from the beginning by the simultaneous attempt to be eternal and up-to-the-minute.

And if the student gets tired of all that, he can always go and start reading some poems.

Chinoiserie, New Idioms,
Middle Biedermeyer

The lesson for today is suggested by some things said in the Introduction to *Twentieth Century Chinese Poetry*, an Anthology Translated and Edited by Kai-Yu Hsu. Of the poetry in this anthology I can't say much: I found almost all of it very dreary, and the worst of it both Red and dead; but translations may be used for information only, not criticism. When Mao Tse-tung writes:

> He who fails to reach the Great Wall is not a man,
> We have, as I count on my fingers, traveled 20,000 li,

My response is a simple un hunh. Some collections in this area give the impression that the original of something like that might be read in several different arrangements of the characters and contain dozens of meanings. But I gather from Mr. Hsu's Introduction that Chinese poetry has largely abandoned the scholarly imperial tradition with its language of learned allusion in which "even a collection of platitudes might be considered a poem." Simple truth is now the thing, though not the only thing, for there is also quantity:

The new leaders in China seem determined to see every front "blossom" at the same rate in the same direction; the rate of dam construction and production increase must be made proportionate to the increase in literary output. Consequently, with every drive to increase the production of steel there has been a comparable effort in the publication of poems. Teams of cultural workers . . . have been visiting the countryside, the factories, the farms, and the frontier areas. Like their counterparts in technological fields, these cultural workers encourage the farmers and laborers to learn reading and writing, and urge them to tell their stories and compose or recite their folk rhymes. The rhymes are then recorded, and, after various degrees of polishing, are published. Literally thousands upon thousands of these verses have appeared in recent years.

That is not all there is to modern Chinese poetry, there are other schools, the Metaphysicals, the Symbolists, and the list of influences upon them is oddly familiar: Verlaine, Mallarmé, Valéry, Rilke. . . . And there are some poets, writes Mr. Hsu, "who have created their own worlds that do not quite fit any of the identified schools," adding with a bland absence of comment which I find very telling, "Some critics refer to these poets as the Independent Group."

On reading that, I supposed for one wild instant that I had solved a literary mystery. Mr. Hsu wasn't writing about them, he was writing about us, and his book was not an anthology of Chinese poetry, but a desperate parody designed to bring us to our senses. Was Kai-Yu Hsu perhaps Harold Rosenberg, corralling his herd of independent minds? The hypothesis had to be abandoned, but the notion of it remains, and I value Mr. Hsu's book not only for the comforting information that things are pretty tough all over, but also for the view it opens up of things nearer home.

The local *chinoiserie* has been with us for some time now. Probably the poets could have been taught how to do it by Arthur Waley, but just as probably they were taught by Ezra Pound that it was worth doing, and *modern* (about 1910).

> Po Chu-i, balding old politician,
> What's the use?

is the way James Wright begins his new book *The Branch Will Not Break*. I mention the matter only because Mr. Wright is a fine poet (right tense?) who is quoted on the jacket as having renounced himself and all his works after his last book: "Whatever I write from now on will be entirely different." Here is a sample of what he is doing now; it is called "In the Cold House."

> I slept a few minutes ago,
> Even though the stove has been out for hours.
> I am growing old.
> A bird cries in bare elder trees.

It is of this kind of work, presumably, that Michael Hamburger is quoted on the jacket as saying: "Wright has completely changed his idiom and style between his last collection and the new one, and it is the new one that is most remarkable. He has absorbed the work of modern Spanish and continental poets and evolved a medium of his own. This medium dispenses with argument and rhetoric, and presents the pure substance of poetry, images which are 'the objective correlative' of emotion and feeling."

I had supposed, and continue to suppose, that the "medium" of poetry is the language in which it is written. And since what revolutions do is revolve, probably the Imagist Manifesto will be here again in a few minutes. A reviewer who liked Mr. Wright's four-line poem might call attention to "the stripped austerity of the notation," and speak of "a new idiom." A reviewer unhappily indifferent to the poem might observe that the idea of "stripped austerity" comes from the words "bare" and "cold" as much as from anything in this already familiar style, and he might add in the spirit of the revolution that for the poet to grow old in a setting of elder trees represents a backsliding into modern poetry, or bourgeois formalism, and introduces metaphysical considerations already condemned in the people's poetics.

I'm not in this to slang Mr. Wright, or even to review his book, but to describe a problem which arises in connection with reviewing poetry, not to mention the related businesses of writing the stuff and teaching it.

"With every drive to increase the production of steel there has been a comparable effort to increase the production of poems. . . . " That is a fair illustration of the unwritten law which says that Americans are perfectly free to do exactly what the Russians and Chinese are compelled to do by their rulers, just so long as we get it done. Our teams of cultural workers went into the colleges, not the countryside, and they went in with the object largely of propagating critical methods which for a time made poems look extremely interesting because of the number of things that could be said about them; but it has been a by-product of that industry to bring forth upon the free world a fair equivalent of what Kai-Yu Hsu calls "the literally millions of verses being composed today by bus drivers, lathe operators, buffalo herders, foot soldiers, and, of course, men of letters."

It would be unbecoming in this old buffalo herder to criticize here, since if our current project is to paper the world with poetry it is clear that I am in there papering with the rest, and teaching into the bargain: the worst sinner of us all. But, speaking now as a reluctant reviewer, I should like to say something about the situation produced in poetry by the meeting of several circumstances which make incompatible demands; these circumstances are: the proliferation of supposed "new idioms," the greatly increased production of verses, and the problematic existence of a criticism based on "analysis" and "explication."

The motto of this criticism might have been, "That poem is best that teacheth best," and in its shabbier aspects it tends to make of the art work, as someone neatly said, an empty space entirely surrounded by opinions. But there remains a good deal of sense to its contention that a poem, whatever else it may be, is something you can use your wits on and get a response from; in some sense, the progressive deepening of that response *is* the poem's value, or excellence.

But it is one effect of so much making explicit, so much making conscious, to turn poetry into the appearance of a series of devices easily mastered by intellectual means alone: any number can play, and a very large number does. For this reason the poets naturally began to cast around for something else, which has often taken the form of a simplicity, or intelligence-defying opacity, of which little or nothing need be said; and a criticism developed, which, being unable to say anything about the poems, talked largely and rather mysteriously and extremely often about a "new idiom"—an epithet whose frequent iteration on dust jackets and in reviews leads me to say that if poems are written by poets, then idioms must be written by—O well, never mind. But it seems that many poets nowadays resemble the Surrealist that Francis Golffing tells of, who when asked what he was doing these days replied, O, the same new thing.

Now it is characteristic of this situation that poetry today has vastly more writers than readers. Nor do I see any particular objection to that. We cannot return, nor should we wish to return, to periods in which the mere possession of literacy conferred magical powers and the land of enchantment was called Gramarye. But if the poetic object be to produce poems about which nothing can be said—and that is a fair enough object—let us acknowledge this change in our situation, and drop the farce of reviewing, teaching, writing about, poetry. You cannot, or at least I cannot, review an idiom. And the comrades ought to show some awareness that it is against the dignity of the Revolution to announce continuous performances.

One word more about the sinister object of increasing poetry production. The arts perhaps always have latent in their power of imitating life a desire to replace it. Schopenhauer's beautiful saying about music, that it is "the world over again," has an unhappy way of being understood literally in the enormities of Richard Wagner, and it may be that something similar happens to painting with abstract expressionism and Action Painting. For the poetry business, Kenneth Koch,

in his new book *Thank You and Other Poems,* has a character called
The Artist, who responds to his first view of the Pacific by ordering
sixteen million tons of blue paint; a very fair diagnosis.

And there is a fable so apposite that I include it although, unhappily,
I cannot remember whose it is. The ruler of a small, backward nation
used Point Four aid to electrify all the prayer wheels in the realm;
they turned at tremendous speed, and more prayers could be accomplished in a day than formerly in many years. But at the end of a
relatively short time the sun and the moon and the stars went out, for
all that was to be done had been done.*

* It seems that the source is "The Nine Billion Names of God," by Arthur C. Clarke
(Ballantyne Books, 1953). In the original, it was a computer print-out of the divine
names that did in the universe, and not electrified prayer wheels; but the result was
substantially the same.

The Theory and Practice of What

Naked Poetry: Recent American Poetry in Open Forms, edited by Stephen Berg and Robert Mezey.

The editors' plan for this anthology, as they explain it in their Foreword, is essentially a simple one: "We decided to cut across the schools, ignoring all feuds and other ugliness of literary life, and simply pick the best poets writing (and three who died untimely and who if this world were better would be living and writing today) and present them in rich and varied selections." A page later they explain that they have succeeded: "We will put aside all the traditional modesties and say plainly what we think, that most of the best poetry written in America during the last two decades is collected in this book."

The best poets are: Kenneth Rexroth, Theodore Roethke, Kenneth Patchen, William Stafford, Weldon Kees, John Berryman, Robert Lowell, Denise Levertov, Robert Bly, Robert Creeley, Allen Ginsberg, Galway Kinnell, W. S. Merwin, James Wright, Philip Levine, Sylvia Plath, Gary Snyder, Stephen Berg, and Robert Mezey.

Nine of the poets have contributed, in addition to their poems, brief essays (from a couple of paragraphs to a few pages) about their own manner of versifying. Most of them do not write iambic pentameter themselves, and would gladly see it suppressed in others: "the rhymed iambics," says one, "which no fashionable poet would be caught dead writing these days."

So now you know what is in this book.

If we look to the editors' prefatorial remarks to find out why exactly these selections from exactly these poets are the best poetry, etc., or what are open forms (epithet from Mandelstam), or what it means to say "naked poetry" (epithet from Jiménez), we do not get much joy.

"What does it matter what you call it?" as they say, having called it that. Griped by revelation, the editors have simply picked the best poems by the best poets, and that's enough about that.

On the other hand, this very circumstance may make the reviewer's job easier. If he wants to show what the best poetry looks like, he may open the book at random and quote some, secure that wherever he looks he will be getting stuff covered by the editorial guarantee. Then if the reader wants to know what the best poetry sounds like, he can read the samples aloud.

Some of it looks like this:

> he hears Blake's disembodied Voice recite the Sunflower in a room in
>   Harlem
> No woe on him surrounded by 700 thousand mad scholars moths fly
>   out of his sleeve
> He wants to die give up go mad break through into Eternity . . .

Other of it looks like this:

> Sometimes on especially
>   warm evenings I
> take a card chair out under
>   the almond tree
>
> and catching the last light, speak
>   to myself without
> words, I try to catch what is
>   behind my throat,
>
> without words . . .

Of course, it will be objected, it is impossible to appreciate the best poetry in little snippets; you have to read the whole thing. That's harder for the reviewer to exhibit with the first sort, because whole things of the first sort may run a dozen or sixteen pages; but here is a whole thing of the second sort:

In a Train

> There has been a light snow.
> Dark car tracks move in out of the darkness.
> I stare at the train window marked with soft dust.
> I have awakened at Missoula, Montana, utterly happy.

So now you know what some of the best poetry looks like. If you have read the samples aloud, you also know what some of it sounds like.

There's no disputing about tastes. And the term "best" does not admit of degree. The editors are within their rights, even to the generous representation of themselves as having written, together, about a tenth of the best poetry. Fair enough, for every poet's middle name is Mimi, and which of us, given command of an anthology, would not have done likewise? Though I like to imagine that there may be poets somewhere who would not make themselves judges in their own cause (nor even, for that matter, commit anthologies at all), because they would not feel the need of doing so.

Altogether, I doubt there can be any useful criticism of this collection on the terms in which it is put forward. Except for the editors, individual poets may not be criticized for being in the anthology, for it is generally true that when a poet is invited to be in an anthology he just says yes and then forgets about it till the postman brings him his tiny check and his two free copies; he does not, as a rule, ask what company his beautiful works will be keeping. As for the editors, the principles which guided them in their selection are expressed in ways which seem to forbid disagreement or even discussion, as they say of their poets:

Everything we thought to ask about their formal qualities has come to seem more and more irrelevant, and we find we are much more interested in what they say, in their dreams, visions and prophecies. Their poems take shape from the shapes of their emotions, the shapes their minds make in thought, and certainly don't need interpreters. In any case, we soon grew bored with our original plan to discuss the theory and practice of what. Our job, we now see, was to imagine the anthology (for there was nothing like it), put it together, and get out of the way. This is an act of silent criticism, is it not? and even a way of theorizing.

(Reader, I can't help it; that's what they say. No need to memorize it on purpose; just stare at it for a bit and it will start beating in your head.)

But I suppose my tastes to be as little disputable as theirs, and it seems to me that several of the best poets are a good deal better than the other best poets. I make these out to be Berryman, Roethke, Lowell, Plath, and Merwin, but have to add that in three and a half to four instances out of five it would be difficult if not impossible to discern their superiority in energy, wisdom, and figure from the selections reprinted here.

Plath is the one to whom that censure does not apply at all; her entire work is too small to be much distorted by the choices of anthologists. And Merwin comes only about half under my aim here; that is, I prefer some of his earlier work over the more recent poems preferred by the editors; but that is again a matter of taste, and not in dispute. (Indeed, had the editors rested their case for the existence and quality of something called "naked poetry" on selections from *The Lice* alone, I would have had to agree that, like it or not, they meant something serious.)

With the remaining three, though, the principle of selection designed to stress nakedness and openness seems to work in a manner not far from being disingenuous. Berryman is represented entirely from *77 Dream Songs,* and the choice of particular items seems designed as much as anything to conceal the fact that the greater number of poems in this and the succeeding volume are written in rhymed stanzas iambically based; of Berryman the author of *Homage to Mistress Bradstreet* we are told nothing.

In similar manner, the selection from Roethke, chiefly late, long meditations (some of which he might have revised had he lived), reveals nothing of the poet who wrote, say, such a small miracle as *Night Crow,* nothing of the poet who so often wrote so beautifully in rhymed stanzas and the derided iambic pentameter. Taste or no, the man who wrote *In a Dark Time* should not be represented—"in rich and varied selections"—as if he never did no such thing.

Lowell, at last, is represented chiefly by translations and imitations. If he is the same Robert Lowell whose originality and energy and strangeness were earlier exhibited by his handling of English heroic line in complex rhymed stanzas, the fact is not allowed to appear in this book.

So now you know something of what is not in this book.

Some way after those five, in my view, there are some good poets, though of a very narrow range as to both subject and tone of voice, and of an appalling sameness of diction. (I'd say here that William Stafford, with his scrupulous modesty and the quietness of his small and finely made poems, is the most surprising choice to be found in a company of naked poets.) And then? Well, then, some distance back, come the rest of the best poems, distinguished chiefly by parataxis and the last refinements of a generous self-pity ("I have awakened at Liverfluke Falls, Idaho, utterly happy," he sobbed).

The impression produced on me by prolonged and repeated exposure to the selections in this book is one of deepest boredom. Dullness and self-indulgence, pretentiousness and triviality, are here in the greatest plenty. The slogan of the poets who write long seems to be, If you can't be immortal be interminable; and some of the poets who write short can be interminable in ten lines.

With that, so much of it is so humorlessly earnest, and so much of it, new as it is, so earnestly derivative. The Blake-fakery! the Whitmania! the riggish ved-antics! the sutras that have come unstitched! Naked poetry forsooth. If there's more enterprise in walking naked (as we are told there is by a poet who habitually wrote in rhymed stanzas), the representations of this book make it out to be private enterprise. And why go naked if you aren't beautiful?

I think I'll go read some clothed couplets, especially if they have a sweet disorder in the dress.

Poetry and the National Conscience

The word *and* is a very good word. It is one of the words that children learn earliest, but its usefulness increases as they grow. One of the best things about *and* is that it is so inconspicuous it can sneak in almost anywhere unnoticed, like a secret agent. Like a secret agent, too, *and* is extremely likely to belong to both sides at once. This property of *and* makes it supremely apt to appear in the titles of discourses, especially learned ones: on the shelf across from me at the time of writing I can see several such: Crowds and Power, Myth and Cosmos, The Raw and the Cooked, Art and Illusion, Permanence and Change . . . I myself am writing a book the chapters of which are about poetry *and* such a variety of other things that I think to call it *Poetry And—*.

What makes *and* so good for titles is its power of putting things together while keeping them apart. It says there is some relation, but is utterly noncommittal about specifying; it is like a marriage service with automatic divorce written into the contract.

An unsuspected fringe benefit to *and* is its power of conferring existence on whatever things stand to either side of it. If one says This *and* That, his hearers are prepared to accept the solidity of both as understood, and to concentrate on the relation between them. Yet I am in some doubts about the useful reality of both the hypostatical entities of our title. Is there, all simply, *Poetry?* Does there exist somewhere, like a Platonic archetype of a rectal thermometer kept in the Smithsonian, *The,* or even *A, National Conscience?* I think not, and will try to say why. But I note first that the passing reference to Plato probably came into my thoughts because Plato actually seems to believe, in a famous place in *The Republic,* that both poetry, or music, and something like a national conscience, or a national morale at any rate, really existed. So strongly did he believe in the relation between them that he banished the poets from the nation, fearing that their libertine and effeminate individualism might impair the soldiers' will to fight (you will remember that in the ideal state a third of the population is army).

There is of course a sense, useful in casual chat, in which both poetry and the national conscience do exist. It is only when you try to specify what they are that you run into trouble. For people who speak English, Poetry will turn out to be the works written by a traditionally sanctioned succession of people named Chaucer and Shakespeare and Milton and so on, with Homer and Virgil and Dante muttering away in the background. The national conscience might be a touch harder to specify, but we probably incline to locate it in what we call *the media* (possibly as inept a term as ever was), and particularly in that section of it, located on the eastern seaboard, that a former governor of Maryland recently said such mean things about. Or you might say that the national conscience was located in the mouth of the former governor of Maryland, rising in righteous indignation against the coalition of the N.A.M., the networks, the *New York Times*, the academic intellectuals, the other intellectuals, the Mafia, the black people, the poor whites, and for all I know the Junior League, who are destroying the country. Someone is always destroying the country.

And whenever we talk about anything big enough and multifarious enough to be invisible when we try to look at it, we are talking mythology. That is not necessarily a bad thing; though I know a teacher who after ten years of explaining to his pupils "When I say Mythology, I don't mean a damn lie" said to me late at night, "You know, Howard, when I say Mythology I mean a damn lie." Not necessarily a bad thing, but necessarily a necessary thing; we simply don't have non-mythological ways of talking.

There is a deeper and more implicit national conscience, though unhappily it is also mythological. If I kick my cat on the front lawn in full view of the neighbors, I shall be reported to the S.P.C.A., and everyone except myself and possibly the cat will feel a touch more righteous; there are things, you see, that simply are not done. The fact, however, that humane societies routinely protect the stray animals entrusted to their care by killing them does not enter the question. In the same way, we are shocked, if we happen to think about it, at societies in which animal sacrifice is an accepted and necessary part of life, and we rather think such horrible things must have happened "in the olden times," as we children used to say. That our own society, for our health and security, tortures and sacrifices animals in numbers exponentially greater than Egypt could have managed in thirty generations, simply never enters in evidence, it doesn't come in the category of conscience but in the category of science. It comes not near our national conscience, which is extremely—and, I should add, necessarily—selective. The great human slogan has always been "After all, we've got to live," and if a shrewd voice murmurs from the shades that he doesn't see the necessity, we shall praise him and honor him and bestow great wealth upon him, but we shall also, just as he did himself, go on trying. And I fear that the national conscience may have to be defined as Mencken defined the individual one: The still small voice that tells you someone is watching.

Now as to poetry. Poets have often behaved, and do now often behave, as though they were, if not a national conscience, at least some kind of capital C Conscience, looking upon the doings of others as surely accursed and bound to lead to eternal perdition in the end. Some poets have made quite a good living at it, for prophecy is powerful magic that can be worked by anyone having sufficient *hubris*, or *chutzpah*. It's almost too easy. Prophets always predict disaster, and disaster unfailingly happens; far as I remember the only exception was Jonah, who succeeded in convincing the people of Nineveh to repent, and therefore failed as a prophet; the city was not destroyed. Jonah was furious, too, and that failure is almost undoubtedly the reason that his book is so much shorter than, say, the book of Isaiah, all three of him.

What fails to be observed in all this is that the world does not respond to these eloquent chidings by getting better; and in view of the continuing state of the world it would be simple prudence for poets to dissociate themselves from the conscience-keeping job entirely and at once, before somebody notices what a complete and utter failure they've been at it.

There has been available for many years now a nice, genteel way in which the poets could be national consciences comfortably, without saying mean things and without getting anybody mad. What we were doing, with our heavenly witch hazel, was "purifying the language of the tribe" (Rimbaud, popularized in English by T. S. Eliot). The argument went on to say that as soon as the language of the tribe had been purified enough, people would be ever so much nicer to one another. I used to sort of believe something of the kind myself, but was finally compelled to admit that we were no better at being this sort of conscience than at being the finger-shaking kind that said *naughty naughty, you mustn't*. Just look at the shape the language of the tribe is in now! The poets might as profitably have put in their time underwater, washing the fish.

All this perhaps will seem sort of unfeeling. I remind you that I am addressing the question of poetry and the national conscience, and trying to do it in a professional way. As a person, as a citizen, I am aware that things are not well with us, and my response to the situation, which is not part of the question here, is made as a person and as a citizen, not as a poet. In the same way, when I did my time in various air forces, several years spent in an improbable state of boredom, confusion and terror all at the same time, I did so as a person and as a citizen, not as a poet.

Before going on to my conclusion, I interject two obituary remarks anent the poet and the national conscience.

He was an advocate of universal peace, that condition wherein the rich might lie down on top of the poor with safety as well as pleasure.

Epitaph on a poet: He appealed to man's higher nature, and nobody bought his books.

To wind up with, I should try to say in a few words what I think poetry actually is able to do for us sojourners in this vale of tears, and why we value it, and why it is proper for us to value it. Poetry, I believe, is neither a sacrament nor a con game. But to say so is to acknowledge the precarious, poised between nature of poetry, and its constant temptation, so often yielded to by the poets, to stray over into sacrament or into con game. Sacred books are written by poets, though also, it appears, by genealogists, priests, merchants and certified public accountants. And the look, the feel, almost the mind of a religion are potently though subtly altered by the becoming almost canonical of its greatest poetry; as *The Comedy* altered Roman Catholicism, so *Paradise Lost* and later on *The Prelude* altered Anglicanism. On the con game side, we have always with us the versifying parsons and riming salesmen of the word so attentively characterized by Macaulay: "venal and licentious scribblers, with just sufficient talent to clothe the thoughts of a pandar in the style of a bellman." He meant the writers most favored in Milton's time, but from no time have they been absent.

At the height of its powers, poetry is—or must we now say poetry was?—a magical means of conferring immunity for a time from the fear of pain and the fear of misery and the fear of death. Poetry accomplished this humane object by homeopathic means; the poets sing of almost nothing but human suffering, cruelty, fear, death, and loss of every kind, and they do this, or did this, in the richest and loveliest and most pleasure-bearing language they could find, so that suffering and loss came to their hearers under their aspects of power, heroism, nobility, courage and courtesy and love – and, of course, illusion. The poise of poetry was to sustain that illusion delicately between the highest truth revealed to the believer and the crummy nature of everyday life, which was and is what Hobbes called it: solitary, poor, nasty, brutish, and short.*

As most great magicks do, poetry operated successfully in this manner only under a certain prohibition, which was that the reality of newspapers must never be allowed to break through except for purposes clearly understood to be satirical and low; this prohibition, I think, must have been behind the unwritten and largely forgotten law of decorum. Of course, when the language and reality of newspapers does in fact replace serious poetry there are always excellent reasons for its doing so; the poetry that sustained the sense of civilization has probably formalized and hardened too far from what people say and think and feel to be how things are. Something like that seems to have happened around 1800 in England, and again around the time of the First World War. And yet, as if by miracle, great poets again arose to find or make a living language, a sweet and lofty style. May it happen again, even out of so unlikely a source as the language of newspapers. Probably, indeed, it has happened again, but we were too busy reading the papers to have noticed.

* Hobbes meant life in the state of nature. But his epithets seem to have become proverbial precisely because writers kept quoting them in application to life in society in their own times.

V

Polonius as Polonius

Polonius Passing Through a Stage

Try to be yourself, they told the child.
I tried. Accumulating all those years
The blue annuities of silence some called
Wisdom, I heard sunstorms and exploding stars,
The legions screaming in the German wood —
Old violence petrifying where it stood.

The company in my Globe Theater rants
Its Famous Histories, the heroes fall
In ketchup and couplets. Ten heavenly don'ts
Botch up a selfhood, but where there's a Will
He's away. Rotting at ease, a ghostly doll —
What is that scratching at my heart's wall?

I tried to be myself. The silence grew
Till I could hear the tiniest Mongol horde
Scuffle the Gobi, a pony's felted shoe. . . .
Then from the fiery pit that self-born bird
Arose. A rat! The unseen good old man —
That sort of thing always brings the house down.

In the course of what is on the whole a very kindly letter about my recent verses, a friend observes: "You leave me behind at times — *e.g.*, I've not the least idea of what's going on in 'Polonius Passing Through a Stage' — and I will not put that down to obtuseness on my part, but to insufficient calculation on yours. . . ."

A poem that needed defending would probably be by definition a lost cause anyhow; and whatever I write about this one will inevitably look like a defense. But if we agree in advance to strip off this poem's buttons and turn it disgraced out of the ranks of Poetry, we get in exchange the opportunity of a pretty adventure in the realm of composition — turning, as Valéry says the philosopher ought to do, a disaster into the appearance of a disaster.

Besides not defending the poem, there is another thing I cannot do, that is, explain it, or explain it away, with reference to the circumstances of its composition, the thoughts which passed through the author's head while writing, etc. Of those thoughts, the poem is the sole remaining record. And if the poem is hard for a learned and intelligent reader to resolve, approaching it freshly, it will be still harder for the poet himself to find a way through it between reading what it says and reminiscing about what he thinks he thought at the time of composition. Such afterthoughts have very nearly a necessity to falsify what happened. For example, it seems plain to me now that I must in some terms have designed to myself a meditation on that famous phrase "To thine own self be true," which when Polonius was a little boy he sometimes heard proposed by his elders as "the meaning" of those three dozen plays and their author; but I have no memory whatsoever of thinking about that phrase.

Yet I do mean to say what I can about the calculation which occasionally appears among the poem's many incoherencies. And I begin with an obvious move: This poem's subject is a certain kind of incoherency, the one that is latent — these days not so latent — in the idea of "character," or, as it is so often and so learnedly called, "Identity."

"Try to be yourself." Children are very often given this instruction, the significantly revised modern analogue of "To thine own self be true." When they come to think about it, which may not be for 20 years, it perhaps seems somewhat problematic in the disharmony it blandly supposes between one's being and one's behavior, its odd relation, or maybe disrelation, between being and seeming, or acting. Being yourself, as against trying to be yourself: It is the difference between lighting a cigarette at home and lighting a cigarette on the stage. But then, a very great modern novelist made nearly his entire *oeuvre* out of the insistence that representing is a higher and even a holier thing than merely being.

Now character must come from somewhere, must find a model to form itself upon, must somehow, to become what it is, become what it is not. This is of course logically absurd, but it happens every day. It would in effect be scarcely extravagant to claim that all behavior is an imitation of behavior; for the origin of behavior, like the origin of almost everything else of interest to us, is hidden in the dark backward and abysm of time.

Given this, the figurative construction of the poem is still rather complicated, perhaps confused, reflecting whether legitimately or not certain confusions of thought attached to its subject. Put it this way, that *character* is a notion belonging equivocally to romance and morality, to history and religion. Once long ago the thought came to me that you grew up, in life, at the moment that, in literature, you began to identify yourself with the villain rather than with the hero. The villain, or else the fool. . . . Perhaps the poem is expressing a disillusion identical with that of Prufrock—I am not Prince Hamlet, nor was meant to be—where he revises himself rapidly downward through the hierarchy of the play, viewing himself as possibly Horatio, Rosencrantz and Guildenstern, maybe even Osric, but finishing up as Polonius. As though to say: I did as I was told, tried to be myself, I ought to have grown up to be Hamlet but turned out to be Polonius instead, and here I am dying of it.

This consideration introduces a further thought or two. Or rather, doesn't introduce, for the further thought or two enters early in the poem, not in narrative sequence as in this account, but more counterpointed and inwoven with other materials.

In some part your character must be received from the past, from tradition, custom, history, and so on. It is transmitted through the parents, chiefly, and a boy may be thought to receive the idea of his character chiefly from the father. Now, besides Polonius himself, who told his son about "trying to be yourself," there are several fathers who briefly and glancingly appear through the confused mutterings of the poem: There is God the Father with his *"ten heavenly don'ts,"* which are of course the Ten Commandments; there is Hamlet's father, who speaks sternly to his son about rotting at ease on Lethe wharf; there is King Lear, who in his madness proposes to shoe a troop of horses with felt in order to steal upon his sons-in-law and kill, kill, kill; finally, there is William Shakespeare, the father of Hamlet and so many others—exactly as, in a famous figure, Jehovah is the father of mankind generally.

About this fatherhood a couple of other things may be remarked. We will allow, for courtesy's sake, that this poem is written by a poet. Well, all poets writing in English have Shakespeare for their spiritual father; that is, they hope to grow up to be Shakespeare, and they never do. Moreover, the parallels between Shakespeare and Jehovah go further than the old metaphor, employed by both, which tells us that the world is a stage. Both of them have spread visibly before us the magnificent manifold of their creation, and about one Divine Will and the Other we know equally nothing: *"Where there's a Will, / He's away."*

Admittedly, interpreting a poem of this sort is a little like interpreting a dream; one proceeds laterally, by association, at first, rather than in the linear sequence of the "plot" (which neverless may exist). But there is a difference: The associations to this dream poem as I have so far teased them out, though they may be here and there a touch recondite, belong to the public domain and are not based on private memories inaccessible to the reader. And it begins to appear that for all its confusions the poem is thinking obsessively, as a dream does beneath its condensations of image and displacements of feeling, a single thought. It is a thought about growing up.

If the reader is able to grant, first that the allusions in the poem are really there, and not merely introduced by me in the way of explanation, and, second, that despite the incoherence of the poem's surface they have a certain consistency of reference, we may speak further about what the poem is trying to say.

"The blue annuities of silence some called | Wisdom . . ." Silence, children are informed, or were, is golden. So keeping quiet for many years ought to be money in the bank, wisdom-wise. But I mean, beyond this, or in counterpoint with it, that if you obey the instruction and try to be yourself, there ought to be some reinforcing response from the world, from the nature of things, that will help you be yourself, and confirm that being as belonging to the world and to the nature of things. Well, you don't get it, at least the queer hero of this poem doesn't get it. Of course, in the silence he hears many things, it is as though both nature and history were a kind of echo of the silence inside his head; but they tell him nothing about how to be, they become *"Old violence petrifying where it stood."* And when this silence returns intensified in the last stanza it is the silence not of wisdom but of insanity, related to images of stealth (Lear's stratagem, Polonius' hiding behind the arras) and the speaker's ridiculous, disgraceful death in the character of Polonius, attended by the same cruel applause as greets the ascent of poetry, its flight as Phoenix, self-born and owing nothing to this world, from the pit—from the unconscious, from the pit of hell itself, or maybe only from the pit of the Globe Theater. The convenient name of that theater, introduced in stanza two, phantasies the drama of history as played out in the world and in the human head at once, just as in Hamlet's pun that says he will remember his father's spirit "while memory holds a seat in this distracted globe." (Some Hamlets, reciting this line, clutch madly at their noggins.)

The first stanza, then, dreams about receiving one's self from nature or history; silence is the result. In the second stanza there appears the more sophisticated, or grown-up, opinion that nature and history are never received directly, but are always mediated by fictions, by drama, artifice, ritual and moral instruction (always negative in form: Thou shall not . . .). By contrast, the greatest creative forces, God the Father and Shakespeare the Father, are a paradoxical contrast of presence and absence, hidden behind their creations as the sun is hidden in his own fire: *"Where there's a Will, | He's away."* This second stanza ends with a confused reminiscence of Hamlet's ghost (*"Rotting at ease, a ghostly doll"*), as though the speaker were guiltily, hence furtively, trying to say that his father in the spirit *is* somehow buried in him, trying to speak but managing only to scratch uncommunicatively on the wall of the heart which is his tomb.

The third and last stanza is indeed made up of wild and whirling words. Beginning in defeated resignation (*"I tried to be myself"*), it insanely confesses the insanity of any such project. Between the insane phantasy of Lear the actor, and the divinely self-begotten phantasy of Shakespeare the maker, our hero is caught: He cannot be either one. Instead of realizing either the youthful dream of being Hamlet or the youthful dream of being Hamlet's creator, William Shakespeare, he dies as Polonius at the hands of one and the other. Even at this desperate moment, a doubt remains as to his identity, for Hamlet in stabbing through the arras cries out, "a rat!," while the Queen a few moments later calls Polonius "the unseen good old man." "Unseen" seems to fit rather pathetically into the poem; as though there had been, after all, a character of goodness in the speaker, but this had remained forever invisible and unrealized.

Finally, *"That sort of thing always brings the house down."* The line seems to come from outside the poem, or from another speaker; it sounds, too, deliberately thrown away. Colloquially, of course, it means that scenes like that, of desperate violence, always get great applause. But it may also mean that the whole house of the world, with its many mansions allotted to so many characters, might collapse utterly, morality, meaning and all, upon any serious inspection of its results, of the catastrophic disrelation obtaining between character and destiny, or chance, and between moral law and poetic phantasy. The other speaker, in this last line, may well be the poet himself, who is merely one of the selves of the speaker throughout: One way regarded, the way of action, he tried to become Hamlet and became an old fool; another way regarded, the way of poetry, he wanted to become a poet, like Shakespeare, and instead became—himself.

And one more thing, fit to come last: the title. Apart from the literal and obvious significations having to do with the theater and the passage from life to death; there is another phrase much applied to growing up. As you try on one character after another before hardening into the one you are condemned to, people will say, whether in rebuke or reassurance, "He's just passing through a stage." That may have some relation to the idea of "states" which Blake, in *Jerusalem*, mercifully substitutes for the cruel idea of "character"; but I wouldn't push it.

Perhaps it may be said that I have won a sort of Pyrrhic victory here. Freeing the poem of my friend's charge that it shows insufficient calculation, I have brought matters round to the point where someone must surely say, "Any contraption as calculated as that can't possibly be a poem."

"The Sweeper of Ways"

About one of his own works the poet can tell the reader three kinds of thing, all of them untrustworthy. First, he can say something about the poem's occasion, about what "real" experience came to him and became a subject. In this instance that element of supposed reality is uninformative: Yes, there was a small mild Negro man with a broom, this happened at a college — something you might or might not gather from the style of address, "Masters," in the third stanza, a point necessary but maybe not sufficient to interpretation . . . and that's about it. For the poem absorbs its occasion, it has to do that or nothing, so that in retrospect the thoughts occurring in the poem are as much a part of the reality represented as the undeniably factual information that this man and I used to exchange casual greetings and remarks about the weather.

Second, the poet can say what he intended to accomplish, what kind of thoughts passed through his mind in the course of composition, why he rejected some and included others. . . . But I think this an impossible task, and suspect that when we seem to be doing it we are deceiving ourselves, if not necessarily others, with mythology after the fact. For, once again, the poem absorbs the thoughts that get into it, and effectively erases the ones that didn't. At least for my own part I cannot remember having had any other thoughts during composition than the ones that appear in the poem; maybe a study of successive drafts would reveal these other thoughts, but I don't have the successive drafts.

The third thing the poet can do, or try to do, is look somewhat coldly at his poem and say what happens in it. He can't even try to do that until he is at a distance from the poem and has forgotten the writing of it and can regard it as scarcely his own any more. In this he is manifestly not to be trusted, for if he cannot remember what he intended he may now, reconsidering, bootleg into the act several new intentions that he thinks he can see and justify. Worse than that, in the measure that he really is able to see the poem as no longer his own, the skill he brings to elucidating it is no greater than that of another reader, and he has no more call to be consulted on the subject than anyone else — less, because there remains the suspicion, which may be correct, that he is fooling himself.

And yet it is just this oblique, entangled, self-referring, self-erasing character in poetry that fascinates and charms and gives to the art its unique distinction in the realms of thought. I know that it is perfectly possible to "have thoughts" and then put the thoughts "in verse," or "give expression to" the thoughts, but it is not so very interesting. My belief about poetry says that you write a poem not to say what you think, nor even to find out what you think — though that is closer — but to find out what *it* thinks.

This belief may rest only on illusion, admitted (it's surprising how much does!); though if you eagerly proclaim that you have seen through the illusion you don't necessarily attain to truth, or reality; perhaps you find only that you have come out of heaven's blessing into the warm sun. But this is no place to start that argument. The belief is there, and among poets it goes so deep that no matter how brilliantly you reason them out of it, no matter how much they may seem to be convinced by your logic, they fall back into it the moment they begin writing the next poem: to find out what *it* thinks, and which way *it* wants to go.

And what is that *it* that thinks, that wants to go one way and not another? The poem, the muse, the holy spirit, the nature of things? The devil, the goddess, the unconscious, the language? The same *it*, possibly, that rains when it's raining.

Maybe this belief about the strangeness of poetry, its otherness, can be clarified by a technical consideration. In a great many sorts of human work you start with idea, plan, plot, blueprint, to be imitated in the material. But in lyric poetry this element may be and often is almost entirely wanting: you have, perhaps, an idea, a thought, a subject, a line . . . but if you say aloud what you begin with, it turns out to be very deficient in the dignified generality that belongs to *idea*. "A small mild Negro man with a broom," is that really an *idea*? So it is as if, or seems as if, the material were somehow forming the idea in the course of composition, hence as though there were no other idea than the whole poem, the poem itself as it finally appears on the page. Some such notion as this might account not only for the poetic belief in the other, the outside, but also for the well-known recalcitrance of lyric poetry to paraphrase, its oracular acceptance of ambiguity as the condition of life, and—in greater examples than we have to do with here—the sheer excess vitality and valency of the text over all its explications no matter how ingenious, no matter how profound, no matter even how accurate.

The Sweeper of Ways

All day, a small mild Negro man with a broom
Sweeps up the leaves that fall along the paths.
He carries his head to one side, looking down
At his leaves, at his broom like a windy beard
Curled with the sweeping habit. Over him
High haughty trees, the hickory and ash,
Dispense their more leaves easily, or else
The district wind, hunting hypocrisy,
Tears at the summer's wall and throws down leaves
To witness of a truth naked and cold.

Hopeless it looks, on these harsh, hastening days
Before the end, to finish all those leaves
Against time. But the broom goes back and forth
With a tree's patience, as though naturally
Erasers would speak the language of pencils.
A thousand thoughts fall on the same blank page,
Though the wind blows them back, they go where he
Directs them, to the archives where disorder
Blazes and a pale smoke becomes the sky.
The ways I walk are splendidly free of leaves.

We meet, we smile good morning, say the weather
Whatever. On a rainy day there'll be
A few leaves stuck like emblems on the walk;
These too he brooms at till they come unstuck.
Masters, we carry our white faces by
In silent prayer, Don't hate me, on a wave-
length which his broom's antennae perfectly
Pick up, we know ourselves so many thoughts
Considered by a careful, kindly mind
Which can do nothing, and is doing that.

Reading this poem of mine over at a distance of several years from the time of writing it, I can almost but not quite see it as not my own. It is still enough my own that I want to think well of it—though even there indifference surprisingly grows; once written, the poem is for the reader, the writer having had his reward in the writing—but this one is far enough away to be a little puzzling; I don't know if I shall be able to think well of it.

The range for interpretation—the number of areas for us to be confused in, or mistaken about—is after all not so very great. It divides up first as inside and outside, and only later does that simple division come to be perplexed and equivocal extremely, as one's experience of the world, poetically considered, appears as a Moebius band, on which you get from inside to outside and back without ever crossing an edge, that is to say without ever noticing the moment of transition. Poetry is a way of doing the inside continuously with the outside, so that the "happening" of the poem, the Negro sweeping up leaves, is really not separable from the speaker's thoughtful perception of him, and the statement of the first two lines is seen as neither more nor less "factual" than such different-looking statements as the one about "his broom like a windy beard / Curled with the sweeping habit."

There is a small drama going through the poem, and it turns on the speaker's problem in getting the Negro identified with reference not only to social questions but also to questions about art and nature. The Negro of this poem is, first of all, a servant, and this gives him a considerable power in thought, the power of embarrassment: anyone who does things for you, whether or not you want the things done, is able to arouse embarrassment, and our problems with both savior and devil often turn out to be servant problems.

The Negro's job in the poem is menial and somewhat futile-looking, like a parody of one of the labors of Hercules: cleaning up leaves that continue to fall from a vast treasury overhead. Yet the title awards him a curious dignity: The Sweeper of Ways; as though he were after all a sort of psychopomp. And while on the one side the futility of his servitude is acknowledged, another line of thought makes him out to be somehow on the side of the leaves, on nature's side, his emblem of office of one stuff with the trees whose leaves he sweeps: "the broom goes back and forth / With a tree's patience."

In stanza two the leaves become thoughts. And in the last stanza the people too become thoughts, the white people addressed as "Masters" perhaps because they are teachers, as well as because they are "the master race."

> . . . we know ourselves so many thoughts
> Considered by a careful, kindly mind . . .

The speaker of the poem, then, is trying to resolve his itch about social inequities and the anguish they cause in two ways, but in such language as shall make the two ways coincide, and his dream—for the poem is in this respect somewhat like a dream, concealing and revealing in the same words, as well as satisfying a wish, in this instance the wish to be reassured about one's responsibility for the naughtiness of a naughty world—might be crudely read in some such way as this:

"This kindly old man exemplifies a wrong in society. I didn't do it, but I have to feel responsible. And I detest about society this constant enforcing upon its members feelings of responsibility which are also deeply hopeless and despairing, so that one guilt evokes another, without remedy or end. For even if you could correct the future, what about the past? Many thousands gone.

"And yet his servitude hasn't embittered him, he remains kindly, there's a feeling of natural wisdom and strength in his patient relation to that broom, to the leaves, the fire that burns the leaves, the sky that soaks up the smoke into invisibility. Of course I should not like to sweep leaves all day for my living. But all the same I should like to be like him, that is, I should like to be able to do my life with the same dignity and patience he brings to doing his. And oddly enough, with all the differences there is something in which we resemble one another, for poetry too is a hopeless sweeping up together of this world's ample provision of fallen experiences, sweeping the leaves might stand as an emblem for any kind of pretension to ordering this chaos; poets also deal somewhat thanklessly with whatever befalls, possibly also with the ambition, after sweeping it together, of seeing it burn— 'O for a muse of fire, that would ascend / The brightest heaven of invention.' And if poetry, by how much the more might teaching be subjected to the same emblem, with the generations of the leaves whispering down as term papers, as the students themselves . . . ?"

So, or somewhat so, it goes. I hope there's more to it than that, but maybe that's part of it.

Attentiveness and Obedience

When I agreed to act as editor of a collection of essays by some American poets on their art, I proposed to the contributors several questions that seemed to me of some interest, with the idea that these might form a sort of thematic center for the book. But because a poet's view of his own work is necessarily personal, I left it to the contributors to decide whether they would be stimulated by the questions, provoked by the questions, or so unaffected by the questions as to pay them no mind. As might have been anticipated, some of the contributors responded to the questions and others did not.

At that time, I did not contemplate being a contributor myself; but now that I find I am one, it seems only just that I thrash around for a while in this labyrinth of my own devising and try to describe my work with reference to those questions I so glibly asked without a thought of ever having to answer up myself.

I

Do you see your work as having essentially changed in character or style since you began?

In style, I hope and in part believe it has, for I began and for a long time remained imitative, and poems in my first books, not to mention the undergraduate work that preceded publication, show more than traces of admired modern masters—Eliot, Auden, Stevens, Cummings, Yeats. I think these reminiscences largely dropped away in later work; though as a corollary to that it should be said that I never consciously sought for what people call "one's own voice," originality, a uniquely recognizable style; so far as anything like all that happened—I am uncertain how far that is—it happened more or less of itself, while I concentrated on writing this or that poem.

Stylistically, I began under the aegis of notions drawn, I suppose, chiefly from T. S. Eliot. Along with many other beginners, I learned to value irony, difficulty, erudition, and the Metaphysical style of composition after the example of John Donne. Again along with many others I learned from William Empson to value ambiguity; it was part of our purposeful labor, in those days, to fill our poems with somewhat studied puns which could be said to "work on several different levels," though often they did not work even on one. I think the direction of my development was away from all these things considered as technical devices; I now regard simplicity and the appearance of ease in the measure as primary values, and the detachment of a single thought from its ambiguous surroundings as a worthier object than the deliberate cultivation of ambiguity.

Yet more than a trick of the old rage remains; as, for example, coming across an abandoned railroad waiting room in which there was a clock with no hands, I came to see that clock somehow as the serpent himself, who initiated human time, and said of "the still mainspring, / Behind the even and the odd," that it "Hides in its coiled continuing / A venomous tense past tense." The difference in meaning, depending on whether you read the first "tense" as adjective or noun, seems to me to belong quite properly to the "tensions" developed by the poem as it reaches that conclusion.

So if character or attitude can be distinguished from style in a technical sense, there has perhaps been not so much change. Brought up to a poetry of irony, paradox, and wit as primary means of imagination, brought up to a view that did not always sharply divide the funny from the serious and even the sorrowful, I continue so, and have sometimes found it a strain to suffer critics gladly upon this issue in particular.

Given so much, however, of consistency in development, I think there have gradually appeared two marked changes in my poetry. The first has to do with the natural world, which I came to rather late, having been born and raised in the city. During the war and since, I have lived in the country, chiefly in Vermont, and while my relation to the landscape has been contemplative rather than practical, the landscape nevertheless has in large part taken over my poetry.

The second change is harder to speak of; it involves a growing consciousness of nature as responsive to language or, to put it the other way, of imagination as the agent of reality. This is a magical idea and not very much heard of these days even among poets — practically never among critics — but I am stuck with it. Trying to say this somewhat difficult idea, I come upon this: I do not now, if I ever did, consent to the common modern view of language as a system of conventional signs for the passive reception of experience, but tend ever more to see language as making an unknowably large part of a material world whose independent existence might be likened to that of the human unconscious, a sleep of causes, a chaos of the possible-impossible, responsive only to the wakening touch of desire and fear—that is, to spirit; that is, to the word.

To put this another way: having a dominantly aural imagination, I not so much look at nature as I listen to what it says. This is a mystery, at least in the sense that I cannot explain it—why should a phrase come to you out of the ground and seem to be exactly right? But the mystery appears to me as a poet's proper relation with things, a relation in which language, that accumulated wisdom and folly in which the living and the dead speak simultaneously, is a full partner and not merely a stenographer.

I once tried to say something of this more or less directly in a poem called "A Spell before Winter." It is about Vermont in late fall, when the conventional glory of the leaves is over and the tourists have gone home, and the land not only reveals itself in its true colors but also, in the figure of the poem, speaks:

A Spell before Winter

After the red leaf and the gold have gone,
Brought down by the wind, then by hammering rain
Bruised and discolored, when October's flame
Goes blue to guttering in the cusp, this land
Sinks deeper into silence, darker into shade.
There is a knowledge in the look of things,
The old hills hunch before the north wind blows.

Now I can see certain simplicities
In the darkening rust and tarnish of the time,
And say over the certain simplicities,
The running water and the standing stone,
The yellow haze of the willow and the black
Smoke of the elm, the silver, silent light
Where suddenly, readying toward nightfall,
The sumac's candelabrum darkly flames.
And I speak to you now with the land's voice,
It is the cold, wild land that says to you
A knowledge glimmers in the sleep of things:
The old hills hunch before the north wind blows.

To see certain simplicities and to say over the certain simplicities — they are in a sense the same thing; a philosopher of language tells us

that see and say come from the same root, "for to 'say' is to make someone else 'see' vicariously that which you have 'seen.' "

II

*Is there, has there been, was there ever, a "revolution" in poetry, or
is all that a matter of a few sleazy technical tricks? What is the relation of your work to this question, if there is a relation? Otherwise
put: do you respond to such notions as The New Poetry, An American
Language Distinct from English, The Collapse of Prosody, No
Thoughts but in Things, the Battle between Academics and—What?—
Others (A Fair Field Full of Mostly Corpses)?*

Because I was the one to phrase this question, a certain surly sarcasm in the asking probably betrays at least the tone of my response
and the somewhat distant attitude I take toward the theater in which
these war games go on in what looks like continuous performances.
But I shall elaborate a little.

I think there was a revolution in poetry, associated chiefly with
Eliot and Pound; but maybe it is of the nature of revolutions or of the
nature of history that their innovations should later come to look trivial
or undistinguishable from technical tricks. I remain grateful to Eliot
and Pound and the others, for winning for poets the freedom to do
anything that seems to them necessary. Nowadays, if you want to
write free verse, or "cadenced verse," or no particular verse at all,
you can do it and no one will object so long as you don't write a manifesto proclaiming your courage and wits to (or against) the world. In
fact it is also probable that no one will even notice what you are doing
unless you write a manifesto, for if the "revolution" won freedom for
poetry it also won for large parts of the world freedom from poetry.
And why poets should still be found, fifty years later, fighting for that
"freedom to experiment" as though they did not have it, is a mystery,
but maybe one of the sillier mysteries.

It is also possible that the revolution produced, as revolutions will,
some bad effects from which poetry can only with difficulty recover;
introducing, among many other things, an extreme insistence on qualities rightly thought to be virtues in the then-obtaining situation—
urbanity, consciousness, control, a certain dryness—its example may
have cut poets off from great ranges of experience that begin and end
in places deeper than consciousness can be happy in. So many people
now concerned with the poetic art are obsessed with technique, even
if the obsession is avowedly directed toward "liberation," that poetry
sometimes appears as a technology, as though the "new idioms," announced with the regularity of new hair styles, were going to make
obsolete everything that preceded them; which for a short, bad time

they appear to do. One might put the point as a riddle: if poems are written by poets, idioms are written by guess who?

I tried to say something of this in a poem, "Lion & Honeycomb," whose title alludes to the riddle wherein Samson asked how from strength shall come forth sweetness. The speaker in this poem is a poet, discontented and somewhat angry with himself and with the other poets, too. It seems he has come to a place where he knows he has lost the way; all his art appears to him merely as skill, or technical virtuosity; he feels especially that he has lost the vital truth of poetry, the great wonder that first beckoned him into its enchanted realm. The process of the poem is the finding his way back to first things and if the poem succeeds, which isn't for me to say, the strength of his angry rejection at the beginning should resolve in the sweetness of the images he comes to at the end, the remembrance from childhood of two instances in particular, soap bubbles and skipping stones, where a certain gaiety, marvelousness, energy, maintained itself against gravity, even against possibility, in a hard world.

Lion & Honeycomb

He didn't want to do it with skill,
He'd had enough of skill. If he never saw
Another villanelle, it would be too soon;
And the same went for sonnets. If it had been
Hard work leaning to rime, it would be much
Harder leaning not to. The time came
He had to ask himself, what did he want?
What did he want when he began
That idiot fiddling with the sounds of things?

He asked himself, poor moron, because he had
Nobody else to ask. The others went right on
Talking about form, talking about myth
And the (so help us) need for a modern idiom;
The verseballs among them kept counting syllables.

So there he was, this forty-year-old teen-ager
Dreaming preposterous mergers and divisions
Of vowels like water, consonants like rock
(While everybody kept discussing values
And the need for values), for words that would
Enter the silence and be there as a light.
So much coffee and so many cigarettes
Gone down the drain, gone up in smoke,

Just for the sake of getting something right
Once in a while, something that could stand
On its own flat feet to keep out windy time
And the worm, something that might simply be,
Not as the monument in the smoky rain
Grimly endures, but that would be
Only a moment's inviolable presence,
The moment before disaster, before the storm,
In its peculiar silence, an integer
Fixed in the middle of the fall of things,
Perfected and casual as, to a child's eye,
Soap bubbles are, and skipping stones.

It goes with all this that I have not much sympathy for either side of the perennial squabble about, most generally, form and content; as a great master said, when you look at a cow, do you see the form or the content of the cow? No ideas but in Things is a slogan having considerable pathos, a brave challenge. But people who try to follow it will find themselves either smuggling thoughts back in, or writing Imagist poetry over again. As for An American Language Distinct from English, if people want to write poems in that language, fine. But if they want to argue with you about it and the room hasn't got a door, you listen to what they have to say as patiently as possible and then ask them to say it over in American. Mostly these slogans amount to edicts decreeing that from now on you should walk on one foot only; when you have got that much of the message you needn't wait around to find out whether they mean the right or the left. The same master I quoted from a moment ago also said, perhaps to artists,

Great things are done when Men & Mountains meet;
This is not done by Jostling in the Street.

III

Does the question whether the world has changed during this century preoccupy you in poetry? Does your work appear to you to envision the appearance of a new human nature, for better or worse, or does it view the many and obvious changes as essentially technological?

This is by all odds the hardest of the questions, for me. I am not even certain now what I meant by it, and perhaps would not have asked had I known a response would be demanded from myself. Probably my secret thought was that the other poets, by their answers, would somewhat illuminate the depths of the question. But I shall have a go.

It sometimes seems to me as though our relations with the Devil have reached that place, so near the end, where paradox appears immediately in all phenomena, so that, for example, the increase of life is the fated increase of mortal suffering, the multiplication of the means of communication is the multiplication of meaninglessness, and so on. At the obsequies for the late President of the United States the "eternal flame" was extinguished by holy water in the hands of children; in the material world that may have been an unfortunate accident, but in the poetic world, where one is compelled to listen to symbolic things, it appears as possibly a final warning, a witty and indeed diabolical underlining of the dire assassination itself.

So if paradox and accenting the hidden side of the paradoxical has always played such a part in my poetry, perhaps the seriousness of that view of life, its necessity even, may now begin to appear. The charge typically raised against my work by literary critics has been that my poems are jokes, even bad jokes. I incline to agree, insisting however that they are bad jokes, and even terrible jokes, emerging from the nature of things as well as from my propensity for coming at things a touch subversively and from the blind side, or the dark side, the side everyone concerned with "values" would just as soon forget. And a commitment to paradox, I think, is liable to be as serious as a commitment to anything whatever else. I shall try to put this in a plain relation with my work in poetry.

In the first poem, "A Spell before Winter," I spoke of "the running water and the standing stone." This distinction of imagery goes far and deep in my poetry and has assumed, over the past seven years, the nature of an antithesis. Long before writing that poem, I had observed in my work a growing preoccupation with statues, with heroic monuments, as representing the rigid domination of the past over present and future; stillness, death, power, compacted into giant forms; the standing stone that looks over the landscape assumes early in history a human face, a frown, even a smile; becomes a god.

The thought of statues as representing a false, historical immortality seems clearly related to the scriptural prohibition against the making of graven images; and the category in which the statues finally come, which I generalized out as "effigies," may include also photographs, mythological figures such as Santa Claus, even mannequins in shop windows, or anything that tends to confirm the mind in a habitual way of regarding the world, which habitual way is, to be short with it, idolatry. There are many examples in my work, and I

have chosen one which represents newspapers, by a slight extension
of the thought, as a sort of verbal effigies, idolatrously confirming
human beings day after day in the habit of a mean delusion and com-
pelling them to regard this mean delusion as their sole reality. I say
this halfway as a joke with the name of a newspaper, *The Daily
Globe.*

The Daily Globe

> Each day another installment of the old
> Romance of Order brings to the breakfast table
> The paper flowers of catastrophe.
> One has this recurrent dream about the world.
>
> Headlines declare the ambiguous oracles,
> The comfortable old prophets mutter doom.
> Man's greatest intellectual pleasure is
> To repeat himself, yet somehow the daily globe
>
> Rolls on, while the characters in comic strips
> Prolong their slow, interminable lives
> Beyond the segregated photographs
> Of the girls that marry and the men that die.

(I might mention for the benefit of foreign audiences that in American newspapers the pictures on the obituary pages are almost exclusively of men, those on the matrimonial pages exclusively of girls.)

It is the contention of my poetry very often that the world is increasingly, and with an increasing acceleration, dominated by habitual idolatry, by images for which my first representation was that of
statues. The extension of the argument to television, for instance, is
not difficult. So that, if my poetry does envision the appearance of a
new human nature, it does so chiefly in sarcastic outrage, for that
new human nature appears in the poetry merely as a totalitarian fixing
of the old human nature, whose principal products have been anguish,
war, and history.

As to the opposite attitude, and the image opposed. Well, if you do
not take your notions of this world from newspapers you take your
notions of this world from looking at this world and listening to what
it seems to say. A great novelist, Thomas Mann, characterized the
religious attitude as "attentiveness and obedience." His illustration
of all that is not attentiveness and obedience is given in his story of
Joseph, where he portrays the mean-spirited businessman Laban as
having buried, according to ancient custom, his first born beneath the

foundation of his house; unaware, so to speak, that the human spirit, with the divine spirit, had moved on from that old-fashioned idea of security. The image that has seemed to me most appropriate for this notion of "attentiveness and obedience" is the image—so dialectical, so subtle, so strange, and yet so evidently an emblem for human life and the life of the imagination—of a stream, a river, a waterfall, a fountain, or else of a still and deep reflecting pool. This image, of the form continuing in the changing material, belongs also to cloud and fire, and I once gave it a somewhat political shape in a despairing epigram: God loves (I said) the liberal thrice better than the conservative, for at the beginning he gave to the liberal the three realms of water, air, and fire, while to the conservative he gave only the earth.

Of the many appearances of this figure of water in my work, I have chosen one that seeks to set the nature of water in relation to human perception and human imagination.

Painting a Mountain Stream

Running and standing still at once
is the whole truth. Raveled or combed,
wrinkled or clear, it gets its force
from losing force. Going it stays.

Pulse beats, and planets echo this,
the running down, the standing still,
all thunder of the one thought.
The mind that thinks it is unfounded.

I speak of what is running down.
Of sun, of thunder bearing the rain
I do not speak, of the rising flame
or the slow towering of the elm.

A comb was found in a girl's grave
(ah heartsblood raveled like a rope).
The visible way is always down
but there is no floor to the world.

Study this rhythm, not this thing.
The brush's tip streams from the wrist
of a living man, a dying man.
The running water is the wrist.

In the confluence of the wrist
things and ideas ripple together,

as in the clear lake of the eye,
unfathomable, running remains.

The eye travels on running water,
out to the sky, if you let it go.
However often you call it back
it travels again, out to the sky.

The water that seemed to stand is gone.
The water that seemed to run is here.
Steady the wrist, steady the eye;
paint this rhythm, not this thing.

In this brief account I have stressed the liberal virtues and neglected the conservative ones, scorning the solids of this world to praise its liquids. That is not the whole truth, for how could you tell the stream but by its rocky bed, the rocks directing the water how to flow, the water—much more slowly—shaping the rocks according to its flow: But maybe I put the accent where I do against this world which so consistently in politics, religion, even in art, even in science, worships the rocky monument achieved and scorns the spring, the rain cloud, and the spark fallen among the leaves.

IV

What is the proper function of criticism? Is there a species of it that you admire (are able to get along with)?

Perhaps my views of the present posture of literary criticism are clear enough already. If I say of that whole area, where busy fellows run about praising this and damning that, that it could do with more patience, more scrupulous attention, and above all more charity, I probably mean "to me," and who needs that?

VI

Speculative Equations: Poems, Poets, Computers

The theme I wish to discuss — Poetry in the New World of Machines — appears to have two main aspects, one specific and one general. The specific one, the question whether machines can write poetry, does indeed look new (although only when first asked) as well as faintly silly; it is tempting to say that the mere possibility is excluded forever by a prophetic remark Yeats made in a diary kept during 1909: "Nobody running at full speed has either a head or a heart." But any prolonged inspection of the question opens out upon the ancient, fascinating general problem of the relation between the mind and machines, the relation characterized by Jonathan Swift as The Mechanical Operation of the Spirit; and from the contemplation of that general question one returns to its particular present application to computers and their artistic or scholarly uses with, after all, one or two things to say. So that is the course of the following observations: from the specific and new to the general and traditional and then back.

I have come across a couple of newspaper reports telling how scientists have programmed computers to do poetry. How serious the scientists were in this project didn't appear very clearly from the newspaper reports, which have a deadpan way of dealing with the wonders of science, a neutral expression that can be taken for reverence if things turn out well or for irony if they don't. In one such instance the scientist protested — although it didn't visibly need much protesting — "I still don't like poetry. I did it as a demonstration to show what this machine will do." The machine would do a hundred and fifty poems a minute, which is enough, I would hope, to make any sorcerer's apprentice stop and think.

I didn't keep or copy out any of that scientist's results, which were not exactly memorable. But I remember programming my own computer to do literary criticism, and in just under a tenth of a second of study it was able to tell the scientist: "You are writing your poems on a late Victorian computer."

So there is one of the difficulties. Supposing it to be technically possible to make a computer write what will technically pass for poetry, we have still to ask about the poetry it grinds out with such frightening industry and at such tremendous speed whether it expresses the soul of the computer or the soul of the programmer, not to mention the degree of his literary sophistication, or in very truth the prophetic soul of the wide world dreaming on things to come. The answer in the present instance is easy: if you bring to the computer a vague belief, derived from memories of high school, that poetry is made mainly of words like *ethereal, refulgent, cerulean,* and so on, the computer will faithfully reflect your belief even while varying the relations of your vocabulary enough that you may be able to suppose it is really writing the poems. The same holds true if you believe that poetry is made mainly of words like *pimple, snot,* and *turd.*

But the answer may not be always so easy, as I shall try to show by extrapolating from this instance a hypothetical instance, or model, in which the computer is given more of a chance—is given, in fact, every chance. I suppose as follows. I put into my computer a vocabulary of, say, two hundred words. Because I am a dour and gloomy fellow, this vocabulary is heavily weighted toward the pessimistic end of the spectrum of feeling, and has ever so many words like *cold, bleak, despair, loss,* and so forth, and relatively few words like *joy, kindness, light,* and so forth. I also provide the computer with certain rules of combination, grammatical, metrical, and, if I want to be very fancy, alliterative and assonant. Then I turn it on, and it rapidly prints out several hundred poems before I have the presence of mind to turn it off. Now I have to read my results, or its results, which takes a good deal longer; for even if I have programmed it to a certain level of what I consider good taste, so that it has rejected a large number of its products, there will still be a great many left over. Most of these seem nonsense to me, even though as the provider of the vocabulary I might be thought to have a predilection for any poems using the words I favored. I warn myself to go slow, however, because some of the effect of nonsense comes from the fact that the computer is set up to do only essential poetic relations and not full sentences, so that its results appear rather like a literal English rendering of a Chinese poem before the translator has supplied the linkages proper to English.

Suppose now that I finally come across something that seems to me very grand and moving indeed. The computer has written:

> Night blindness world.
> I darken in.

I respond with sympathy and a sharp pencil, and see that the machine's intention is to say:

> Night is the blindness of the world;
> I darken from within.

Never mind just now whether literary criticism would certify these phrases as the real thing; the point is that I am moved by them, I say them over to myself for days, they yield that troubled exaltation that for me has always signified the presence of the real thing—I have still to ask myself what has happened, what is the nature of the transaction that has taken place among myself, the computer and the language.

I provided the machine with a basis for making statements, and in doing so predetermined to a certain extent the range of its feelings. But within this range it is the machine, and not I, that has produced a statement that, let us suppose, I do not think I could have made up myself, a thought that I had not thought before and which overtook me with that sense of recognition that for Keats characterized the highest poetry.

The instance, I repeat, is hypothetical. But supposing everything to turn out as I have said, the result is remarkably like the process of poetic composition as we know it quite apart from computers: the poet combines in various ways the familiar materials of the world-in-language, and once in a great while he surprises himself, or it surprises him, with thoughts beyond the reaches of his soul. The self, working happily along with its rhyming dictionary, is suddenly invaded by the Other, the Outside, and it is tempting to believe that the computer has acted here as the true agent of poetry however named: inspiration, the Muse, trance, ecstasy, the Holy Spirit. I observe, however, that it still takes a human being to decide that in one instance out of hundreds this is what has happened, for I assume that the computer has not been programmed to be moved by its own poetry, or even to read it with the highest discrimination. And I observe also that there is no guarantee that other human beings would agree in being moved by the lines; that too is rather like the situation in poetry at present.

Leaving that fictive instance now, I turn to my second example, which concerns the use of computers for studying poetry. Under the headline, "COMPUTERS TURN TO POETRY STUDY: Milton's

Influence on Shelley Appraised Through Tapes" (*New York Times,*
September 11, 1964), the essential claim is reported as follows:

> The diction of *Paradise Lost* was organically used in *Prometheus Unbound*
> and its presence can be detected only by techniques beyond unaided human
> capacities.

Heaving mightily, this mountain produces the following mouse:

> Through his computer studies, Professor Raben believes he has produced a
> new understanding of what the poets were trying to say. He believes that it
> has never so clearly been shown before that what Milton is saying is that God
> is good but that man's inadequacy brings his doom; man knew no wickedness,
> then he meddled, and learned of sin and death.
>   Shelley, Professor Raben believes, is saying according to the computer
> studies, that man is good but that God created an environment where man has
> difficulties; that if there is love in human environment then all man's experi-
> ences will be better.

Perhaps one's most charitable response to this trivial nonsense is to
think that the reporter must have got it all wrong, every word of it; that
must happen as often as not. But how dreadful, to have to rely on
newspaper accounts for so much misinformation on so many things
you have no chance of testing out for yourself.

Even supposing the Professor's computer had produced, instead of
this series of sophomorics that contrive somehow to be simultaneously
platitudinous and inaccurate* — you would almost certainly fail a

---

* In general, I find, scholars in the humanities who apply to computers tend to get
carried away by enthusiasm or else slightly fuddled by the heady atmosphere of "Science," so that they neither make the best claims for their results nor produce the best
evidence for those claims. Witness the following unexplained sentence in the report of
a computer's study of the Baconian authorship of The Plays: "It ruled out Bacon as the
author but was unable to say flatly that Shakespeare wrote the plays either." Surely, if
this means anything whatever, it is the ancient and feeble academic joke that says The
Plays were written either by Shakespeare or by another man of the same name. Witness
also the following: "From the study has come new understanding, for example, of what
St. Thomas meant when he wrote the Latin word 'virtus.' In English the word means
'virtue,' which is understood to mean self-control. But Father Busa said that computers
had found that St. Thomas intended the word to mean strength or driving power." I had
supposed, and continue to suppose, that this revelation reveals a simple fact that cannot
fail of being perceived and understood by a beginning student of St. Thomas or for that
matter of any author whatever writing in Latin. One assumes the machines can do more,
and better, than such examples show; but there remains considerable doubt just what it
is. (These examples were supplied me by the kindness of William G. Mount, News Bu-
reau Supervisor of the IBM Data Processing Division.)

student who deposed in that manner about either poem—something quite revolutionary, what then? For whatever it says is beyond question by "unaided human capacities," including in this instance, I guess, the unaided human capacities of Milton and Shelley. And if traces of Milton's influence on Shelley cannot be detected without a computer, are they in fact there?

The question whether the influences are there invisibly is the kind of question Galileo opened up by training his telescope upon the heavens and finding for science, as Hannah Arendt says, its Archimedean Point. But there is a peculiar poignancy to this application of the question, for what will become of people who sit down to read poetry with techniques beyond unaided human capacities? Will they not be in peril of pride, and liable to treat the rest of us with superb scorn? Will the computers learn to sorrow and delight? More importantly, will poetry, for so long the illuminating witness of familiar nature, now retire into the invisible and problematic realm of inferred nature,* exhibiting, so to say, only its subatomic properties, and these only to the readings of a machine under the prompting of an expert?

I mean to say that the example appears to me as a parody of scientific understanding, as false science and misdirected scholarship; in effect, as idolatry. And when I say "idolatry" I am compelled to see that what this sort of thing offers its priesthood is not a new dream in the least, but a very old one indeed, the dream of divination and esoteric oracular utterance, not from the flight of birds, the entrails of animals, or the cracks on the shells of tortoises, but from the more prestigious authority of the machine and the language of numbers.

But to see this is also to put away one's indignation and even acknowledge a remote sort of sympathy. For whatever its particular folly in this instance, the dream behind the professor's attempt, like that behind my hypothetical attempt to write poems by computer, is the ancient and heartbreaking dream of poetry itself, to persuade an indifferent and mighty Nature to respond to the human, as it does in these absurdly lovable lines of Shakespeare:

> For Orpheus' lute was strung with poets' sinews;
> Whose golden touch could soften steel and stones,
> Make tigers tame, and huge leviathans
> Forsake unsounded deeps to dance on sands.
> *(Two Gentlemen of Verona,* 3.2.78)

* The antithesis of familiar and inferred nature is from Owen Barfield. See *Worlds Apart, passim.*

My two examples, with what I have said about them, have put me in difficulties. For my own wish would be to say flatly that poetry is an intimate, a vital, secret of the human spirit (if not of another also), and that consequently, no matter how sophisticated the procedures to be developed, poetry written by a machine will always be inferior poetry and imitation poetry, whether it imitates a particular poet's style or merely a vague idea of "poetic" style in the mind of the programmer.*

But the logic of the argument, while it doesn't altogether forbid my saying some of that, warns me that the development of the theme is by no means simple or to be handled by a flat "No" any more than by a resounding "Yes" (it is worth noting that these two responses alone are shared by the mind and the computer: the power of being on or off but not between). To see this development clearly it will be useful to stand well off and take a fresh look.

Our ideas of what poetry does and how it does it split into two substantive positions, usually identified with the names of Plato and Aristotle. The main point of contention — whether poetry is good for the citizenry or not — doesn't concern me here, but a subordinate and related difference does, for the argument about the morality of poetry rests in part upon a difference of opinion between Plato and Aristotle as to how poets do their work. On this question, Plato is quite explicit: the poet must be in ecstasy, literally outside himself, his own spirit replaced for the time by that of his god, who dictates the words. Aristotle is so thoroughly of the opposite persuasion that he doesn't even deal with the question directly; but everything he says in the *Poetics* simply assumes our agreement that the poet is a rational and conscious craftsman, a working member of the *polis* for whose citizens he writes plays characterized by constructive thought. Of inspiration, or possession by a divinity, I believe nothing is said.

Now this disagreement can never be settled conclusively in favor of one side or the other, and I do not mean to debate it now. All I mean to take from this passing reminder that the disagreement exists is the somewhat surprising conclusion that the computer, which one would have thought should be on the side of rational constructiveness, turns up not on that side at all but on the other, the side of Plato, where

* This is not to say that computers, even present ones, "can't write poetry." For nine-tenths of the poetry in the world, past and contemporary, is of a dullness and mechanic servility so appalling that if it has to be written at all it certainly ought to be written by computers, although only on condition that other computers be instructed to read it.

the poet is regarded as oracular, vatic, not speaking so much as spoken through by something other than himself. This Other has usually been thought of as a divinity, the Muse, the Goddess, the Holy Spirit, God telling the prophets what to say: "Son of man, stand upon thy feet, and I will speak unto thee. And the spirit entered into me when he spake unto me . . ." (Ezekiel, 2, 1–2). But in point of the poetic function of this Other, it may make little or no difference whether we characterize it in human, divine or cosmic terms, as a person, as the wind, or as a machine—all are equally names, metaphors for something mighty and secret—for the sole requirement of the Other is simply to be other, hence to guarantee that the poet shall express not his silly little personal consciousness but the vast consciousness open to the Other.

The idea of the Other is a somewhat dangerous as well as a tempting idea, magical, religious, superstitious, according to your point of view. Even supposing that poetry represents a connection with the Other, and that such a connection might be made by means of a computer, we should still have the same problem about the Other that the Church had with Joan of Arc: admitted that she had made her connection, was it with the right party? Alternatively, we may believe that this connection, this idea of a connection, is neither with heaven nor with hell, but is merely the ultimate refinement of the solipsism from which we have no escape but by delusion into illusion; however that may be, and leaving the question open, I am compelled to conclude that in both my examples, grotesque and parodied as they seem, the computer stands for the Other, the Outside, or our delusion concerning it. In the first, hypothetical example it makes the programmer surprise himself, in the second it makes a professor of English preen himself upon being put in possession of knowledge no human being could have gained by himself. On the evidence of such powerful impositions I may not simply dismiss out of hand the computer's pretensions to poetry, but must turn instead to ask why such a relation should ever have come up at all and become a subject of interest; what is the real nature of the combined affinity and antipathy between the various arts and machinery?

For many people, caught in an unexamined romanticism, the idea of art is utterly remote from the idea of the machine; any hint of mechanism, formula, device, in the art work is repugnant to them in their blessed simplicity, and their attitude is summed up by a sign I once saw in a drugstore window advertising "genuine hand-painted oil paintings." You can't argue with people who feel this way, although you might suggest to them that if they stand under the windows of the Conservatory of Music on a nice warm day they will learn something; or you might ask them which came first, pianos or piano music.

A machine reproduces somewhat abstractly in inanimate materials some bodily or mental motion. The feelings we associate with the machine are far from simple or unambiguous: we may admire its economy of motion, its obedient and predictable regularity, its tireless performance; we may view its repetitiousness and noise and brute incessance as emblems of a world gone mad; we may be impressed, for good or ill, by its quality of relentlessness, its character as a mindless fate and a senseless predestination. The steam locomotive became for a whole age the epitome of blind power not only on account of its quite real strength but also because this strength, by being confined to a track, appeared as a thunderous necessity going for no particular reason where it had to go. Even now, with even greater powers, aircraft and steamship have not attained this symbolic property, because they are uncommitted externally with respect to direction.

Consulting one of the earliest and best of analogue computers (nonelectronic), the unabridged dictionary, we can add to the range of associations. A machine, in a first, archaic meaning, was the handiwork of a divine or supernatural being, and the word was used to characterize the human frame. The meaning of the Latin and Greek antecedents is double: a means or an expedient, an engine or a device or trick; and our shrewd sense that there is in the magic of machinery something uncanny and not quite honest survives in a couple of expressions: machination, and, in politics, the party machine.

Several usages point up the closeness and ambiguousness of the relation between art and the machine. *Deus ex machina* is perhaps the best known, and a closely related one is the idea of the *machinery* in an epic poem, meaning in general the supernatural agents invented or received from tradition and supposed the real movers behind the doings of the human characters (for example, Pope's sylphs and salamanders, *et cetera*, in *The Rape of the Lock*). Finally, in painting, a *machine* is the cant term for a big bad picture got up chiefly for exhibition purposes.

Now the machine has the distinctive trait of fixing and regularizing a human motion so that it will always be the same. Dante described Nature, in relation to God, as "an artist that hath the skill of his art, and a trembling hand"; the machine would have the skill of the art, and exclude the trembling of the hand. We have now to inquire whether and to what degree that characteristic has been and is at present desirable in the arts. Some of the evidence appears to suggest that the ambition of a mechanical and tireless regularity, like many another human dream, was a wonderful and benign ambition indeed — until it showed signs of becoming a daily reality.

Music, so widely regarded for a couple of centuries as the liberator of the human spirit, as instigating the most daring and subversive flights into the contentless anarchy of the forbidden, is at the same time full of indications having the opposite sign, the sign of a mechanical servitude. Schopenhauer in a beautiful phrase characterized music as "the secret history of the will," but I suppose that a compulsion to regularity, to formula, to repetition, to simple fractions and perceptible symmetries, must also be included among the will's secrets.

For an example, take the slow movement of Beethoven's Seventh Symphony, where the beautiful lonely lost lament soars and falls over a ground where the same motif has more the sense of the turning of, say, a camshaft. Take the opening of the Waldstein Sonata op. 53, or of Mozart's A-Minor Sonata (K. 310), it's the same story: individuality, you might say, belongs to the right hand, mechanic regularity and relentless drive to the left. And if you go back to an earlier period, before "polyphonic objectivity" — the phrase is Thomas Mann's — with its equally rigorous treatment of the several voices had split into the detached notions of "melody" and "accompaniment" or harmony, you see that fugue, canon, chaconne, and passacaglia express very fully a will to mechanism and its determinations. In fact, a useful pun makes it possible to say that the cathedral organ was the first great digital (not to mention pedal) computer, programmed by J. S. Bach to exhaust the possibilities of the then obtaining tonal language.* A composer of my acquaintance, looking over the score of a chorale prelude, said with a somewhat lofty disgust, "Why does he hoke it up like that? He'd already said all that was necessary in the chorale." "Why?" I said. "Why else but that he *could?*" The same answer as that given by the scientist in my first example: "I did it as a demonstration to show what this machine will do."

Now as to painting. Leaving aside what is called Abstract Art, if only because all art is, we very quickly learn that between us and

---

* Bach's great contemporary, Jonathan Swift, also had a computer; it was explained and demonstrated to Lemuel Gulliver by a Professor at the Grand Academy of Lagado, and while his description is too long to be appropriate here, the Professor's claim for his machine is worth having: "Everyone knew how laborious the usual Method is of attaining to Arts and Sciences; whereas by his Contrivance, the most ignorant Person, at a reasonable Charge, and with a little bodily Labour, may write Books in Philosophy, Poetry, Politicks, Law, Mathematicks, and Theology, without the least Assistance from Genius or Study." See *Gulliver's Travels*, Book III, Chapter V.

the direct transcription of the landscape we had perhaps naïvely hoped for, there is interposed a formidable body of language and mechanisms for using it, mysterious yet systematic transformations whereby the sight of the eye is translated through a turn of the wrist to a mark on paper. E. H. Gombrich, in his *Art and Illusion,* convincingly shows by history and analysis that the artist's transcription of nature is always mediated by a scheme, which he learns first: he doesn't directly copy the human head, he does an egg which is something like it but simpler and more compassable, then he refines and articulates and individualizes and maybe even addles his egg till it becomes the illusion of a human head; and perhaps the achievement of Cézanne and later of the Cubists was the removal of this procedure from the classroom and its location in the vision itself.

From the Far East we have similar testimony in Mai-Mai Sze's *The Tao of Painting,* some four hundred pages of illustration and commentary from a seventeenth-century treatise, elucidating the elements of style in the use of brush and ink as applied by the various masters to natural forms: seventy-three illustrations, for example, of the methods of drawing trees, ninety of methods of drawing rocks, clouds, running water, two dozen on the bamboo alone, and so on. Only by years of repetition of gestures might one learn how to paint mountains with brushstrokes like ax-cuts or brushstrokes like raveled rope, or to distinguish and perform some thirty ways of dotting foliage (like mouse tracks, pine needles, *sharp* pine needles, a sprinkling of pepper . . .). Gradually, perhaps, one's own style would reveal itself, but it would have been formed by conventions become second nature. And the treatise adds, about those exceptional masters who began without any particular habit of technique but made up what they needed as they went: "One need not, however, make things more difficult by following such a procedure, which would be like imitating the man who made a hole in the boat to mark the spot where his sword had dropped into the water."

A recent book from Germany, *Creative Drawing: Point and Line,* by Ernst Röttger and Dieter Klante, illustrates with student work the fantastic potential of this approach to drawing by means of porism, or problems having fixed conditions capable of an indeterminate number of solutions. One fascinating by-product of such procedures is the discovery that figuration by point or line according to very simple rules ever so often unintentionally produces forms that resemble the forms of nature. Without meddling my ignorance into the mysteries of physics, I should like to suggest on the model provided by this book that perhaps the wave-particle question is but one more reflection of the way in which point and line compose the visual world. We see the curve of the shoreline—or we begin counting the grains of sand that make it up. We see the line formed by the hills, and might paint it against the sky in a single sweep, or else we might build it up pointillistically by dabbing in at one distance every tree, at another every leaf. We play this world legato or staccato, according to directions from the composer, who thought in phrases, maybe, but built with notes. We speak in waves what we write in particles. Perhaps nothing we do with point or line is ever, in the common meaning of the word, "abstract": the simplest formula or the most abstruse, carried through, turns out to imitate some piece of nature. Or not to "imitate," since that was not included in the intention, but to correspond with, or resemble, or suggest.

There has recently been some striking confirmation of this bond between imagination and mechanism, or thought and the world, a little more mysterious than it may at first appear. The invention and development of photography was widely thought to have been a powerful influence in turning the art of painting away from representation of the visible world and toward abstraction, geometry, the nonrepresentational; as though the artists were "refusing to compete" against the camera on its home ground. But now, many years later, comes electron microphotography, and it turns out that between many paintings done in the interim and the photographs at very high magnification of all sorts of fine structure in nature there are numerous and rather precise resemblances. It is not always possible, in books of reproductions, to distinguish painting from photograph, art from science, nor does the judgment as to which of two paired examples is more "beautiful" produce much illumination; the entire question of beauty and the beast, in the face of these evidences, becomes almost impossible to ask intelligibly, much less to answer. And if the camera can do that, is there any reason why, for better or worse, the computer should not be able to learn to write poetry?

In the arts of language it is, curiously, just the addition of mechanisms and mechanical requirements that traditionally distinguished poetry from prose, and it will be remembered in this connection that *versus* meant returning, or recurring, while *prosus* meant going straight forth. The idea of a couplet, of a quatrain, of a sonnet, appears to be the imitating, or modeling, of the abstract invisible process of thought by simplifying, refining and mechanizing procedures for illustrating what kind of thing a thought is. Even the idea of a line, in poetry, to a certain extent mechanizes not simply the form alone, but also the thing said and the nature of expressiveness itself. For

example, William Shakespeare wrote a very large number of lines that
might be thought ideally suited to production by computer:

> Increasing store with loss and loss with store . . .
> > (sonnet lxiv)

> With eager feeding food doth choke the feeder . . .
> > (*Richard II*, 2.1.37)

> > Love is not love
> Which alters when it alteration finds,
> Or bends with the remover to remove . . .
> > (sonnet cxvi)

In these and ever so many similar examples there is a suggestive
resemblance to the programmatic proceeding by opposite states:
yes-no or on-off. It may be even that effects of mere mechanism are
avoided in such places only by the circumstance that the line has an
odd and not an even number of feet.

Perhaps an unreckonably large part of the pleasure to be had from
poetry in our tradition resides in this kind of mechanism wherein
by formal means antitheses are sharpened and precised and thought
reveals itself as moving by a kind of alternating current.

A quatrain by Frost expresses, as it illustrates, something of this
affinity of poetry for mechanism as a way of securing that quality in
art that we are accustomed to call, somewhat helplessly, inevitability,
or rightness:

> In a Poem

> The sentencing goes blithely on its way,
> And takes the playfully objected rhyme
> As surely as it keeps the stroke and time
> In having its undeviable say.

That is only half the story, for there is among poets at present the
most grievous division of opinion and practice on just this point of the
line, the stanza, the poem, considered as a mechanism or as something
else; here is William Carlos Williams, in *Paterson*, proclaiming the
view opposed:

> Without invention nothing is well-spaced,
> unless the mind change, unless
> the stars are new measured, according

                    to their relative positions, the
                    line will not change, the necessity
                    will not matriculate: unless there is
                    a new mind there cannot be a new
                    line, the old will go on
                    repeating itself with recurring
                    deadliness . . .

One can see from this that the relation of the line to the sentence structure, if it makes any sense at all, deliberately doesn't make the same sense it did before and continues to do for someone writing, as Frost does, in traditional measures.

Opinion among the masters, on this question of composition as mechanism, is as usual both divided and confusing; not only are there two sides, but theory and practice do not always or even very often coincide in one man's work. For Paul Valéry, *"To write* should really mean to construct, as solidly as possible, a machine of language in which the force of the stimulated mind is used in overcoming real obstacles; hence the writer must be divided against himself." That, again, is not a view that would be entertained, even as a metaphor, by everyone. Yeats, for instance, thought that art should be "a Centaur finding in the popular lore its back and its strong legs," and despised logic for being a machine: "unhelped it will force those present to exhaust the subject, the fool is as likely as the sage to speak the appropriate answer to any statement . . . You throw your money on the table and you receive so much change." And yet the poetry of Yeats, like that of Shakespeare, seems to me characterized by the most relentless pressure of logical force and coherence, and although he affected to dislike machinery he surely, in *A Vision* and the related poems, invented a vast deal of it.

A good deal of evidence—from science fiction to schizophrenic fantasies—suggests that our tensions about the machine became immensely aggravated when machines began to become our substantive daily reality. As many fairy tales will show, and some of them are scientific and technological fairy tales, the sudden transformation of a dream into a reality deprives the dream of much of its charm. So I suspect that all the to-do about "free verse" that has both blemished and adorned poetry in the present century may be not unconnected with a fear of the role of scientific technology in reducing to a mechanic regularity one area of life after another; poets would rebel in the only way professionally open to them, by stripping poetry of all

the traits that made it resemble mechanism, such as regular measure
and rhyme; even their visions would stress the irrational, irregular,
and unpredictable. The one significant exception that I am aware of,
anticipating the modern revolt by almost a century, is William Blake,
and he really does appear to prove the relation rather than deny it,
for it was *Jerusalem,* composed 1804–1820, that he did in free verse,
and both his practice in that poem and his justification in its preface *
relate to the fact that the theme of *Jerusalem* is the rebellion of the
poet, or fourfold human, against machinery, against all geometric
regularity and repetition, for which the poet's symbols are the mill,
the loom, the water wheel, and so on, on up to the "starry wheels"
of Jehovah's or Urizen's dead or dying universe, locked "in single
vision & Newton's sleep." In this Blake was again by many years
prophetic, not only in what he had to say but in the poetic means he
devised for saying it.

But the assertion that the interest in free verse may have had its
origin in some part from feelings of discomfort about machines may
not stand alone, for the opposite line of thought is also highly suggestive: there is at least enough synchronicity between the development
of free verse and the coming into wide availability of typewriters to
make me wonder if the machine, in this instance, might not have provided exactly the freedom it was thought to be taking away — because
on a typewriter you can write lines and strophes (or "verse paragraphs," as they significantly began to be called) having a rationalized
appearance on the page (by making the lines all about the same
length, for instance) even though neither the foot nor the number of
feet be counted at all; you can get the appearance of measuring without doing any measuring. Picasso said that the nail was the great en-

---

* "When this verse was first dictated to me, I consider'd a Monotonous Cadence,
like that used by Milton & Shakespeare & all writers of English Blank Verse, derived
from the modern bondage of Rhyming, to be a necessary and indispensible part of
Verse. But I soon found that in the mouth of a true Orator such monotony was not
only awkward, but as much a bondage as rhyme itself. I therefore have produced a
variety in every line, both of cadences & numbers of syllables. Every word and every
letter is studied and put into its fit place; the terrific numbers are reserved for the
terrific parts, the mild & gentle for the mild & gentle parts; all are necessary to each
other. Poetry Fetter'd Fetters the Human Race. Nations are Destroy'd or Flourish in
proportion as Their Poetry, Painting and Music are Destroy'd or Flourish! The Primeval
State of Man was Wisdom, Art and Science." *Jerusalem, To the Public,* p. 434 in the
Nonesuch edition of Geoffrey Keynes. What Blake meant by science is not easily
settled; how difficult the settlement might be is perhaps indicated by two notes from
The Laocoön Group (1820): "The Gods of Greece & Egypt were Mathematical Diagrams — See Plato's works." "Science is the Tree of Death."

emy of painting; maybe the typewriter has the same relation to poetry.

The relation of the arts to machinery, then, has always been ambiguous, containing both fascination and fear of being enthralled; in a sense its closest analogies are the relation between the spirit and the body, and now, with the advent of computers, the relation between the mind and the brain. It is true that minds without brains have not been observed to exist; yet I think it would be overhasty, on that account, to follow those philosophers who tell us that the term "mind" is a redundancy and a merely hypostatical entity, and that it therefore must be given up. For the brain, we are told, is an immensely complicated affair, having billions of relations; while the mind, like poetry which gives us one of our images for the mind, proceeds by thinkable simplicities, and out of those billions of possible relations can handle perhaps no more than two or three at a time without becoming lost, without being, in effect, taken over by the brain. There may, of course, come unforeseeable changes in the relation of the arts to machines; but if my analogies are in any degree accurate, the ambiguousness of the relation will remain, as they say, invariant under all transformations. I mean only that for every computer busy turning out beat poetry, another computer will be doing rhymed hexameters with a quill pen and possibly a flowing tie.

I don't see any way out of that impasse, and suspect there isn't one. You might, I have now and then idly thought, program a computer to make all possible metaphors on the common form a:b::c:d. Simplest example:

> So are you to my thoughts as food to life . . .
>
> (sonnet lxxv)

You would do this, relying upon the computer's immense speed, in the most wasteful manner possible, by instructing it to put together every possible combination of four words existing in the unabridged dictionary. The possibility of insanity here is very close: *fluff* is to *did* as *hippopathology* is to *reverse*. You would, I suppose, provide the computer with certain parameters of relevance, so that it would at once reject such figures as have no visible significance at all (these would rise into the billions of billions easily). But when the computer had printed out and preserved its few hundred beautiful and strange figures (presuming there would be some), and printed and thrown into the wastebasket its silly and useless figures, you would not be surprised to see, phoenixlike, a new school of poets arising from the wastebasket, for that or something like it appears to be the relation of poets at present to limits, órder, meaning, good sense, parameters, and all that.

Thus far my own sleeveless speculations, leading to the not particularly striking conclusion that computers could possibly write poetry if programmed by poets. But poets do not know how to program, and programmers do not, on the evidence thus far, know poetry; we are in the same sorry case with translators of the Greek drama, who appear to know either Greek or English but never by any chance both. Before adding a few remarks on the desirability of the culture's having its poems written by machines, however, I should seek the help of someone who, unlike myself, knows something on the technical side, and say a little about how the feasibility of the project stands at present.

From a recent book, *Computers and the Human Mind* by Donald G. Fink, I learn that the best opinion here also is as usual divided. In a discussion of Illiac music composed on a computer by Hiller and Isaacson a decade ago, Mr. Fink observes that in three out of the four experiments the program was "essentially imitative, not original," and he seems to regard this as possibly an intrinsic limitation, for he goes on to say: "Whatever originality appears in the Illiac music rests ultimately on random searching, which is, of course, the antithesis of artistic purpose."

I am in grave doubts about that easy "of course," and the conclusion to which it leads. Art cannot—and I am tempted to say "of course" myself now—consist entirely of random searching; yet the very phrase irresistibly suggests to me Keats's phrase, "Negative Capability," which he defined as "when a man is capable of being in uncertainties, mysteries, doubts, without any irritable reaching after fact and reason." And I have always supposed this component of Negative Capability or random search, to be somewhat higher in lyric poetry than in the other arts of language, and to have been considerably increasing during the present century; increasing, maybe, more than it ought to have done. Yet there certainly remains a force to Mr. Fink's argument, if I read him right, for if musical composition is subject to this limitation of the computer, that it must always be—to put the matter extremely— either imitative or foolish (reminding me of Dr. Johnson's finely saying of the disciples of Locke that "Truth is a cow will yield no more milk, and these people are gone off to milk the bull"), the same limitation will apply more strongly in literature, where, Mr. Fink says, "the scope of the symbols and the range of their combination are vastly greater," adding that "the range of concepts and relationships used . . . in composing poetry (which must take account of the sounds as well as the meanings of words, and must depart from normal modes of expression) may forever transcend the bounds of computer science."

Myself, I rather incline to hope so, for the following possibly sardonic, possibly funny, but not frivolously intended reasons. Thus far, that is, I have tried to do my duty by the subject, but now, with a deep breath—back to reality.

1. In a world where practically no one reads poetry, it is not really desirable, and may not even be sane, to increase exponentially the number of objects called poems, thus giving some poor idiot the task of deciding whether in fact they are or aren't.

2. The dullness, the want of gaiety and charm in the idea, are as appalling as the absence of sanity. The advantage claimed for the computer is its immense speed, but programming it, on the other hand, looks to be a slow and laborious and rather uninteresting business; in witness whereof, one anecdote.

A little book appeared a few years back called *Poetry: A Closer Look*, but the subtitle, "Programmed Instruction With Selected Poems," gives a clearer idea what it's up to. It seems to me clearly designed to teach computers, not people, to read poems, but its pretense is that it is addressed to the human student (the flap copy begins, chummily, "How long is it since you read a poem?") and I should not be surprised if the pretense had actually imposed on some teachers so that they imposed the book on their pupils. Some idea of the tedium that would result from following its procedures by nonelectronic means may be got from a few questions about the first poem it has programmed us to read:

What line in stanza one tells us that the man is watching the woods − − with snow?
The title tells the reader that the evening is snowy. Line − of stanza one also indicates that it is snowing.
Scene Two (stanzas two and three) introduces a new character: the "little −," who, according to his driver, must think this stopping by the woods a queer business.

The book goes on in this manner for a heartrending eighteen pages. This is reading poetry? I like poetry tolerably well, but I cannot imagine that after enduring an infliction like that I would ever willingly read another poem.

3. Why should the idea ever have come up at all? To what need in the human spirit does it respond?

This is a terrible thought, for a law formulated by me a moment ago in the course of writing the last sentence states that people get the poetry they want, and it always turns out to be the poetry they deserve. If their minds seem to them compassable even by very sophisticated machines, then their poetry inevitably will be written by machines. If you consider, too, that the great continuing epic poem of the present age, overlooked because omnipresent, is the daily newspaper, that sordid miracle, you must acknowledge that our real poetry is already reckonably nearer to being written by machines than it formerly was. And the need of the spirit to which, not in the area of our subject alone, the machines are responding, is a very ancient one: the curious compulsion upon the mind to literalize its metaphors and reify its symbols, to the end of turning the whole world, if possible, into *things;* and the further compulsion upon the mind to turn these dead things into ghosts, spirits, demons, divinities. So that once we have a machine that in certain respects functions after the model, much simplified, of the brain, it follows inevitably and ever so soon that the brain will be declared to be like that machine, and the machine will presently be referred to as The Brain. In a splendidly funny discussion of this theme of the introjected machine, Nigel Dennis says that such metaphors characteristically are first introduced in single quotes to indicate awareness, distance, even irony; later the single quotes get left out.

This process of "real-izing" notions will go forward in spite of numerous warnings against its being allowed to happen at all by people intimately acquainted with the actual workings of whatever machine is in question. Probably any number of lyre players could have given Pythagoras their opinion that the soul really wasn't very much like a tuned string; he would not have listened. And by the time Aristotle mentioned some important objections, it was too late; the idea had become fixed. Metaphor is a mighty power, the mightier perhaps for its property of being at the best imperfect; as Coleridge said, no comparison goes on all fours. But people are so taken with similarity that they refuse to see it is grounded in difference.

So if poetry did come to be written by computers, and people read and even declared they loved that poetry, one would still have to suspect that what had happened was not so much that the machine had imitated the subtlety of the mind, but that the mind had simplified (and brutalized) itself in obeisance to its idol the machine; on the model of the programmer who was asked if the computer could think, and replied: I compute it can. As Hannah Arendt says on this point: "The trouble with modern theories of behaviorism is not that they are wrong but that they could become true, that they actually are the best possible conceptualizations of certain obvious trends in modern society. It is quite conceivable that the modern age—which began with such an unprecedented and promising outburst of human activity—may end in the deadliest, most sterile passivity history has ever known." And, putting that warning in direct relation with our theme, "Thought itself, when it became 'reckoning with consequences,' became a function of the brain, with the result that electronic instruments are found to fulfill these functions much better than ever we could." It may indeed be that the fate of poetry, which only a short while back set itself the task of "absorbing the machine," will be to be absorbed by the machine; well, let determin'd things to destiny hold unbewail'd their way. But in the interval the poet's attitude will be, I suspect, compounded of amusement, keen interest, and, at the end, defiance. I close with one more gloomy warning.

Some time ago, I wrote of the poet as "the respected proprietor of an industry making, to the highest standards of craftsmanship, a product which has just been superseded by something more modern." A little later, maybe, his work will be valued as an antiquity; meanwhile it is merely obsolete.

More recently, during the night of the great power failure over the Northeast, while we did not know either the extent or probable duration of our calamity, I remember thinking that this would be a hell of a time to find out that all the candle factories had been fully automated.

Computer Poetry

A few years ago I wrote a lecture called "Speculative Equations: Poems, Poets, Computers." I did this without more knowledge of what computers had actually done about poetry than a vague memory of examples quoted in newspapers, and without other knowledge of what they might possibly do than the opinion of a competent authority writing, however, for the lay audience (Donald Fink). Probably the technically initiated will consider these handicaps as fatal to my attempt. But my hope is that I remained within the limits of my modest competence by speaking first theoretically about what sorts of things a machine would have to learn in order to write poetry, and second historically, about the long-standing traditional relations between arts and machinery.

Since then I have had only one more active relation to a computer. My wife and I bought a plastic, manually operated model of a digital computer; it came in the mail; we opened it. The instructions were admirably clear, and in about half an hour we had put it together and checked it out so that it said in its binary language that it was fit and ready to be put to work. But then we found we had nothing to ask it, and the poor thing stood on a shelf till a cat knocked it off and it fell into, well, bits. It was a very pretty-looking machine, though, and I remember it with affection.

When I first gave my lecture on computers and poetry, Professor Isaac Asimov was in the audience, and during the question period he came up with what seemed a telling criticism of my view. He asked me at what age I had begun writing poetry. About age seventeen, I said. And was my poetry at seventeen, he wanted to know, was it any good? I allowed it probably wasn't. And he said I ought to remember that the computer is scarcely older now than I was at seventeen.

But now, owing to the kindness of Professor Robert Dana of Cornell

College, I have some samples of computer-written poetry to exhibit to you; and by accident I have come again into the possession of some poems I seem to have written at ages seventeen to twenty-one or so; and with these as a basis I may hopefully go somewhat beyond my earlier remarks, and be a good deal more particular, as well as somewhat ruder.

The samples of computer poetry I now have come from two computers, and are quite different in kind. Though the machines used in both programs were IBM 360s, it turns out I wasn't wrong in raising an anticipatory question in my first attempt, saying that "for every computer busy turning out beat poetry, another computer will be doing rhymed hexameters with a quill pen and possibly a flowing tie." For one IBM 360 is a moralist, while the other is an aesthete. The aesthete seems to me more gifted, although or because very derivative. And possibly I am prejudiced here, for the aesthetically minded machine shows passing evidence of having read a phrase of mine, among many other phrases.

On the basis of these materials I think to defend the following positions.

Either the computer's ability to write poetry was abysmally more inadequate at the time of my earlier essay than I had supposed it to be—my criticisms at that time look to be mild, charitable and, as Hans Christian Andersen says, stupider than the law allows—or in the interval the computer has not been growing up with respect to poetry, as Professor Asimov supposed it would, but growing down into a savage illiteracy and idiocy that would be difficult to believe, were not the evidence to hand. Were a human being responsible for this garbage, we should have to forgive him while throwing it away, on the excellent principle of detesting the sin but loving the sinner. But what attitude are we to take toward a machine? I am indignant at its imposture and imposition, but it will not be affected by my indignation unless I go to Nebraska and take an axe to its memory. And even then, it would not be affected in the direction of reform. What would be most grievously affected, I submit, would be the tempers of its friends and employers—for even a machine may have friends as well as employers—who would no doubt have me put in jail for damaging valuable property. So you see that in such an eventuality, no matter what is claimed for the machine (and it is by turns little and much), human beings would still be in the act, taking ultimate responsibility for answering to my ultimate act of literary criticism with an axe. Therefore, while illustrating my contentions—and they are going to be fairly contentious—from the samples supplied by the computer, I shall also illustrate from the programmer's prefatory notes what the trouble, or anyhow a few of the troubles, seems to be.

In my earlier essay I outlined in a most moderate and even gentle way what one of our critical problems would be: "Supposing it to be technically possible to make a computer write what will technically pass for poetry, we have still to ask about the poetry it grinds out with such frightening industry and at such tremendous speed whether it expresses the soul of the computer or the soul of the programmer, not to mention the degree of his literary sophistication, or in very truth the prophetic soul of the wide world dreaming on things to come."

On the basis of the examples to hand, my supposition looks absurdly generous, for this IBM 360 has not been taught to write anything that will technically pass for poetry unless among such as are willing to jettison the past of that art entire—including the entire range from *The Iliad* to *Mother Goose*—and start all over again with redefinitions to fit their results.

Here is an example. The programmer quotes it at the end of his preface with the following encomium: "Perhaps the following poem, which was produced by the first successful run of the program, is more poetical than later works."

Monsters

They fight beans to her wires
Fred's Greek often creates her.
Irving's devil mainly angers her!
Whee! Ouch, aha!
Black the green void appears.
Their pig computes behind her
I dive and those hangmen move to us
Ouch! Exist of the void
Some birds release poisons
Which green wise poets convince Fred's ugly flower?

After a moment of silence, and before saying anything off my own hat, I shall remind us by a few brief instances of some of the things poetry sounds like.

If the Sun & Moon should doubt
They'd immediately go out.
                                    Blake

Slow, slow, fresh fount, keep time with my salt tears;
   Yet slower, yet, O faintly gentle springs.
List to the heavy part the music bears;
   Woe weeps out her division, when she sings.

                                        Jonson

Things out of perfection sail,
And all their swelling canvas wear,
Nor shall the self-begotten fail
Though fantastic men suppose
Building-yard and stormy shore,
Winding-sheet and swaddling-clothes.

                                        Yeats

The ebb slips from the rock, the sunken
Tide-rocks lift streaming shoulders
Out of the slack, the slow west
Sombering its torch; a ship's light
Shows faintly, far out,
Over the weight of the prone ocean
On the low cloud.

                                      Jeffers

The hand that signed the paper felled a city;
Five sovereign fingers taxed the breath,
Doubled the globe of dead and halved a country;
These five kings did a king to death.

                                 Dylan Thomas

   These five samples come from three different periods of poetry in English. I have taken three of them from the present century, because I believe that part of the programmer's difficulty comes from an opinion that what is called "modern poetry" is, in contrast to earlier poetry, wild, mannerless, free as to measure, and "obscure" — leading on directly to the fallacy I see among my students, that if you write something you yourself cannot understand you must thereby have been extremely profound.

   I enjoy shooting fish in a barrel as well as the next fellow, but I shan't make particular criticisms of the computer's effort because where nothing is right there's no point in trying to say what's wrong. Nor do I want to argue with my readers on the subject. If the computer's poem pleases you, well, that is one of the liberties guaranteed to you by the Constitution, and I would not abridge it if I could. And if you do not see and acknowledge some immense differences between the computer's poem and *all* of my five examples, you are beyond the point of no return, not so much because you do not think but because you cannot hear.

The chief differences, to me, are these. The computer has not been told about, or what they call "programmed for," scanning its verses; consequently it cannot write verses. A human being could write verses rejecting every known principle of scansion, but he would know that he had to supply some principle in their stead; and this the computer does not know. The computer has in any event been taught to write not poems, but statements, which can only by courtesy of an extreme kind be thought of as lines; one line succeeds another in time and on the page but never in sense. Finally, what the computer has been taught to do is what children begin doing about age two to three, make independent use of that marvelous carrier wave the sentence, which is capable of accommodating an indefinitely large number of messages as long as they accommodate themselves to its various but relatively few forms. The child, by the way, does this without being taught; he makes up sentences of his own, which by and large make excellent sense. The computer makes up sentences which are grammatical but on the whole remarkably avoidant of meaning; a human being attempting to be nonsensical, inconsequential, and irrelevant for ten whole lines would find the attempt a very great strain indeed; for most of us I venture to say it would be impossible. Truly it might be said of the computer what Settembrini said of Naphta, "His form is logic but his essence is confusion."

It has learned to make grammar without having learned to make sense, which is if you think of it a pretty remarkable achievement all by itself.

There is one other point. The computer has not learned the tradition of poetry in English; it shows no sign even of having learned that there is a tradition of poetry in English; consequently it does not write poetry in English; oddly enough it cannot even decide to be untraditional or antitraditional. Remembering Mr. Asimov's joke, I shall introduce for contrast an undergraduate poet writing about 1940; the example later appeared in *Poetry*, not through any will of his own—he was away at the wars—but through the well-meaning officiousness of a friend:

Sigmund Freud

Each house had its ghost. Graves opened to his voice,
The dead lived in him by his grave consent:

He was, by their constraint upon his choice,
Orpheus of all the lonesome, spent
His evenings charting out a private hell,
The spaceless realm that all the puzzled caught,
The swamps that made their frightful towns unwell: ·
He chained his life to theirs, was like them lost.
Perhaps unwillingly he did this, became
Laureate of those who were afraid.
For himself assumed them as a native guise,
Entered their warring lands as one of them,
Employed their rhetoric and blague to raid
The towers of their most strategic lies.

Now this undergraduate bard, unlike the computer (which *pace* Mr. Asimov may be of a generation, but cannot be of an age), knows all too well what he is doing, and anyone at all acquainted with the history of the matter can see very clearly what he is doing. He is writing a sonnet, and doing it with on the whole tolerable skill at filling out forms, a fairly humble enterprise in itself but of some moment to the art of poetry; and he is imitating W. H. Auden, who at that time had just come out with a number of poems about famous writers, sages, and so on, such as Melville, Voltaire at Ferney, and even Sigmund Freud. Our young epigone has in a couple of places pretty cutely caught the Auden manner—a manner that Auden in his turn had caught and modernized from the Eighteenth Century. Consider:

The swamps that made their frightful towns unwell . . .

or

The towers of their most strategic lies.

And place them next to a couple of characteristic lines by Mr. Auden:

That neither the low democracy of a nightmare nor
An army's primitive tidiness may deceive me . . .

or

To vilify the landscape of Distinction and see
The heart of the Personal brought to a systolic standstill,
The Tall to diminished dust.

It is fairly plain, then, what this young poet was doing; he was trying to learn to write poetry. In order to come to even so humble a

stage he had first to acknowledge that a sort of stuff called poetry
existed, that it had been in the world for a long time before his appearance on the scene, that it had ways of its own that had to be mastered, and that possibly—though by no means certainly—the way to
mastery was at least in part, as Ben Jonson had suggested so long ago,
through the imitation of beloved and revered masters whose own
works enthralled him. The same master, Mr. Auden, once suggested
that in any school for poets operated by himself the only sorts of criticism allowed would be parody and pastiche; and it looks as though
our young poet had already decided that for himself; had he had a
teacher, that teacher's appropriate response would have been neither
"this is wonderful" nor "this is atrocious" but a smile and a pat on the
head: "Bien, bien. Continuez." For sometimes out of such stuff as this
sonnet, and by means entirely mysterious, may come a mastery of
one's own, a thing so unbelievably strange and simple that when a
master says something as near as not absolutely indistinguishable
from what anyone might say we hear it in his voice—

So what said the others and the sun went down—

yes, of course, we say at once, Wallace Stevens. What's so strange
about that? But it is, it is very strange. Nothing like it has been taught
the computer under discussion, and subject to the correction of the
learned I incline to doubt anything like it can at present be taught to
the computer at all.

Before it tries to write poetry the computer has in a sense to be told
what sort of stuff poetry is, as well as how to write it. This teaching, I
venture out of my ignorance long enough to say, has little or nothing
to do with the technical art of programming, for it consists of assumptions as to what poetry is that are largely unconscious in the programmer (at least according to the present example) and of course
completely unconscious in the computer, which does not have consciousness.

For this reason I am most grateful to the programmer for his prefatory "Notes on this Computer Poetry," and I am going to show my
gratitude by saying some rather mean and nasty things about some
of the statements made therein. I am grateful because the "Notes"
show, as the poems don't at all, what the programmer believes about
the art of poetry, and I am mean and nasty because what the "Notes"
show is that he is wasting his time and mine, as well as constituting
a threat to an art I care for.

Most of the "Notes," all the same, are technical ones descriptive of the procedure of programming and some of its limitations; with these I am not concerned. But there do occur at least two places at which the programmer allows us to see a little what he thinks he is up to. I shall take the last one first, as being the shorter:

It is difficult to discuss the poetic merit of such computer poetry, for this is not an area in which the ordinary standards of "greatness" apply. We do not claim that these works are particularly good literary creations, only that they are literary creations, and that they were produced by a human artifact rather than by a human.

Would but ask the programmer beseechingly: If it is difficult— what you really seem to mean is *impossible*—to discuss the poetic merit of these things, why do'em? Either you are doing poetry or you are not doing poetry; if you cannot decide, what is the aim of the exercise? But in fact it is difficult to discuss the poetic merit only because it isn't there. Demonstrably, your examples contain no external, mechanical feature that can be shown to characterize poetry in English for several centuries; would you claim it is on that account that they are in some intrinsic and spiritual way poetic? I do not think you can avoid your difficulty by the seeming modesty of your claims; the moment you take the poem out of the machine and present it to another person as a poem you are in an area in which the ordinary standards of "greatness," whatever those may be, apply, in an area indeed in which no other standards can possibly be allowed to apply. Ruskin, in speaking of several kinds of first-rate poetry, pauses to say, rather loftily, that with other than the first rate no one ought to be allowed to trouble the public; even making allowances for somewhat lower but still pleasant slopes of Parnassus, how can we admit for a moment the need to attend to what your silly machine has done? Even on that, I own to some unscientific doubts. For what, after all, did the machine do? You say that your procedures "demonstrate the ability of a simple algorithm to create images independently of any human being," and argue that "Ha ha, the arid riders oppose merry robots"— your best line, by the way, in several pages—"produces a meaningful (though not useful) image in the mind of the reader which was not previously in the mind of any person on earth." But what I seem to see is that you put the structures of simple sentences into the poor beast's head and then filled up the syntactical forms with irrelevancies, so that silliness was bound to come forth.

As to the programmer's second point. Some of the poems have what he calls "a special improvement."

In these works the vocabulary was arranged with an ethical structure as well as a syntactical one. Simply, this means that "bad" individuals are always associated with "bad" adjectives and verbs. . . . Actually, the situation is not this simple, for some words are neither "good" nor "bad," and the use of transitive verbs depends on the moral quality of the object as well as the subject.

The classification of individuals as "good" or "bad" is rather arbitrary and may confuse some. Though some may disagree, Henry V, Mr. Zip, St. Joan, LBJ, Tarzan, Fillmore, and Ivanhoe are included in the "good" category, while Dracula, Mao, Napoleon, Goliath, Scrooge, and Godzilla are "bad."

I can agree with the programmer, though on other than linguistic grounds, that "actually, the situation is not this simple." Even if from the technical side it is permissible to begin with crude approximations — to verse, to metaphor, to meaning — and hope to refine them progressively by experience and the use of more capable machines, I do not believe that model is applicable to the making of ethical judgments, which if they are crude to begin with are almost bound to become more so with use, instead of less.

Poetry is often and defensibly said to have to do with moral judgment; someone once defined it as "the charity of the imagination," meaning I suppose that though we might ultimately have to condemn a man's action flatly we shall do well to let ourselves be instructed also concerning his struggles in deciding on that action and his torments and doubts following it; as Donne said about a suicide, "Thou knowest this man's fall, but not his wrastlings."

Since the computer's list of heroes touches on a hero of poetry only at one point I may as well comment on the comparison. Here first is the computer on Henry V.

> Superman planned for kind patriots promise
> Near the milkman and two vicious vandals
> seventy kind allies respect the hero
> my virtuoso loves brown suitors
> bold allies fought the vicious rogue
> though the oracle will be Tarzan
> superior martyrs accused your guilty demon
> their champion and their friends worship readers
> ah, bold Ivanhoe forgave one bad werewolf
> dracula pursues the enemies
> my vampire bothered noble St. Joan
> peerless creators condemn each corrupt traitor
> and this savior was Arthur
> since your paragon is St. Joan.

My first observation is that this is not identifiably about Henry V except possibly for half of one line; he did condemn some traitors before embarking for France (*Henry V*, 2, 2). Nor do I at all see in what sense any moral judgment whatever, on anyone, can be made to emerge from these incoherent ramblings; we are told nothing of a moral nature about either the Henry V known to history or the mythological one poetized upon by Shakespeare. But even supposing, as the programmer's preface supposes, a moral judgment to have been made pronouncing Henry V "good," that judgment remains without content of any kind; we have yet to ask what he did, that was good or bad. About this, both history and Shakespeare, in very different ways, are less decisive. History, of course, knows nothing of a Prince Hal who got drunk, roistered with Falstaff, robbed travellers, was rebuked by the Lord Chief Justice and dramatically reformed upon ascending the throne. Quite the contrary, Henry was already conducting his father's wars by early adolescence, was made Warden of the Cinque Ports at fifteen, and is known for having a dour and pious disposition, as well as for cruelty.

But that is only history; what of poetry?

Shakespeare's tetralogy about Richard II, Henry IV, and Henry V is his attempt at a national epic. In Hal he inherited a hero around whom mythological traits had assembled themselves in traditional and sequential fashion; these were believed to be true, they were in the histories the poet had to hand. All the same, Shakespeare is in doubts about his Hal; even at the beginning of the first play he may be suspected of coldness, cynicism, and hypocrisy to his friends. His genial and engaging style deteriorates considerably from the first play to the second, in which indeed the moral character of all the persons has become considerably worse; and when we first see him as king he is being legalistic, when we next see him as king he is hanging some traitors; then he rises in our sympathy during the scene on the eve of Agincourt, going anonymous among his soldiers and meditating the awful burden of the kingship; he rises again in the stirring invocation to battle, and he is a charming gallant in his courtship of the French princess afterward, and his marriage to her is represented most movingly and piously in the tradition for heroes of romance as the bestowing of peace and prosperity on the war-ruined realms of France and Britain. Shakespeare breaks off on this high note, omitting the epically inappropriate circumstances that Henry died only a few years after Agincourt and the wars thereupon began again.

The point is not to compare Shakespeare's adequate with the computer's inadequate versification but to consider poetry in relation to morality. Shakespeare, being a man, thought, and he thought in rela-

tion to history and tradition. In these plays he thought nearly two
centuries into the past, but what he thought about was painfully near
in his own time also: rebellion, legitimacy, peace and war, the replacing of an old style of life, of character, of belief, with a new one.

Now of all this the computer does not know. It has been programmed with a vocabulary suitable to its condition, and the decision
as to this suitability was made by the programmer, who no doubt deliberately omitted from consideration this simple thing, that before
you judge someone good or bad you should know what he has done.
You must also have some feelings toward what he has done, and these
feelings may be very complex, and far from unequivocal. So far as the
present examples suggest, the computer may be able to change its
mind serially, that is, to think two successive but different and possibly opposed thoughts upon the same subject; but it is not able to hold
two—or three or a good many—thoughts in the solution of a great
style, which is what poets attempt to do.

But according to the present examples the computer can neither
write verse, make sense, nor stay with a subject for longer than half a
breath; it should go back to school and study again. Or, and this is the
preferable alternative, the whole business should be dropped at once.

For what seems to me to emerge from the whole discussion is that,
even granting the ultimate technical improvements, the computer can
never do more than imitate from the outside certain imitable characteristics of art; but in spite of all the agonizing doubts of art and doubts
of self by artists in the present century, art comes from inside and outside at once.

Poetry tells us stories deep and rich with experience, with thought,
with language. The technological—I would not say the scientific—
pretension is that all this is artificially imitable; and technologically
that might one day turn out to be true. And then?

I close with the wise words of an anthropologist, Paul Riesman,
writing on "The Eskimo Discovery of Man's Place in the Universe."
After remarking upon the cruelly minimal character of Eskimo life so
far as concerns material comfort and safety, and upon the remarkable
fact that in these circumstances poetry is to them of the highest importance, he has this to say:

. . . when we ask of science the question "Why are we here?" or "What is our
place in the universe?" the probabilities and equations we get for answers do
not satisfy us.

They do not satisfy us because we feel somehow that the question has not
been answered. After all, what we want to know is something quite definite:

"Where are we?" . . . Science tells us that our place in the universe is no-where in particular . . . or anywhere. I think that this is the best that science will do for us. No amount of research will effect a qualitative change in that answer. For it is true; it is the correct answer. It has stared us human beings in the face throughout our history. Think of all the natural calamities that we know about in history: the comings and goings of the ice age, the volcanic eruptions, the earthquakes, the floods, the droughts: do not these things tell us that the universe does not know that we are here, that whether we exist or not does not matter? Or consider any historical event, such as a war: in a sense the more we investigate it the less we know about it with certainty: the recent proliferation of works on our Civil War, for example, suggests to me that the closest we can come to understanding it is to consider it as something that "just happened" to us, rather than as something we did for such and such reasons.

All that modern science has done in this situation is point out the facts more clearly. Conventional reactions to science, for example, our faith in it, our belief in progress, together with social and technical developments . . . have made it difficult for people to understand what is going on or what they can do about it. And yet in all times and places human beings have resisted the idea that they are nowhere for no particular reason and for no particular purpose. They have almost always managed to find a somewhere to be, and a reason to be there. The finding of these somewheres is an activity which is crucial to human life, for people seem to go to pieces when events force them to contemplate the ultimate nowhere of their lives. Then they act in ways which the majority of mankind would consider inhuman, ways which they themselves would have considered inhuman from the point of view of some-where.

from *Sign Image Symbol*, ed. Gyorgy Kepes.

Poetry, Prophecy, Prediction

The first effect of writing on the theme of "Educating for the Twenty-First Century" is to remind me that I shan't be around to see the twenty-first century, whose habits in teaching and learning will not be judged primarily by their success in matching any predictions I might make for them. But then, I don't expect to be making any predictions. For one thing, if I were to do so I should be doing black magic. For another, I should be improperly trespassing on the territory of a good many specialist experts who are fairly competent at this kind of black magic as long as they keep within their specialized domain. That leaves it a question what I may properly discuss. And you can see to begin with that a man who begins by saying he doesn't know what to write about, much less what he will have said when he's through, is scarcely a man to tell you much about educating for the twenty-first century.

To be, asked to do so, moreover, because one writes poems, is an instance of a temptation the world offers in ever so many ways: one's supposed competence at something in particular turns into an invitation to have opinions about everything in general; we all have opinions, and are most of us fond of delivering them on a good occasion. But poetry is not opinions.

What is poetry? Hard or impossible to say, for if one minute poetry is saying things like "Fara diddle dino, This is idle fino," at the next minute it may be found saying things like,

> When time is old and hath forgot himself,
> When water drops have worn the stones of Troy,
> And blind oblivion swallowed cities up,
> And mighty states are grated characterless
> To dusty nothing . . . ,

contemplating as it were with a lofty equanimity and impersonal grandeur the End of Days; not, however, because the poet was announcing the End of Days as imminent, but rather because such expressions seemed to suit his subject (someone swearing undying love), and because he knew, without probably thinking about it, that we, his hearers, rather like listening to such sublime and solemn magnitudes as go with the falls of cities, states, princes, and so on. There was a Chinese painter who for effects of mist-enshrouded steepness became known as The Master of the High and Distant Style, and that might do for the poet in this instance, too. But I am told that the Hindu God Siva, he of the seven arms, when he does his dance of the destruction of the universe, always keeps one of his seven hands extended toward the beholder, in a gesture whose conventional meaning is "Fear not." And so the poet, in imprecating oblivion and dusty nothing on civilization in general, and doing it in the loftiest language he can find, may also be whispering in an aside, "Fara diddle dino, This is idle fino."

Poetry, however, has through most of its long tradition been closely akin to prophecy, for the poet, on one widespread and enduring view of him, sang not from his personal thought or mind but from the mind of a god or goddess who had for the time being driven him out of his personal thought and mind; so it was with the prophets of the Old Testament, and with Plato's god-drunken poet in the "Ion." In the Middle Ages, Virgil's reputation was primarily that of a sorcerer, and people read the future by using verses of the "Aeneid" somewhat as people continue to read the future from the arrangements of the "I Ching," or "Book of Changes." And at least as late as Sydney's "Apologie" the poet in English is regarded as a vates, or vaticinator, which can mean anything from vulgar soothsaying to true prophecy.

If we think entirely in prose, we reject that relation of poetry and prophecy altogether. Yet the relation may remain, though in hiding from what is ordinarily thought in prose, or, rather, in the language of this world. There is another world, however, in which the highest poetry may and sometimes does have a truly prophetic sense, and that will be my theme.

But because in poetical thought the shortest way between two points is through a labyrinth, I am to approach this theme not directly but variously, by forthrights and meanders. I shall introduce it, then, by giving you first a statement, an incomplete statement, by a poet who is also a prophet, who says: "We who dwell on Earth can do nothing of ourselves; everything is conducted by Spirits. . . ." and by giving you a pair of riddles to mull over for a while until I announce the return of the theme by completing the poet's sentence and answering the riddles.

> I am the combination to a door
> That fools and wise with equal ease undo.
> Your unthought thoughts are changes still unread
> In me, without whom nothing's to be said.
>
> Without my meaning nothing, nothing means.
> I am the wave for which the worlds make way.
> A term of time, and sometimes too of death,
> I am the silence in the things you say.

And now, entering the labyrinth that dances us away only to dance us back to the beginning in the end, I shall try to say a number of things about the world, about time, memory, history, that impose their strange conditions on all that we do, including predicting the future and prophesying.

The things I have to say will look random indeed, for it is of the nature of poetical thought to weave up its reality gradually, and to produce its justice retrospectively. To say the most arbitrary thing you can dream of, and then to sing up around it a world in which it will look perfectly at home, that is what poetical thought chiefly means to do; in which it somewhat and surprisingly resembles mathematic thought. If the poet should begin to philosophize he must needs do so as a beginner, as a pre-Socratic, and think in fragments. And professionally, his motto might be that expressed by a modern philosopher: "If a man doesn't contradict himself, maybe he isn't saying anything" (Si un hombre nunca se contradice, sera porque nunca se dice nada—Unamuno, in conversation with Erwin Schrödinger).

II

I remember that a vision concerning the future of education did once happen to me. It was ten or eleven years ago, and the Dean of the Graduate School at one of our great Universities (that is a conventional expression, but it certainly was a very large university) was showing me through the buildings belonging to his domain. We were in a long corridor with glass doors at either end. From behind the closed doors on either side came the mumbling of innumerable phrases, none of them distinctly to be heard. At that moment there came into my mind a picture: The same corridor, the glass doors broken, silence at either hand save for the noise made by the wind blowing bluebooks and dust along the rubbled floor.

That experience impressed me deeply, for it had a number of characteristics that seem to belong to vision and prophecy rather than to anything we usually identify as thought. It came unbidden; I had not been thinking about education or its future at all. It came as a picture, not as a thought. It did not offer any explanation of itself. It could not refer to past or present, hence it had to refer to the future . . . or to nothing at all. It did not set a date for the pictured event, nor offer any cause for the reduction of a thriving enterprise to the condition it pictured; indeed, it was repugnant to reason, and had I mentioned it to the Dean I should probably have done so as a rather feeble joke, and that is certainly how he would have received it. In fact, I did not mention it, for the good reason that to have done so would have seemed bad manners (another trait that usually goes with prophecy) and an abuse of my privilege as a guest. And the whole episode came and went in perhaps a second or so.

This happened in 1959. That university, and universities in general, are still here and still very largely prospering. There is only this to be observed, though, that what in 1959 would have been prophecy, to be received with a passing smile as beyond thought incredible, would ten years later look not like prophecy at all but like a reasonable though perhaps unduly pessimistic extrapolation of likely futures from present happenings. So that is how I missed my chance to be numbered among the prophets.

But while I was writing this essay there came to hand another instance that seems to belong with the one just given. *Esquire* for December, 1969, adventured into the future, not quite so far as the twenty-first century, and brought back to its readers a copy of the *New York Times* for Wednesday, November 3, 1976.

Now this was a very cute idea for someone to have had, and the execution of it must have involved great ingenuity and artifice, as well as a deal of hard work and good fun for the participants. Given the idea, however, one has to say that the project is for the most part polemical and satirical rather than prophetic, as you can see from a sampling of headlines such as: Agnew Proclaimed President . . . Rusk Concedes Bitter Contest, and Good News on Vietnam Voiced; Defense Chief Sees U. S. Pullout by '78; U. S. Casualty Rise Smallest of Year, and so on.

But there was at least one piece that seemed poignantly to illuminate, in contrast to satire, the prophetic voice. The headline reads: "BEWILDERED ADD TO PEOPLE HERDS; Nomads Have Little Contact With Residents of the Area." I shall quote a few passages that seem particularly striking:

Las Cruces, N.M., Nov. 2—The days are shorter and cooler here now in the Jornada del Muerto. The morning sun, rising over the San Andres mountains to the east, no longer turns this rocky, sandy, hundred-mile-long valley into the dusty hell of full summer. But the real sign of oncoming winter is the arrival in the Jornada of the nine-million-strong People Herd from its summer range in Eastern Utah. The herd will linger here a month or so, perhaps more, before turning westward toward Yuma on the never-ending annual cycle of migration. So it has been for the last five years, since the Department of Health, Education and Welfare handed over the population problem to the Department of the Interior; and so it will continue in the foreseeable future. Only one thing sure: the herd will grow. In 1971 there were fewer than one million Groupers, as the herd members are called; by the end of the decade, according to herd officials, there will be at least forty million.

The news item goes on to record with devastating accuracy the kinds of thing we should probably learn of such an event, should it ever happen, by reading the *New York Times*. For instance, "It isn't true that they can't talk," adds Kelley. "They just don't have much to say. I've talked to some of them myself. At night, sometimes, they sing." And for instance again:

No signs of cultural or social development have yet been noted among the herds. "How so many people can remain socially static for so long is a mystery to us," says Professor Roland Thorn of the University of New Mexico's sociology department.

My singling this bit out from the rest as prophetic seems when I think about it to have several causes. What is prophetic will have to do with the vast and meaningless and confused—"migrations that must needs void memory," said Hart Crane; what is prophetic is so because it projects upon the modern and up-to-date future images of what is primitive and archaic, boding of "great tribulations such as were not from the beginning of the world" (Matthew 24.21); finally, what is prophetic is a matter of style. The sinister, ominous, brooding quality of the vision, which goes quite unforcedly with its humor, comes as much as anything from the miming of the imperturbable voice and attitude of the newspaper of record, which does for modern times what the recording angel was supposed to do for biblical times, that is, record. This item and one or two others contrast decisively with the vision of the rest of *Esquire*'s parody, in which the future is simply the present, doubled and vulnerable, the only question being who is holding the Last Trump.

One more point about the instance should have separate notice,

because it belongs to that relation of poetry and the prophetic I mentioned earlier, and to which in the usual labyrinthine manner we are
returning. Like my vision of the university, this vision does not explain itself, nor offer to reconstruct the stages that led from here to
there. But the poetic thing about this vision of the people herd is that
it comes not from looking into the future so much as from looking at
the present and seeing it clearly, that is, with eyes not under the spell
of the languages — such as the language of the *New York Times* — that
customarily tell us what we believe about, or what is the meaning of,
the things that are happening in the present. Enlightened by this
poetical prophecy of annual and aimless meanderings on the part of
millions of persons, we may see that what we are told to look at is
not — or not only — a hypothetical and more or less probable notion
about the future, but what is accepted at present as one of the routine things that happen: the millions of airline miles, of automobile
miles, annually clocked by millions of people across the country and
up and down the country, save that in the parody this amazing phenomenon is given dramatic as well as statistical bulk and dramatic
power (in part by analogy with the migrations of hordes of buffalo and
bison); whereas when we are told of such things by the *real New York
Times* we are led to believe that behind the statistical form are individuals like ourselves, moving where they do for good and sufficient reason, even if only to move back the way they came — for good
and sufficient reason — the following year. As if history should provide us with the image of Ostrogoth and Visigoth, Vandal and Hun,
rolling back and forth across Europe season to season and year to
year, instead of coming once only in successive waves of conquest
and settlement. Or as if Krishna's instruction to Arjuna, so eloquently
moralized by T. S. Eliot, had read: "Fare Forward, Voyagers, in all
directions at once."

III

Digressive Note. Prophecy, Prediction, and the Idea of Cause.

Owing to the one-directional nature of the Arrow of Time, prophecy
is always of disaster, and as a good many people are always prophesying, one or another prophecy will always be seen as having come true.

Seeking the simplest and most general expressions for this twinned
truth, I found them not in Isaiah or Jeremiah or any other voice crying
in the wilderness, but in the seat of government, in the Capitol and in
the White House.

1. A General from the Pentagon testifying before a Congressional
Committee on Defense Appropriations said decisively: *The period of*

greatest danger lies ahead. That remark has the granite simplicity of
a fundamental law.

2. President Eisenhower is reported to have said: *Things are more
like they are now than they've ever been before.* That, one may say,
is why prophecies are always coming true: because things are always
being more like they are now than they ever were before. That is,
contrary to common supposition, you do not really remember the past
better than you foresee the future; a surprising disadvantage of the
arrow of time is that it can also goose you feather-end first. Nor do you
generally see visible things more clearly than invisible things, nor
things near you more clearly than things far away. This has to do essentially with the idea of civilization, but instead of explaining civilization I shall illustrate by a couple of small stories.

One year a village had its crops destroyed by a plague of seventeen-
year locusts. The people, after they had picked up the pieces and got
things going as best they might, went to their local shaman, or prophet,
and asked him if they should expect the same to happen next year. He
replied: "No." And it became part of ritual that they should ask him
this question at the appropriate time each year; his No, you see, was
not only predictive but magically protecting, which is truly what
prophecy ought to be though it mostly isn't. So year after year the
wise man kept replying: No. And for sixteen years he was right as
right could be. Even in the seventeenth year, though, when the
plague of locusts came again, his reputation scarcely suffered at all.
Most people, even if they had been alive during the earlier disaster,
quite failed to remember it, or if they did remember it they remembered it so vaguely and with so many distortions that they thought the
present disaster something altogether different from the former one;
and to the odd skeptic who dared to attack the prophet's reputation
the faithful had a ready answer: "Could you do better as a prophet,"
they said, "than our prophet who has been right sixteen times out of
seventeen?"

I think it was in Freud that I read a related story, wherein, however,
distance in time is replaced by distance in space. There was a rabbi of
Lodz who during service in the synagogue had a vision, which he reported to the congregation: He saw (he said) his colleague the rabbi
of Cracow in bed and dying, nay, now dead. Which was the more wonderful as there was present at the service a man from Cracow who only
a day or so before had seen the rabbi there in excellent health. So the
fame of the rabbi of Lodz for his feat of what may fittingly be called
television got noised about the town — until the next week, when a
second visitor from Cracow said that the rabbi there was not dead,

was not even sick, he didn't have so much as a head cold. But again the faithful had a ready answer: "Even so," they said, "it's not every rabbi who could see from Lodz to Cracow."

Though I couldn't resist adding the second story because it made such a pretty balance, I think it's the first one that makes the main point: Prophecy and prediction are often taken to be two words for the same thing, but they aren't. Poets occasionally—very rarely, I believe—are prophets and I shall illustrate this contention at the end of the essay. But if they set up for predicters of the future they do so not as poets but in their spare time and, of course, at our own risk. Prophecy is a much more awesomely mysterious business, but prediction has its little mysteries too, and of these I shall speak first.

Predicting the future—knowing which horse is going to win, or whether rain will spoil the picnic—is an immensely powerful idea because it draws its powers from so many sources commonly thought to be rather at odds than in cahoots with one another. It is the most ancient and enduring dream of magic, but in its new scientific form it is amazingly practicable and productive of most marvelous results, such as putting people on the moon and getting them back to earth. As the first object of civilizations, predicting the future—which one does by making it oneself—is also immensely successful, except for those times at which it doesn't succeed. The possibility of perfect prediction and perfect control draws upon one of the most magical dreams human beings have ever had, the ideal of a mechanic rationality to all the billion bits and pieces of the universe; the ideal of an earlier and simpler science, still so much with us (though not with the scientists), that enabled Laplace to say with a kind of dunderheaded audacity that if you knew where every little bit and piece was right now you could say where the whole business would be later on.

Finally, the appeal of predicting the future draws upon an incredibly simple, powerful, and inadequate phantasy about the world, whose name is Cause and Effect. It is the phantasy of an active, aggressive, outgoing people in a world which allows them to suppose that when they press a switch and a light goes on it is their pressing the switch that has *caused* the light to go on. If you object that this account of cause is not altogether adequate, the likeliest response is a blank stare of incomprehension; or they may say, "I pressed the button, didn't I? And the light went on, didn't it? What more do you want?" O, a great deal more than that, you say, handing them a switch to which no light happens to be connected: Try pressing that. "But it doesn't have a light," they will say . . . and slowly you watch their eyes light up with the dawn of thought, followed by the dawn of a certain horror, as they make a bare beginning at enumerating what sorts of thing might have to be included among the *causes* of the light's going on when they press the button: Edison, of course, not to mention Con-Ed, and billions of dollars, and waterfalls, and coal miners and copper miners, natives tapping trees for latex, ancient Phoenicians transmuting sand into glass . . . until the web of causes spreads quite beyond anyone's understanding or control and becomes, quite simply, quite impossibly, civilization altogether, or maybe one had better say merely IT.

And yet it is almost always with this primitive and unexamined notion that to each effect there is one cause and to each cause one effect that it is proposed to harness the tides of historical change. How odd, too, that David Hume should have been fond of playing billiards, thus by inadvertence presenting the general mind with an image of cause as one ball striking another ball whose movement was called effect! For it was the same David Hume, on whose arguments I have been drawing, whose devastating analysis of the nature of cause has been, so far as I know, neither surpassed nor answered.

To acknowledge the argument is not in the least to deny or even diminish the impressive triumphs of science and technology operating on simplified models of process and isolated systems; it is only to suggest the need of a good deal more clarity than we presently have about where such things fit with the universe in general, including ourselves, and where they not only don't fit but throw sand into their own gears. Which brings me at last to poetry as a kind of prophecy.

At the end of the beginning I gave you an unfinished sentence and a couple of riddles, promising to come back and complete the one and answer the others at the beginning of the end.

The sentence was William Blake's, and he will be very much the subject of my concluding observations. The incomplete form of his sentence might easily tempt us to ill thoughts and dark mutterings about these airy-fairy poets and how far out of touch they are with the real world, and so on. But here is the complete form:

We who dwell on Earth can do nothing of ourselves; everything is conducted by Spirits no less than Digestion or Sleep.

That proud fellow the Mind, who sits up in the top of the house and thinks, is properly rebuked. He may not believe in Spirits, but he has to believe in Digestion and Sleep, and if the management of either were entrusted to that reason that he believes is the ruler of the world neither of them would work at all, and no more would the world, if so entrusted.

Now as to my riddles.

> I am the combination to a door
> That fools and wise with equal ease undo.
> Your unthought thoughts are changes still unread
> In me, without whom nothing's to be said.

Answer: the alphabet. It is possible that the alphabet is really our "I Ching," our "Book of Changes." Imagine how such words as "infinitesimal calculus" and "psychoanalysis" could have hidden themselves for centuries and millennia among a mere twenty-six elements! It suggests the not unpleasing phantasy of some future Swiftian Academy of Lagado in which the philosophers would set themselves the task of combining and recombining the letters to make new words, to which, hopefully, some new thought about reality might correspond. Though reason tells us the idea is nonsense—for it is in general the *meanings* that are new, the words, or at least their molecules (such as "psyche" in "psychoanalysis") being very old—yet there is a teasing possibility that the thing happens after all, and that if enough children played long enough with enough alphabet blocks they would build the Tower of Babel, or derive "Finnegans Wake."

> Without my meaning nothing, nothing means.
> I am the wave for which the worlds make way.
> A term of time, and sometimes too of death,
> I am the silence in the things you say.

Answer: the sentence. But maybe this one wants a little clarifying in the details. Line three is merely riddling, and should give the answer by word-play alone: a life sentence, a death sentence. "I am the wave for which the worlds make way." The sentence may be likened to a carrier wave capable of accommodating an indefinitely large number of messages, so long as they accommodate themselves to doing their variations upon its fundamental and simple requirement of noun-verb-noun. "The worlds"—I mean the world inside the head and the world outside the head. "I am the silence in the things you say." Well, perhaps by now that is obvious. But still it is odd that we go on talking sentences all our lives without ever noticing the matter after being once compelled to do so in grammar school; and if all that while we hope that our sentences say something and mean something, it remains constant that the sentence itself never does either.

I mean by these instances that an occult part of the poet's relation with prophecy is a relation with language.

IV

If the poet ever prophesies, what he does therein is caught in a marvelous phrase of Shakespeare's, who begins a poem so appallingly obscure that no one has more than a general idea of its meaning with "the prophetic soul of the wide world, Dreaming on things to come." The phrase honors an ancient and traditional view of the poet as speaking not from his personal mind (which may be as silly or stupid as you please), but from a universal mind, or, as Shakespeare prefers to call it, soul.

This kind of prophecy does not predict, it is never precise, it does not specify particulars or give dates; it dreams on things to come. And dreams, as everyone knows so well these days, do not work by fact and reason but by wish and fear, by wish inseparable from fear.

If the poet so far mistakes his calling as to predict, even his doing so in verse won't save him from error. Ezra Pound was wrong about the Unholy Roman Empire, but no more than Dante was about the Holy one. (See my poem "Maestria" on this subject.) It is not in that way that the poet's art relates to prophecy.

But that false though common idea of the way in which the poet sees into the future may lead us by reflection to see the true way, or a couple of related true ways. The poet is in the ancient word for him a *maker,* and he doesn't foretell the future, he makes it, he brings it to pass, he sings it up. It becomes his dream.

It would be an error, again, to see the poet as doing this either consciously, of set purpose, or with respect to the future as fact (facts being *facta,* anyhow, things done, there can in strictness be no future fact). What the poet does is not to invent the world that will be there in the future, but to bring into being the mind that will be there in the future, the mind that will alone be able to see the future world because that world will be in its present and past. When Shakespeare wrote *Hamlet* we do not suppose him to have had any thought of the future, or indeed any thought other than the thoughts that might pertain to writing *Hamlet.* And yet it is clear that *Hamlet,* once it had been brought into being, affected the future in unpredictable but important ways by making available, among the models for human character, Hamlet Prince of Denmark. That this influence on the general mind of the world was immense, we know; that it was unforeseeable, we suppose; that the reach of its effects may be multifarious and still proceeding now, we surmise. So that in writing *Hamlet* Shakespeare may have been doing two things that are to the purpose of my argument. One was diagnostic: by his art, bringing together characteristics available to observation only as it were in solution, he precipitated out the solid of new character emergent upon the stage of the world. The other was prophetic: once that character existed in the play, he became a model upon which people in the world might form, and did form, their characters, their ideals, their beliefs about themselves, and perhaps even to a remarkable extent their ideas. One can read some large part of the literature of the nineteenth century as a series of variations on the figure of Hamlet, and maybe someone with a vast enough learning could trace the influence of the Prince upon history as well.

I don't mean to exaggerate, save to make the point more plain to the mind's eye for a moment. For there were many other influences that went to form our minds such as they are. But the poet's peculiar power, it may be, is over the voice in which people will afterward repeat the most solemn, sublime, and intimate things they are able to say about themselves.

The idea that diagnostic and prophetic work together in the maker's making leads on to a second true idea of the poet's relation to the future, and this one was given the best expression by William Blake, who said, in effect, that prophecy was a very simple thing, it meant saying to people, "If you go on doing thus, the result will be thus." The true prophet, if he be a poet, need not bother his head over the future, but his whole endeavor will be to see the present with absolute clarity. Blake would probably have called it seeing things as they are in eternity, and doing that, you will realize, is no easier than foretelling the future. Which may be why it is done so rarely.

Two main elements in Blake's prophetic writings seem to me most striking as a demonstration of what prescience seems to have been attained by a man who, whatever his oddities and cranks, was utterly sane in his ability to see with a purified vision that penetrated quite beyond what people said they were doing to what, essentially, they were doing—whether they knew it or not. One is his absolute certainty that the world before our eyes, the world we habitually see as "other" and "out there," is to an unimaginably large extent a mental world, wherein what we see is the result of how we see, and not the other way round. The other is his grasp and development, about a hundred years before Freud published *The Interpretation of Dreams*, of the idea of unconscious mental process, especially as it affects vision, of the part played by compulsive mythological phantasies in the construction of what we glibly refer to as reality. He saw clearly and proclaimed with outspoken obstinacy that the look of life was changing because thought was changing, and that thought was changing as and because perception, or vision, was changing. "The eye altering alters all," he says, and, repeated through *Jerusalem*, the refrain, "You become what you behold," "They became what they beheld."

What it was we beheld, what it was we became in Blake's prophecy, or realized dream, I shall try to express in the most summary way. Experiencing the essence, or god, of the universe as other than human, men began to imagine the meaning of this other on the model of astronomical and inexorable order; this imagining began to make possible the invention of machines, for which the images available to Blake may seem to us ludicrously homey—the loom, the mill, the clock—though they notably didn't seem so to him, but, on the contrary, ominous, hostile, vast as the planetary model on which they were constructed. It may be observed in passing, that although machines do real work the image they most often present as what it looks like to do real work is going round in a circle. The invention of machines in its turn produces the image of a giant machine as a metaphor for the universe; but also, inevitably, as a metaphor for the mind, whose servile ambition henceforth will be the progressively perfected imitation of relentless and mechanic order without other purpose than the maintenance of its sterile circularities, from which soul, spirit, mind itself at last, will be progressively excluded. The summa of all this imagery is realized as a cold sky god, who if he is not dead is hopelessly insane and unreachable by love and prayer—because he is human phantasy itself. To this god, whom Blake calls Nobodaddy and Urizen—Horizon, Your Reason (but also, whether in his hellish or his redeemed form, You Risen)—and to his vicegerents who rule on earth, humanity exists only to be enslaved in school and factory and sacrificed in war.

Blake's vision does not stress the beneficent powers of machinery. Neither is it meant to be a Luddite instruction to abolish machinery. But it is a severe warning against our allowing mechanical ideas to become, as they so largely have become, our supreme and at last our exclusive ways of seeing ourselves, our experience, and the world.

I may leave it to the reader to decide for himself in what ways and to what degree Blake, standing in the first decades of the nineteenth century, looked at what was and extrapolated to what would be. Not, again, by thinking of the future; but by seeing what was to him the present and common circumstance. For the true prophet does not say "It will be," but "It is; it is here, it is now, if you will only look." The realization of his prophecy would not, for Blake, be a matter of waiting around for the coming of the bulldozer, the bomb, the drug, the electronic calculating machine, for it was there already, to anyone with eyes to see, in the mill, the loom, the clock; in the Industrial Revolution, the crowding of the newly dispossessed in towns and cities; in child labor and in the government of England. It was among his hopes for humanity that the American and French Revolutions might signify the end of tyranny and oppression, the redemption of the world by freedom and lovingkindness, but the clarity of his vision made him write:

> The iron hand crush'd the Tyrant's head
> And became a Tyrant in his stead.

To conclude. I remind you again that Blake did not directly picture the world as it would be a century and more after he lived. But he confers upon his readers a language whence he is able to derive a series of striking expressions which make it possible for them to think about what has been happening, and what is happening, in a way we could not have invented for ourselves. This is another thought that makes prophecy so tricky a thing to understand: that the prophet can come to be known as such only when what he sees as present has actually entered the future — which is to say, has become our present and past. It is not the coming on of event as such, in the outward world of history, but rather the coming on of new mind and new vision, made available by the poet's words, that makes him appear as a prophet to those who live later.

For most of the nineteenth century almost no one read Blake's Prophetic Books; and indeed not very many read them now. But they are read and studied, by those who do read them now, with a seriousness that perhaps they could not have inspired earlier, before the unfolding of event began to make their meaning overwhelmingly significant, and before another prophet, Freud, had made explicit and put into more or less scientific terminology some of the things that in oblique and hidden ways were present in the poet's thought. For scientific language, among the many other things it is, is also the language in which we tell each other myths about the motions and the purposes of mind disguised as world, as time, as truth. It scarce needs saying, that myth believed is never called a myth.

The Protean Encounter

Poetry is the other way of using language. Formally, it is recognizable by its dependence on at least one more parameter, the *line*, than appears in prose composition. This changes its appearance on the page, and you will observe that people take their cue from this changed appearance on the page and read poetry aloud in a very different voice from their habitual voice, possibly because, as Ben Jonson said, poetry "speaketh somewhat above a mortal mouth." If, by way of testing this description, you show people poems printed as prose you will find that in the main people read the result as prose, simply because it looks that way; that is, they are no longer guided by the balance and shift of the line in relation to the breath as well as the syntax.

That is a minimal definition, though hopefully not uninformative. Perhaps it is all that should be attempted in the way of definition. Poetry is the way it is because it looks that way, and it looks that way because it sounds that way, and vice versa. It is hard to imagine anyone who had never read a poem as consulting dictionary or encyclopedia on the subject and receiving much joy of the result; here is a standard dictionary definition:

1. The art of rhythmical composition, written or spoken, for exciting pleasure, by beautiful, imaginative, or elevated thoughts. 2. literary work in metrical form; verse. 3. prose with poetic qualities. 4. poetical qualities however manifested.
— The Random House Dictionary of the English Language.

These definitions offer the dictionary's usual solemn reassurance, while leaving us uninformed where we have not been misinformed. If we inquire, for example, what qualities are *poetic,* and look under that word, we get: "possessing the qualities or charm of poetry"; which puts us back where we were. When the dictionary is not in this way describing circles, it is describing externals which may or may not be of the essence, as in definition 2 above: "literary work in metrical form; verse." That is true in the usual dictionary sense that it is one of the ways in which people commonly use the word *poetry;* but as Aristotle observed some time ago, if you versified the *History* of Herodotus the result would not be poetry.

Poetry & Prose

People's main reason for wanting a definition is to take care of the borderline case, and this is what a definition, as if by definition, won't do. That is, if a man asks for a definition of Poetry, it will most certainly not be the case that he has never seen one of the objects called poems that are said to embody poetry; on the contrary, he is already tolerably certain what poetry in the main is, and his reason for wanting a definition is either that his certainty has been challenged by someone else or that he wants to take care of a possible or seeming exception to it; hence the perennial squabble over distinguishing poetry from prose.

Sensible things have been said on this point. T. S. Eliot suggested that the trouble lies in our having the technical term *verse* to go with the term *poetry*, while we lack an equivalent technical term to distinguish the mechanical part of *prose* and make the relation symmetrical. Valery, picking up a simile used by Malherbes, said that prose was walking, poetry dancing. Indeed, the original two terms, *prosus* and *versus* meant, respectively, "going straight forth" and "returning," and that distinction does point up the tendency of poetry to incremental repetition, variation, and the treatment of different themes in a single form. Robert Frost said shrewdly that poetry was what got left behind in translation, which suggests a criterion of almost scientific refinement: when in doubt, translate; whatever is left over is poetry, whatever gets through is prose. And yet even to so cagy a definition the great exception is a resounding one: some of the greatest poetry we have is in the Authorized Version of the Bible, which is not only a translation but also, as to its appearance in print, identifiable neither with verse nor with prose in English but rather with a cadence compounded of both.

There may be a better way of putting the question. One of my students showed by a simple test that when people are presented with a series of passages drawn indifferently from poems and stories but all printed as prose they will show a dominant inclination to identify everything they possibly can as prose. This will be true, oddly enough, even if the poem rimes, and even if the poem in its original typographical arrangement would have been known to them. The reason seems to be absurdly plain: we recognize poems by their appearance on the page, and we respond to the convention whereby we recognize them by reading them aloud in a quite different tone of voice from that which we apply to prose (which indeed we scarcely read aloud at all). I would add here that we make the distinction even without reading aloud; even in silence we confer upon a piece of poetry an attention that differs from what we give to prose in two ways: in tone, and in pace.

Instead of niggling further with definitions, I shall be somewhat bold now, and exhibit the plain and mighty differences between prose and poetry by a comparison. In the following a prose writer and a poet are talking about the same subject, getting older.

> Between the ages of 30 and 90,
> the weight of our muscles falls by
> 30 per cent and the power we can
> exert likewise . . . the number of
> nerve fibres in a nerve trunk falls
> by a quarter. The weight of our brains
> falls from an average of 3.03 lb. to
> 2.27 lb., as cells die and are not
> replaced. . . .

> Let me disclose the gifts reserved for age
>   To set a crown upon your lifetime's effort.
>   First, the cold friction of expiring sense
> Without enchantment, offering no promise
>   But bitter tastelessness of shadow fruit
>   As body and soul begin to fall asunder.
> Second, the conscious impotence of rage
>   At human folly, and the laceration
>   Of laughter at what ceases to amuse.
> And last, the rending pain of re-enactment
>   Of all that you have done, and been . . .

Before you object that this comparison cannot possibly cover all the possible ranges of poetry and prose compared, consider for a moment what differences are exhibited. The passages are oddly parallel in a formal sense, for both consist of the several items of a catalogue under the general title of growing old. The significant differences are of tone, pace and object of attention. If the prose passage interests itself in the neutral, material, measurable properties of the process, while the poetry interests itself in what the process will feel like to someone going through it, that is not accidental but of the essence; if one reads the prose passage with an interest in being informed, noting the parallel constructions without being affected by them either in tone or in pace, while reading the poetry with a sense of considerable gravity and solemnity, that too is of the essence. One might say as tersely as possible that the difference between prose and poetry is most strikingly shown in the two uses of the verb "to fall."

> the number of nerve fibres in a nerve trunk falls by a quarter

> As body and soul begin to fall asunder

It is observable too that though the diction of the poem is well within what could be commanded by a moderately well-educated speaker, it is at the same time well outside the range of terms in fact employed by such a speaker in his daily occasions; it is a diction very conscious, as it were, of its power of choosing terms with a peculiar precision, and of combining terms into phrases with the same peculiar precision, and at the same time of combining *sounds* with the same peculiar precision. Doubtless the precision of the prose passage is greater in the more obvious property of dealing in the measurable; but the poet attempts a precision with respect to what is not in the same sense measurable nor even in the same sense accessible to observation. In *Biographia Literaria*, chapter I, Coleridge tells us what he chiefly remembers having got from his schoolmaster Dr. Bowyer:

> I learnt from him, that Poetry, even that of the loftiest and, seemingly, that of the wildest odes, had a logic of its own, as severe as that of science; and more difficult, because more subtle, more complex, and dependent on more, and more fugitive causes.
>
> Also: In the truly great poets, he would say, there is a reason assignable, not only for every word, but for the position of every word.

That last saying illuminates the same author's terser formulation in *Table Talk*, 12 July 1827: prose is words in the best order, poetry the best words in the best order.

Happily, if poetry is almost impossible to define, it is extremely easy to recognize in experience; even untutored children are rarely in doubt about it when it appears:

Little Jack Jingle
He used to live single,
But when he got tired of this kind of life,
He left off being single, and liv'd with his wife.

It might be objected that this verse is not of significant import and
weight to be an exemplar of poetry. Remember, though, that it has
given people pleasure, so that they continued to say it until and after
it was written down, nearly two centuries ago. It has survived, and its
survival has something to do with pleasure, with delight; and while it
is still with us, how many more important works of language – epic
poems, books of philosophy and theology – have gone down, deserv-
edly or not, into dust and silence. It has, obviously, a form, an arrangement of sounds in relation to thoughts which somehow makes its
agreeable nonsense closed, complete, and decisive. But this topic
should have a heading and an instance all to itself.

Form in Poetry

People nowadays who speak of form in poetry almost always mean
such externals as regular measure and rhyme, and most often they
mean to get rid of these in favor of the freedom they suppose must
follow upon the absence of form in this limited sense. But in fact a
poem having only one form would be of doubtful interest even if it
could exist. In this connection the poet J. V. Cunningham speaks of
"a convergence of forms, and forms of disparate orders," adding: "It
is the coincidence of forms that locks in the poem." For a poem is
composed of intellectual forms also, and these are sufficient without
regular measure and rhyme; if the intellectual forms are absent, as in
greeting card verse or advertising jingles, no amount of thumping and
banging will supply the want.

Form, in effect, is like the doughnut which may be made either by
putting some nothing into a circle of something or by closing some
something around some nothing: it is either the outside of an inside,
as when people speak of "good form," or the inside of an outside, as
in "the soul is the form of the body." Taking this for a principle, we
may look at a very short and very powerful poem with a view to
distinguishing the forms, or schemes, of which it is made. It was
written by Rudyard Kipling, and its subject is a soldier shot by his
comrades for cowardice in battle.

I could not look on Death, which being known,
Men led me to him, blindfold and alone.

I find this admirable, and more moving the more I say it over and ponder what it says. One reason for my response must of course be in the grimness, horror, and sorrow of the subject itself, and that is reason enough to carry me for a first few readings. But as I question the poem, and ask further of it how it can so please me even while remaining so stark an account of so cruel a theme, my delight increases; and this is the delight in art itself, which makes it possible for us to contemplate the world's awful realities without being turned to stone.

There is (1) the obvious external form of a rhymed, closed couplet in iambic pentameter. There is (2) the obvious external form of a single sentence balanced in four grammatical units with and against the metrical form. There is (3) the conventional form belonging to the epitaph, terse enough to be cut in stone and tight-lipped, perhaps, for other reasons as well, such as the speaker's shame. There is (4) the fictional form belonging to the epitaph, according to which the dead man is supposed to be saying the words himself. There is (5), especially poignant in this instance, the real form behind or within the fictional one, for we are aware that in reality it is not the dead man speaking, nor are his feelings the only ones we are receiving, but that the comrades who were forced to execute him may themselves have made up these two lines with their incalculably complex and exquisite balance of scorn, awe, guilt, and consideration even to tenderness for the dead soldier. There is (6) the metaphorical form, with its many resonances ranging from the tragic through the pathetic to irony and apology: dying in battle is spoken of in language relating it to a social occasion in a drawing-room or court, the coward's fear is implicitly represented by understatement as the timorousness and embarrassment one might feel about being introduced to a somewhat superior and majestic person, so that the soldiers who put the coward to death are seen as sympathetically helping him through a difficult moment in the realm of manners. In addition, there is (7) a linguistic or syntactical form, with at least a couple of tricks to it: the second clause, with its reminiscence of Latin construction, participates in the meaning by conferring a Roman stoicism and archaic gravity on the saying; remembering that the soldiers in the poem had been British schoolboys not long before, we might hear the remote resonance of a whole world built upon Greek and Roman models; and the last epithets, "blindfold and alone," while in the first acceptation they clearly refer to the coward, show a distinct tendency to waver over and apply mysteriously to Death as well, sitting there waiting, "blindfold and alone." One might add another form (8), composed of the balance of sounds, from the obvious likeness in the rhyme down to subtleties and refinements beneath the ability of our coarse analysis to discriminate. And even there we should not quite be at an end, for there remains an overall principle of all these forms, the implication of what might have been epic or novel or five-act tragedy into two lines, or the poet's precise election of a single instant to carry what the novelist, if he did his business properly, would have been hundreds of pages arriving at.

It is no part of my intention to suggest that the poet composed in the manner of my laborious analysis; no, the whole point is that he didn't catalogue eight or ten forms and assemble them into a poem; much more likely it "just came to him." But the example may serve to indicate how many modes of the mind go together in this articulation of an implied drama and the tension among the many possible sentiments that might arise in response to it.

In this way, by the coincidence of the forms that locks in the poem, we may see how to answer a question that often arises about poems: their thoughts are commonplace, but they mysteriously are not. We answer that a poem is not so much a thought as it is a mind: talk with it, and it will talk back, telling you many things that you might have thought for yourself but somehow didn't until it brought them together. Doubtless a poem is a much simplified model for the mind. But it might still be one of the best we have available. On this great theme we shall do best to proceed not by definition but by parable and interpretation.

The Protean Encounter

In the Fourth Book of *The Odyssey* Homer tells the following strange tale.

After the war at Troy, Menelaus wanted very much to get home but got held up in Egypt for want of a wind, because, as he later told Telemachus, he had not sacrificed enough to the Gods. "Ever jealous the Gods are," he said, "that we men mind their dues." But because the Gods work both ways, it was on the advice of a Goddess, Eidothea, that Menelaus went to consult Proteus the Old One of the Sea, as one might consult a travel agent.

Proteus was not at all easy to consult. He was herding seals, and they stank even through the ambrosia Eidothea had thoughtfully provided. And when Menelaus crept up close, disguised as a seal, and grabbed him, Proteus turned into a lion, a dragon, a leopard, a boar, a film of water, and a high-branched tree. But Menelaus managed to hang on through all this until at last Proteus gave up and was himself

again; whereupon Menelaus asked the one great question: How do I
get home? And Proteus told him: You'd better go back to Egypt
and sacrifice to the Gods some more. (My paraphrase follows the translation by T. E. Lawrence.)

We may take this as a parable about poetry. A man has an urgent
question about his way in the world. He already knows the answer,
but it fails to satisfy him. So at great inconvenience, hardship, and
even peril, he consults a powerful and refractory spirit who tries to
evade his question by turning into anything in the world. Then, when
the spirit sees he can't get free of the man, and only then, he answers
the man's question, not simply with a commonplace, but with the
same commonplace the man had been dissatisfied with before.
Satisfied or not, however, the man now obeys the advice given him.

A foolish story? All the same, it is to be observed that Menelaus did
get home. And it was a heroic thing to have hung on to Proteus
through those terrifying changes, and compelled him to be himself
and answer up. Nor does it matter in the least to the story that Menelaus personally may have been a disagreeable old fool, as well as a
cuckold.

A poet also has one great and simple question. Chaucer put it as
well as anyone could, and in three lines at that:

> What is this world? What asketh men to have?
> Now with his love, now in the colde grave,
> Allone, withouten any companye.

And a poet gets the simple answer he might expect, the one the
world grudgingly gives to anyone who asks such a question: The
world is this way, not that way, and you ask for more than you will be
given. Which the poet, being no more a fool than his fellows, knew
already. But on the path from question to answer he will see many
marvels, he will follow the metamorphoses of things in the metamorphoses of their phrases, and he will be so elated and ecstatic in this
realm of wonders that the voice in which he speaks these things, down
even to the stupid, obvious and commonplace answer, will be to his
hearers a solace and a happiness in the midst of sorrows:

> When I do count the clock that tells the time,
> And see the brave day sunk in hideous night;
> When I behold the violet past prime,
> And sable curls all silver'd o'er with white;
> When lofty trees I see barren of leaves

Which erst from heat did canopy the herd,
And summer's green all girdled up in sheaves
Borne on the bier with white and bristly beard,
Then of thy beauty do I question make,
That thou among the wastes of time must go,
Since sweets and beauties must themselves forsake
And dies as fast as they see others grow;
   And nothing 'gainst Time's scythe can make defence
   Save breed, to brave him when he takes thee hence.
                   —Shakespeare, Sonnet 12

Like Menelaus, the poet asks a simple question, to which moreover he already knows the unsatisfying answer. Question and answer,
one might say, have to be present, although of themselves they seem
to do nothing much; but they assert the limits of a journey to be taken.
They are the necessary but not sufficient conditions of what really
seems to matter here, the protean encounter itself, the grasping and
hanging on to the powerful and refractory spirit in its slippery transformations of a single force flowing through clock, day, violet, grey-
ing hair, trees dropping their leaves, the harvest in which by a peculiarly ceremonial transmutation the grain by which we live is seen
without contradiction as the corpse we come to. As for the answer to
the question, it is not surprising nor meant to be surprising, it is only
just.

On this point, that the answer comes as no surprise, poets show an
agreement that quite transcends the differences of periods and
schools. Pope's formula, "What oft was thought, but ne'er so well
expresst," sometimes considered as the epitome of a shallow and
parochial decorum, is not in essence other than this of Keats:

I think poetry should surprise by a fine excess, and not by singularity; It
should strike the reader as a wording of his own highest thoughts, and
appear almost a remembrance.
                   —Letter to John Taylor, 1818.

Both are in substantial agreement with a remark of Robert Frost's in
the present century:

A word about recognition: In literature it is our business to give people the
thing that will make them say, "Oh yes, I know what you mean." It is never to
tell them something they don't know, but something they know and hadn't
thought of saying. It must be something they recognize.
     —Sentence Sounds, in *Modern Poetics*, ed. James Scully, N.Y., 1965.

And John Crowe Ransom gives the same formulation a cryptically elegant variation: "Poetry is the kind of knowledge by which we must know that we have arranged that we shall not know otherwise."

There is another part of the story of Menelaus and Proteus, for Menelaus asked another question: What happened to my friends who were with me at Troy? Proteus replies, "Son of Atreus, why enquire too closely of me on this? To know or learn what I know about it is not your need: I warn you that when you hear all the truth your tears will not be far behind. . . ." But he tells him all the same: "Of those others many went under; many came through. . . ." And Menelaus does indeed respond with tears of despair, until Proteus advises him to stop crying and get started on the journey home. So it sometimes happens in poetry, too: the sorrowful contemplation of what is consoles, in the end, and heals, but only after the contemplative process has been gone through and articulated in the detail of its changes:

> When to the sessions of sweet silent thought
> I summon up remembrance of things past,
> I sigh the lack of many a thing I sought,
> And with old woes new wail my dear time's waste;
> Then can I drown an eye, unused to flow,
> For precious friends hid in death's dateless night,
> And weep afresh love's long since cancell'd woe,
> And moan the expense of many a vanish'd sight:
> Then can I grieve at grievances foregone,
> And heavily from woe to woe tell o'er
> The sad account of fore-bemoaned moan,
> Which I new pay as if not paid before.
>   But if the while I think on thee, dear friend,
>   All losses are restored and sorrows end.
>   — Shakespeare, Sonnet 30

This sonnet might be taken as condensing into its fourteen lines the whole mystery of the art of poetry. To elucidate that statement I must for a moment be personal.

When I began to read poetry, as a boy of seventeen, Shakespeare's Thirtieth Sonnet moved me to tears. When I began to study poetry, a little later, it seemed to me not only a masterpiece but a marvelous display of virtuosity. A quarter-century later, having sorrows now to match its sorrows, it moves me to tears. And I still, or again, see it as a masterpiece and a marvelous display of virtuosity. These attitudes have coalesced, so that while the page is wet with tears I can marvel at the fourth line, the only ten-syllable line of my acquaintance to have seven accents.

It brings up what may be the deepest and hardest question we ask of poetry: Is it a sacrament or a con game? Echo answers.

Or Rilke answers: Works of art are of an infinite loneliness, and by nothing so little able to be grasped as by criticism. That statement gets itself quoted ever so often, together with the sequel telling us that love alone is capable in these things; but as often as it is quoted you will find it is a critic who is doing the quoting.

Shakespeare's sonnet is not even at all points very attractive. "Then can I drown an eye, unus'd to flow." Surely that is Poetry Itself, at or near its worst, where the literal and the conventional, whatever their relations may have been for Shakespeare and the first readers of these sugared sonnets among his friends, now live very uncomfortably together ("Drink to me only with thine eyes" is a like example of this bathetic crossing of levels).

Moreover, while the whole is uniquely Shakespearean, the bits and pieces are many of them common property of the age, what one writer called "joint stock company poetry." And the tricks are terribly visible, too; art is not being used to conceal art in such goings-on as "grieve at grievances" and "fore-bemoaned moan."

Nor is that the worst of it. This man who so powerfully draws my sympathies by lamenting what is past manages to do this by thinking obsessively about litigation and money; his hand is ever at his pocketbook, bidding adieu. He cannot merely *think* sweet silent thoughts about the past, no, he has to turn them into a court in *session,* whereto he *summons* the probable culprit *remembrance;* when he *grieves,* it is at a *grievance,* and we are back in the hands of the law again; finally, as with Dante's sinners, his avarice and prodigality occupy two halves of one circle: he bemoans his expenses even while paying double the asking price.

And yet . . . *eppur si muove.* It is still beautiful, it still moves, I remain grateful to the man who made it. As between confidence game and sacrament there may be no need to decide. If it could be plainly demonstrated to us that poetry was metaphorical, mythological and delusive, while science, say, or religion, or politics, were real and true, then we might throw poetry away and live with what is left. But, for better or worse, that is not the real condition of our lives in this world; and perhaps we care for poetry so much—if we care at all—because, at last, it is the only one of our many mythologies to be, and to make us, aware that it and the others are mythological.

I. A. Richards, in a deep and searching consideration of this matter, concludes: "It is the privilege of poetry to preserve us from mistaking our notions either for things or for ourselves. Poetry is the completest mode of utterance."

The last thing Proteus says to Menelaus is strange indeed:

You are not to die in Argos of the fair horse-pastures, not there to encounter death: rather will the Deathless Ones carry you to the Elysian plain, the place beyond the world . . . There you will have Helen for yourself and will be deemed of the household of Zeus.

So the greatest of our poets have said, though mostly nowadays people sing a different tune. To be as the gods, to be rejoined with the once-beloved, the world forgotten . . . Sacrament or con game? As impossible as unnecessary to decide. The greatest poetry sees clearly and says plainly the wickedness and terror and beauty of the world, while at the same time humming to itself, so that we overhear rather than hear: All will be well.

ABOUT THE AUTHOR

Howard Nemerov was born in New York City in 1920 and received his A.B. from Harvard in 1941. During World War II he served as a pilot with the Royal Canadian Air Force, with the United States Army Air Force, and on detached service with the Royal Air Force.

He has taught at Hamilton College, at Bennington College, and at Brandeis University. He has also been Visiting Professor at the University of Minnesota, Poet in Residence at Hollins College, Consultant in Poetry to the Library of Congress, and Hurst Professor of English at Washington University, St. Louis. He is presently on the English faculty of Washington University. He is also a member of the National Institute of Arts and Letters and a Fellow of the American Academy of Arts and Sciences.

Nemerov's publishing career began in 1947 with the publication of his first volume of verse, followed by six additional books of poems. He has also published three novels and two collections of short stories. The Rutgers University Press published his *Poetry and Fiction: Essays* in 1963 and *Journal of the Fictive Life* in 1965.

The text of this book was set in Caledonia Linofilm and printed by Offset on P & S Special XL manufactured by P. H. Glatfelter Co., Inc., Spring Grove, Pa. Composed, printed and bound by Quinn & Boden Company, Inc., Rahway, New Jersey.